Justifiable Conduct

TEMPLE UNIVERSITY PRESS
Philadelphia, Pennsylvania 19122
www.temple.edu/tempress

Published 2013

Library of Congress Cataloging-in-Publication Data

Goode, Erich.
Justifiable conduct : self-vindication in memoir / Erich Goode.
pages cm
Includes bibliographical references and index.
ISBN 978-1-4399-1025-2 (cloth : alk. paper)
ISBN 978-1-4399-1026-9 (pbk. : alk. paper)
ISBN 978-1-4399-1027-6 (e-book)
1. Deviant behavior—History. 2. Conduct of life—History. 3. Deviant behavior in literature—History. 4. Autobiography. 5. Sociology—Biographical methods. I. Title.

HM811.G6657 2013
301—dc23 2012041438

♾ The paper used in this publication meets the requirements of the American National Standard for Information Sciences—Permanence of Paper for Printed Library Materials, ANSI Z39.48-1992

Printed in the United States of America

2 4 6 8 9 7 5 3 1

Contents

Preface

HALF A CENTURY AGO, during my first semester of graduate school, I enrolled in a course taught by Robert King Merton—then the most eminent sociologist in the world—entitled, as I recall, "Analysis of Social Structure." The inaugural lecture was packed, as virtually all of his were, with fifty or sixty students in rapturous attendance. Merton began the course by explaining that in *Leviathan,* Thomas Hobbes argued that humans are naturally selfish, unruly, and individualistic and that if each one of us pursued what he or she coveted without respect for the rights of others, such behavior would engender a "war of all against all," in which life would become "solitary, poor, nasty, brutish, and short." Hobbes raised what eventually became the foundational question of sociology: "How is social order possible?" The answer the English philosopher offered was that societies demand that their members agree to an unspoken social contract: Abandon your natural, selfish desires, submit yourself to the rule of the sovereign, and what you receive in return is—life itself. Protection. Nourishment. Association. Connubiality. Intimacy. But, Merton added, when some of the society's members stray too far from its rules—which we sociologists call norms—members of the society will formally or informally sanction them and oblige them to account for themselves. He encouraged us to answer Hobbes's question in a more satisfying, persuasive, and analytically powerful manner: How is such a social contract carried out today?

The question Merton mooted in his inaugural lecture stewed in my brain for five decades, and this book is the product. I wonder if he would have approved of my distillation of Hobbes's argument. (Merton died in 2003, at the age of ninety-two.) Perhaps not. Though he was a seductive encourager of student research, Robert K. Merton was an extremely exacting and demanding critic.

That some—or many—members of the society violate one or more of its norms, or those of its constituent collectivities, is hardly news. That people who do so blab at length about their transgressions, and on the scale that currently prevails, is a fairly recent development, although widely known. That violators who blab about normative violations do so in interesting and revealing (and not entirely predictable) ways is, in my estimation, an underreflected-upon phenomenon. Yes, social psychologists and sociologists have extensively investigated apologies (Tavuchis, 1991; Lazare, 2004), excuses (Snyder, Higgins, and Stucky, 1983; Maruna and Copes, 2005), confessions (Brooks, 2000), and scandals (Adut, 2008; Kipnis, 2010)—not to mention any and all manner of cognate verbal processes. But, for the most part, their inquiries focus mainly on violators who have been found out and are forcibly and rudely called upon to explain themselves—human deer, as it were, caught in the headlight of exposure.

Instead, here, I explore transgressors' well-thought-out and carefully constructed accounts of normative violations and their mostly self-serving interpretations, directed at audiences who may (or may not) endorse such presentations. My informants, if they may be called that, describe their deviant behavior (whether initially known or unknown) in a crafted, stage-managed fashion. Laura Kipnis (2010, p. 21) refers to "the hollowness of redemption" of these trapped human deer who clumsily (in her cases, unsuccessfully) attempt to bamboozle a vindictive audience into refraining from tearing them apart. But the targets of scandal have stepped into a mess—of their own making—on which social headlights have suddenly and inadvertently focused. Instead, my cases are made up of transgressors of *someone's* norms who have gone on at length self-revealing—and, for the most part, exculpating—their selfsame putative violations. My authors have framed their discussions in ways that are very different from those of transgressors who are frozen in the act when the curtain is pulled back and the audience is aghast at or derisive about the discovery. In short, most of my authors have spent a substantial part of a lifetime reflecting on their putative transgressions and have crafted a mostly positive spin on what these acts mean, attempting some measure of vindication and redemption. Indeed, some do not even regard what they have done as wrong, do not even feel that they belong in the company of other miscreants, though they feel that explaining themselves is nonetheless necessary—and they are usually sincere in their belief in the truth of what they are saying and often prove persuasive in their rationales. As receivers, connoisseurs, and appreciators of such accounts, we should take such narratives seriously. In short, I do not believe that these authors' redemptive accounts are "hollow" at all, and they clearly reveal how a major feature of our society works. But it is they, the authors, who recognize discrepancies between their self-image and their described actions, and it is they, the authors, who have constructed a reconciliation that smooths over this seeming contradiction by means of a verbal construct.

This book focuses on the process by which autobiographers and memoirists explain, justify, exculpate, excuse, and warrant their putatively untoward, transgressive, non-normative behavior. By "untoward," "transgressive," and "non-normative" behavior, I mean acts that are likely to attract condemnation among identifiable and relevant, actual or potential audiences, such as peers and associates, friends and acquaintances, and relatives—or enemies, rivals, and competitors—and editors, readers, the general public, and law enforcement officers. Sociologically, deviant/deviance is not an identifiable *thing* in the world, like an oak tree or an Apple computer; it is a *label* that designated collectivities apply to a person, a set of acts, or an expressed belief. It is important that I stress this point, since several critics of what I say here have already reacted to the term "deviant" or "deviance," taking the lay meaning as *my* meaning, or as some abstract, indwelling, essentialistic meaning—thereby committing the fallacy of reification. Such critics' imputation is very far from the truth. Sociologists teach courses entitled "Deviant Behavior"—with robust enrollments, I might add—and they teach from texts entitled *Deviant Behavior,* some of which sell well. Half a century or more ago, sociologists abandoned the archaic notion that the word or the concept "deviance" is pejorative, that it has anything to do with psychiatric pathology or immanent sin (Becker, 1963); unfortunately, however, much of the public and some misguided critics still cling to this antiquated, reified definition. We would love to abandon the term for a less clumsy one, but no one—not even those who have objected to such use—has suggested a viable alternative. "Unconventional," "regarded as transgressive to certain audiences," "non-normative within a specific context," and "supposedly untoward" are insipid, flabby, namby-pamby, milquetoast, and verbally contorted attempts. We are still waiting for that better term; in the meantime, we will have to continue to use the word "deviant" to describe that which is *situationally objectionable to specific audiences.* Proof of the pudding—a "definition in use."

The sociological definition of deviance is relativistic; it relies on how designated *audiences,* real or potential, react to behavior, beliefs, or characteristics. Certain observers react in such a way that it is clear they have decided that someone has violated their normative system so egregiously or chronically that the person *deserves* to be condemned or punished. This definition says nothing about who *ought* or ought *not* to be so treated, but it does insist that such treatment in response to perceived violations against a normative system is a social fact. By their reactions to the behavior of our actors in question, designated audiences make announcements such as these: Jordan Belfort is not to be trusted with our money; Eddie Bunker deserves a prison sentence; Roman Polanski is not to be trusted with our daughters; Elia Kazan is a rat and should be avoided; Malcolm X is a troublemaker and a rabble-rouser; Melissa Febos should not be taken home to meet Mother; Norman Podhoretz is a right-wing nut case. The sociology of deviance does *not* valorize these judgments; it recognizes that some observers have made these judgments about our authors. And such judgments may have real consequences. Moreover, these author-actors, recognizing that some observers have condemned them or their actions, take such judgments into consideration. Consider these quotes from some notable memoirs: "The theory circulated that I had gone mad" (Norman Podhoretz); "I was notorious, an informant, a squealer, and a rat" (Elia Kazan); "If you behave like a man, you are doomed" (Jack Henry Abbott); "Why so much anger?" (Jim Bouton); "What else could I do?" (Edward Bunker); "I had crossed the fine line between decent folks and scum" (Roman Polanski). Their words constitute that *they* recognize that they have been tagged with the label "deviance"—that is, what *sociologists* mean by a "deviant"—and they encapsulate their defensive reaction to their own designation.

This recognition is not simply cognitive; it is emotional as well. Bill Clinton's sense of entrapment at the charge that he had engaged in sex with Monica Lewinsky must have amounted to the feeling of holy terror—that his presidency was at an end; that history would judge him a foul, depraved, out-of-control profligate; that his wife might leave him and his daughter would not respect him. He was desperate to do something—tell a feeble lie, make up a distinction that would delay his impeachment, do *anything* to avoid being kicked out of the White House. "I did not have sexual relations with that woman" was the verbal neutralization, and *My Life* (2004) was the memoir that enshrined that emotion. Feeling that he is "doomed," Abbott not only knows he must react to avoid said doom—he *feels* a sense of terror, knows in his bones that he must act a certain way, but he cannot think his way out of the Minotaur's Maze in which he is trapped. James Frey, a *novel* manuscript in hand, is given a book contract for a *memoir* that would make him rich and famous. What to do? *What the hell!* he tells himself, with a dry throat and trembling hands. *I'll fake it—I'll* call *it a memoir and see how far I can take this ride.* Polanski's awareness that friends and acquaintances, moviegoers, supporters and enemies alike felt he was *pond scum,* set off tremors of fear throughout his psyche, backed him into an emotional corner, forced him to devise legal, logistical, and verbal schemes to escape this collective judgment. Saturated with hormones, the mind does not always come up with sound solutions, but they are nearly always interesting to the student of human behavior.

Kipnis describes the "ongoing battle between the anarchy of desire and the sledgehammer of social propriety" (2010, pp. 19–20)—a graphic and apposite phrase. Rules are ubiquitous, their violations are ubiquitous, and society's punishments—though contingent—are likewise ubiquitous. Deviance is the unruly side of social life, and its social control is the subject matter of Hobbes's formulation—which becomes necessary when the social contract breaks down—and the attempt at exculpation following a violation is its inevitable love child. As sociologists and anthropologists have learned, societies can thrive on fairly high levels of normative violation, provided certain conditions prevail, and perhaps one of those conditions is how transgressors frame their acts to audiences.

Authors keep audiences or significant others in mind when narrating their life stories; they anticipate criticism from these relevant audiences as they unfold the details of their lives. To fashion an acceptable persona, as characters or actors in their own life drama, memoir writers couch the details of their transgressions in more or less acceptable (or less unacceptable) fashion and typically receive responses that are more positive than they would without such verbalizations. These verbalizations often come naturally to authors, so we need not impute or attribute, as Kipnis seems to, sly or cynical manipulation at work here. I walk away from my memoir authors' self-exculpations with exactly the opposite feeling from Kipnis's. I sense that most of these authors have gotten themselves into all-too-human jams or have interacted with dubious companions, and I *empathize* with their feelings about the experience of being reproached. I feel that *I* could have engaged in many—though not all—of the condemned activities in which they participated. I try to avoid the term "rationalizations" when referring to deviance neutralization inasmuch as this is a loaded, pejorative term that implies that such accounts are "hollow," illegitimate, cynical, crass manipulations of the sympathy of the intended audience. Yes, what persons who use such verbal strategies as are often *labeled* "rationalizations" engage in is rhetoric, though I assume some measure of heartfelt emotion in such strategies—for the most part, their users *really do* believe that the acts they exculpate are not as bad as their detractors say they are. Yes, such articulations are verbal "strategies," devices," "contrivances," and "techniques," which terms sound as if their authors use them to induce audiences to react in a certain way to them, their books, and the acts they describe. And yes, actor-authors often exaggerate or sweep damning details of their lives under the proverbial rug. All of this is true, as it is common to all social interaction, but this in no way detracts from the sincerity of these authors. I argue that the narrators typically project anticipated negative reactions *by* their audiences *to* the revelations of untoward behavior and find it necessary to explain and contextualize said actions in certain ways—hence, these contrivances. These are not simple lies to get away with something; they are efforts to ingratiate themselves with audiences.

In addition, different memoir authors address, seek out, or have attracted particular audiences or circles of readers. Hence, in any array of writers, the vocabulary each author uses to frame, explain, or contextualize the acts and their meaning will differ, one from another; moreover, the type of behavior in which each engages will occasion each one to construct a distinctive house of stigma verbalizations. Here, I address the processes by which some memoir authors seek to win over generic audiences; others court more specialized or *subcultural* readers, social circles, or collectivities; and still others woo those that are both generic and specialized.

I am not saying that the only motive that drives people to write memoirs, especially "deviance" memoirs, is to square accounts with their past and neutralize the stigma that readers might attach to them and their transgressive acts—but it is a major, and a powerful, motivating factor. More important is the fact that the manner in which authors narrate their transgressions, or supposed transgressions, *functions* as a mode of neutralization, regardless of why people write or utter the narrations. Readers can more readily appreciate why someone may have engaged in behavior that they regard as untoward if the author supplies an account for it, and they will condemn him or her less and like the book they are reading more. The more readers know about the specifics of the acts in question, *as they are interpreted by the author,* the more empathetic they feel about the enactment of the behavior and the actor and the less judgmental they are about both. I argue that what sociologists refer to as "deviance neutralization" should be hugely expanded to include factors that make for emotional identification with the actor and causal and descriptive accounts given by the actor for why the behavior was enacted and what it was like. These may be literary or storytelling devices—but they *serve* to mitigate condemnation of the narrator/actor.

* * *

SHORT OF READING every memoir and autobiography ever published, how does the conscientious researcher find a few dozen interesting but more or less representative pebbles strewn along this seemingly endless stretch of beach? Diane Bjorklund, a sociologist, examined over a hundred autobiographies published during the past two centuries so that she could lay bare society's efforts to define the self (1998). In conducting her research, she systematically selected a random sample of volumes from a well-defined and clearly laid-out universe of books. Contrarily, I have not followed a systematic selection process, short of choosing from among those that fall into the "deviance" genre, sociologically speaking. Frankly, my selection was somewhat haphazard. I have stuck with American memoirs, and I have chosen the fairly well-known over the obscure and the fairly recent over older samples; the median date of publication for the volumes I examine is 2000. I have included one non-book example (a magazine article [Van Doren, 2008]—in fact, a book-length memoir in process) because it is so delectable that I felt compelled to sample the tasty feast it offers. In any case, memoir aficionados will no doubt feel that their favorite and, on my part, neglected paragons deserve attention, but with so many to choose from, this consequence is inevitable. These restrictions limit the variability of cultural convention in shaping deviance neutralization. For instance, I do not treat historical time as a factor because my time frame is so narrow, though the impact of how history plays a role in the shaping of both narrating and exculpating deviance would constitute a fruitful and enlightening line of inquiry.

A major feature of the narrative of a memoir is detail, and narrative entails *storytelling*. The same applies to deviance disavowal, which cannot be understood apart from the events of the lives that actors narrate. In the past, analysts of the exculpation of transgressive acts have ignored context, as if these verbalizations dropped down from the skies virtually intact. What their authors have avoided, some observers aver, is the *circumstances and sequence of behaviors* that led the self-absolver to downplay the seriousness or impropriety of the acts. In order to grasp how such verbal formulations come to be made, critics argue, we need to engage the unfolding of these events, as the actor interprets them, in all their fullness. This enterprise entails allowing actors to have their say in quite a bit of detail—hence my inclusion of much of the narrative of the stories they tell. Most of the authors whose memoirs I discuss are consummate storytellers, and following the tales they spin is worth the rides we take. But in addition to sharing with us their *narrative arc* (a beginning, middle, and end) our authors reveal a *process*—namely, how, when, and sometimes why they devised the mechanism of deviance neutralization. The story and its dynamic role in downplaying a social blemish are intertwined.

It seems intuitively obvious that social *context* shapes the content of deviance neutralizations. Norm violators "spin" their narratives and the justifications for their misdemeanors according to the setting in which they find themselves. Though not all the memoirs I look at here were published during the author's lifetime, and not all were written solely by the subject, all are published memoirs. Hence, the influence of setting for the rendering of *oral* accounts may have only oblique implications for accounts lodged in books; the dissimilarities of the two settings are so significant as to generate substantially different types of narrations. Even with that strictive, our accounts make up a mixed bag in terms of composition, execution, and production. As I said, only one (Charles Van Doren's) is a less-than-book-length confession, though the author says he is working on a full memoir (Anonymous, 2008, and personal communication). Four (the memoirs of Jim Bouton, Joe Bonanno, William Cope Moyers, and Malcolm X) were coauthored with or edited by a journalist or professional writer. For instance, Malcolm X's amanuensis, Alex Haley, toned down the radicalism and anti-Semitism of the subject's narrative (Biddle, 2011), as I discuss in Chapter 7. It is entirely possible that John Herman, Bonanno's editor, and Sergio Lalli, his collaborator, toned down Joe's elaboration of the heinousness of his own crimes. One (Abbott's memoir) is a gathered-together collection of articles first published in a literary magazine, and one (Kirk Read's) was originally self-published and then picked up by a major commercial house. The remainder were produced by means of the more conventional route, though some were put out by large, commercial houses (e.g., Susan Cheever's), while others were issued by smaller, more specialized publishers (e.g., Cathy Wilkerson's).

It seems almost superfluous to say that the relationship between the editor and the writer is crucial in shaping and producing the final manuscript. Though authors tend to be a feisty, independent-minded bunch, editors and publishers are acutely aware that publishing is a commercial enterprise, and any author who puts on a sour, cynical, or excessively reprehensible face on the page is likely to be told by the publishing "gatekeepers" that changes need to be made. Nonetheless, self-exculpation is the inevitable offspring of a confluence of multiple forces, and here I focus on the author as agent. A study of the role of editors and publishers in adapting the content and tone of deviance authors' memoirs would be worthwhile, and I invite the critical reader to conduct such a study; I would read it.

Hence, it is a virtual truism that what we say cannot be removed from time and place; circumstance must be factored into the equation. Making a certain statement is partly dependent on *the circumstances* under which we make it. What we say here would never be uttered there, and vice versa. A statement is not a simple reflection of who we are, brought out of us like a vial of blood; it is rendered by the narrator under stipulated circumstances. This generalization is self-evidently true and goes almost without saying. Gresham Sykes and David Matza's well-known discussions of deviance neutralization among juveniles (1957) make no mention of circumstance; their analysis is virtually *contextless.* We have no idea how these two sociologists reached the conclusions they drew; neither author refers to his own research and, though they cite a few boilerplate slogans that anyone might make in neutralizing conventional norms, they quote no actual juvenile delinquents. Certainly *written* deviance disavowals are likely to be quite different from *oral* ones, if only because authors have more space, especially in the book-length memoir, to flesh out a verbal defense of their actions (Kahl, 1984). Lois Presser (2004, p. 82) insists that different social settings elicit very different narratives about the self—one does not *have* a life story, she argues; one *makes* one, within a particular context. True enough. Still, Mary Kahl and Lois Presser do not offer a systematic comparison among the apologies that different settings are likely to elicit. And it is difficult to imagine any sensible research program that would have drawn out of Presser's violent offenders a Little Boy Blue image—though she does admit that the accounts she generated are "tethered" to the brute facts of her respondents' lives. Other things being equal, virtually all life narrators manifest a systematic tendency to underplay or explain away the horrendous atrocities they have committed, but the issue of *how* and *where* they narrate their tales does *not* produce unlimited variation. We take it for granted that context counts (Presser, 2004; Agnew and Peters, 1986) and move on to more substantial matters.

Apologies are widely understood to represent an acknowledgment, by an actor, of having committed a transgression, along with an expression of regret at having done so. They are likely to work *to the extent that* the offender promises not to commit the same sin in the future, convinces audiences (especially the offended) that the apology is sincere, is observed as having suffered, and establishes a meaningful dialogue with the offended (Lazare, 2004). Apologies represent a particular subtype of deviance neutralization device; they are an attempt to wipe the slate clean and start again on the basis of a ritual of debasement of the offender. At the same time, because observers, especially victims, are on the lookout for an insincere or phony apology, their devisers are motivated to fashion convincing-sounding ones. But first they have to satisfy *themselves* that they are convincing, by making a sincere effort in this fashioning process to inhabit the skin of the other. But the point is that not all deviance neutralization devices are apologies, and not all persons who have offended others think that they have done anything wrong—nonetheless, they know that *others* about whom, presumably, they care in one way or another will object to what they did and said. Herein dwells the nub of the tale that unfolds in this book.

Acknowledgments

I AM GRATEFUL to the memoir authors I interviewed—some face-to-face, some on the phone, and some via e-mail—for a different but related project: David Carkeet, Donna Gaines, Steve Geng, Richard Goodman, Jeffrey Hammond, Marya Hornbacher, James Lang, Larry O'Connor, Emily Rapp, Richard Shelton, and Gordon Shepherd. These interviews stood me in good stead while I read and analyzed the works on which this book is based. I also thank the instructors with whom I took courses on memoir, who taught me how the genre is put together: Bill Loizeaux, at Johns Hopkins University, and Pat Willard and Kelly Caldwell, at the Gotham Writers Workshop. Likewise, I am grateful to David Greenberg, Temma Kaplan, Iona Man-Cheong, and Dorrie Olds for assisting me in one way or another; Susan Cheever for her advice; and Charles Van Doren for his encouragement. My essay on Eddie Bunker originally appeared in *The Angolite,* November/December 2006. I borrowed and adapted four paragraphs from several editions of my book *Deviant Behavior.* I thank my lovely, brilliant, and charismatic wife, Barbara Weinstein, for her wisdom, insights, and patience, and my good friend Nachman Ben-Yehuda for all manner of helpful suggestions. I also thank the anonymous readers of the original manuscript of this book; their suggestions were extremely constructive, and I took them very seriously in making my revisions. Throughout this volume, I have observed the "fair use" doctrine, as I have construed it.

My weightiest debt of gratitude is to the writers whose memoirs I discuss here; I have learned enormously from them. These writers' courage in revealing the intimate, sometimes formerly secret, and potentially discreditable details of their lives sets a high bar for the rest of us.

* * *

DEAR AUTHORS, please, *please,* understand that I am not the one who refers to what you did as "deviant"; *you, yourselves,* are telling *us* that others, persons whom you designate, regarded your behavior or your views as unacceptable, worthy of condemnation and punishment—in short, however mistaken, a form of deviance. These critics expressed disapproval of your behavior, and so you wrote accounts of your lives—"apologias"—that defended you against that disapproval. You do not necessarily use the exact word "deviant" (Jim Bouton does, but he received a lecture from his wife, a social scientist, about the significance of the condemnation he experienced), though from a sociologist's perspective, you use the exact *meaning* of that word. I *observe* that self-reference, take note of it, and write about it; *I* am not labeling you—you have *already* expressed that you have been so labeled. Perhaps you mistakenly conflate the popular and clearly archaic connotations of the word with its contemporary sociological meaning; what I emphasize throughout this book is that these two meanings are not the same. I admire your courage and candidness, and I am extremely grateful to you for supplying me, possibly against your will, with your literary material so that I may make *sociological* use of it. I am extremely respectful of that material, of your talent, and of you, you writers, even though you did not create your work for what must seem to you an incomprehensibly strange and esoteric purpose.

Justifiable Conduct

1
Introduction

THOUGH NARRATING life stories is a universal human enterprise, such tales are expected to unfold in a certain way and according to certain conventions. Memoirs represent *accounts* rather than *reflections* of reality. And yet, they offer a stand-alone *dimension* of reality. The reality they present *is* the constructed account. You would be wise to be suspicious of the assertion, in that presidential memoir you're reading, that the chief executive never lied to the American people—but the fact that the author *said* it is a fact, and a reality in its own right. All humans tell stories about their lives because, as social creatures, we are quintessentially empathetic: We anticipate reactions from our audiences and attune our behavior accordingly. Hence, we tell stories *in a certain way.* True, some of us miscalculate and become crashing bores—narrating stories only the narrator finds interesting—or sickeningly offensive, but the enterprise of storytelling tilts more toward narrators who anticipate and take into account audience reactions. *Which* audience we address is an essential element of the equation, but *an* audience, *some* audience, nonetheless. If we anticipate that during our telling, particulars of an event will put us in distinctly bad odor with audiences whose opinion we care about, we ignore those details, or lie about them, or narrate them and then offer an explanation or justification for engaging in or chronicling them. In spite of their bad odor, we may be motivated to disclose such details anyway because they are more interesting than bland, cardboard cutouts that do not offend. And memoir and autobiography brim with recitations of self-exculpation for one's sins and transgressions; they carry the tale forward, bring the audience into the narration, and lift a sickly pallor from the narrator's person. Some of our life stories are written with a specific audience in mind, while the authors of others imagine a more generic audience—but all entail picturing a writer-to-reader communication.

And yet, not all self-exculpations are created equal; they represent a coat of many colors, and their variety is as revealing as their overriding mission. It might seem contradictory to say that in *violating* social norms, narrators *conform* to the norms, but that is true. To introduce how deviance memoirs are narrated, I would like to introduce an erstwhile dishonest quiz show contestant and a washed-up baseball player. The tales these two tell exemplify the *spin* autonarrators put on their accounts of wrongdoing by engaging self-absolution before a potentially critical audience. These illustrations manifest both the generic and the idiosyncratic character of instances of deviance neutralization.

Charles Van Doren, "Herb Stempel Was the First to Agree to the Fix"

During the summer of 1955, CBS Television launched a quiz program it called *The $64,000 Question,* which proved an immediate and enormous success, capturing, at one point during its initial season, 85 percent of its time slot's audience. Within four years of *Question*'s first broadcast, Revlon, the show's sponsor, had multiplied its profits by ten times. Network executives scrambled to produce more of the same, and by 1958, CBS, NBC, and ABC were broadcasting two dozen quiz programs a week. But the soil that produced this rich harvest also hatched corruption, scandal, and, eventually—worst of all from the networks' perspective—cancellations.

On the night of September 10, 1956, NBC produced its own version of a prime-time quiz show, *Twenty-One.* The initial broadcast honestly and fairly pit one contestant against another, and may the most knowledgeable contestant win. It proved a disaster, the contestants embarrassingly revealing their predictable and inevitable broad patches of ignorance. The sponsor, Geritol, a vitamin tonic, threatened to pull the plug on the show. NBC producers decided to "fix" *Twenty-One* by coaching its contestants, feeding them answers, and prearranging winners and losers.

The quiz show rigging raises the following inevitable question: Why did producers and contestants alike, willingly, some, almost unthinkingly, dive into the cesspool, only to emerge, stinking, humiliated, humbled, forced to answer sharp, probing questions from friends, relatives, district attorneys, grand juries, even congressional committees? And why did the producers so blatantly rig the show, bringing the whole enterprise crashing to the ground?

Why did you do it? How could you have been so *stupid*? The simplest and most obvious answer—"money"—is too glib. In any case, even if it had been the major motivating factor—it was—that was not a sufficient justification, at least in the eyes of audiences who sought redemptive apologies from transgressors. The contestants did not want to seem *in the audience's eyes* quite so venal and crass. Other, very different answers were likely to—and did—tumble from their lips or issue from their typewriters and pens. *How did they justify what they did?* More specifically, since he was the most visible and puzzling figure in the drama, how did *Charles Van Doren* neutralize the deviance of his collaboration in the cheating scheme and explain his elaborate lying about it afterward? The answers he offered in congressional testimony in 1959 and in a *New Yorker* article almost half a century later (2008) prove revealing and instructive.

Enter Herb Stempel. Among the show's early audience was one Herb Stempel, a twenty-nine-year-old undergraduate attending the City College of New York on the GI Bill. Unaware that the show had been rigged, Stempel applied to NBC to become a contestant. He scored higher on the program's qualifying exam than any other previous applicant. Dan Enright, one of *Twenty-One*'s producers, explained to Stempel that the show was dishonest and that he would have to agree, in effect, to be an actor, not a contestant, enticing him with the possibility of winning twenty-four thousand dollars; Stempel nonetheless agreed to participate. Enright taught Stempel how to act, what gestures to use, when to pause, and what answers to give and how to give them; before each broadcast, the two of them rehearsed the evening's script. Even the presentation of Stempel's character was scripted. He was supposed to come across as an oaf, a savant, and a smug know-it-all by wearing an ill-fitting suit, a cheap, loudly ticking watch, and an ugly haircut.

Van Doren's seduction. Twenty-One introduced Herb Stempel as a contestant on October 17, 1956. Not only did he win that night; his skein of victories continued until December 5. But the show's audience had reached a plateau, and the producers felt they needed a boost in the ratings. In the meantime, Charles Van Doren, then an instructor in the English department at Columbia University, had inquired about appearing on another of NBC's programs, *Tic-Tac-Dough*. Van Doren was urbane, suave, articulate, and telegenic—everything Stempel was not. Van Doren took and excelled on the entrance exam, but instead, the producers invited him to appear on *Twenty-One,* and he accepted. Before he appeared, however, one of the show's producers, Al Freedman, explained the nature of the show to him and that the current champion, Herb Stempel, was unpopular and probably unbeatable in a fair contest. To increase the entertainment value of the show, Freedman said, Van Doren would have to receive answers in advance, initially tie

Stempel, and then proceed to defeat him. Van Doren has gone on record as saying that he balked at first, then "unfortunately agreed, after some time," to Freedman's proposal (1959). Freedman offered Stempel a substantial sum of money, as well as the lure of a lucrative job, to agree to lose; Stempel agreed.

The story breaks. Stempel and Van Doren appeared on *Twenty-One* on November 28, 1956, and, as scripted, their first encounter resulted in a 21–21 tie. But it was time for Herb Stempel to get yanked off the stage, and so, on December 5, as previously agreed upon, he missed an absurdly easy question—what movie had won the Academy Award for best picture in 1955 (*Marty,* a film Stempel loved and had seen three times)—thus ending the savant's reign. But by early 1957, Stempel had spent all his money and, distressed by Van Doren's popularity and resentful that he had not been sufficiently compensated, regularly showed up at Enright's office, demanding more money. At about the same time, Edward Hilgemeier Jr., an aspiring contestant for *Dotto,* came across answers to the program's questions in the possession of one of the show's contestants. He informed a *New York Post* reporter about his discovery, but the paper refused to publish the story for lack of corroboration and fear of lawsuits. A year later, however, Stempel informed a reporter at the now defunct *New York World-Telegram* about the rigged shows, and the paper ran a news story about the same allegation. In 1959, Congress investigated the charges, questioning seventeen witnesses, among them Van Doren and Stempel, both of whom had appeared on *Twenty-One.* The investigation destroyed the quiz show empire.

Van Doren denied before a district attorney and a grand jury that he had received prearranged answers. But in November 1959, more than a year after the story broke, when he was called upon to testify before Congress, he spilled the beans about the nature of his participation in the rigged show. In so doing, Van Doren admitted to a crime—lying to a grand jury—and so was opening himself up for prosecution, conviction, and imprisonment. Clearly he gave his congressional testimony in exchange for immunity from prosecution. Eventually, all the other contestants, also perjured, confessed; none was prosecuted for a crime, and none served any jail or prison time.

Who could have imagined that Charles Van Doren, in the words of *The New York Times* (July 21, 2008), would plummet from *Time* magazine cover boy to "tabloid humiliation as one of the most reviled men in America"?

Van Doren neutralizes. NBC's producers' excellent sense of theater aside—a genuine, live television quiz show is *boring,* while a fake show such as *Twenty-One* is exciting, dramatic, and profitable—what does Van Doren, the most famous of the program's contestants, have to say about his collusion in dishonesty? What neutralizations does he use? Here's how Van Doren explains his decision to participate in the rigged quiz show in his testimony to the House Committee on Interstate and Foreign Commerce, Investigation of Television Quiz Shows, in November 1959 (http://historymatters.gmu.edu/d/6566). Note that in 1958, Van Doren lied to the press ("It's silly and distressing to think that people don't have more faith in quiz shows"), lied to Manhattan District Attorney Joseph Stone, and lied to the grand jury investigating the case. While the facts of the matter of his testimony are likely to be true—he was, after all, under oath and subject to prosecution for perjury—the more subjective aspects of his statement are less verifiable. But in a sense, whether or not he is telling the truth about how he feels regarding the malfeasances he committed is not the central issue. We can never know how he felt at the time of the occurrence of these events or at the time when he testified before the congressional subcommittee (November 1959) or at the time of the writing of his 2008 *New Yorker* article. The house of contrition Van Doren builds is a construction of materials lying at hand. *Of course,* Van Doren is contrite: He got caught, and his relevant others—his vast audience, his academic peers, his family—disapproved of his cheating and subsequent lying about it. Still, this house of contrition holds many rooms, and the configuration of each is distinctive and tells us a great deal about its builder.

Van Doren testifies in his congressional testimony that Albert Freedman, a producer at *Twenty-One,* told him that Herbert Stempel, the current champion, was unpopular, was defeating opponents "left and right," which hurt the program, and so the sponsors wanted Van Doren to defeat Stempel (2008, p. 63). As a favor to him, Van Doren said Freedman told him, he would tie Stempel and thus increase the entertainment value of the program. "Do they have a right to do that?" Van Doren asked. "Hey, come off it, Charlie," Freedman chided. "Don't be naïve" (p. 64).

Freedman ran through Stempel's drawbacks as a contestant. Though his answers seemed based on "genuine knowledge," his "posture and gestures were awkward, his clothes were too tight . . . his speech was wooden. . . . I've thought about it, Charlie," Freedman said, "and I've decided that you should be the person to beat Stempel. And I'll help you do it" (p. 64).

Freedman requested Van Doren's cooperation in the rigging scheme as it were a virtue rather than a vice, but his next statement contradicts that and attempts to exonerate his virtue. He says he asked Freedman to let him go on the program "honestly, without receiving help." Freedman said that was impossible. "He told me that I would not have a chance to defeat Stempel because he was too knowledgeable. He also told me that the show was merely entertainment and that giving help to quiz contestants was a common practice and merely part of show business." Van Doren's next sentence is significant: "*This of course is not true, but perhaps I wanted to believe him*" (1959; my emphasis). It was one among an array of armaments Charles used in attempting to justify what followed. Even more interestingly, and perhaps more revealingly, Van Doren stretched his vice-as-virtue justification to embrace the academic community at large: Freedman, Van Doren said, emphasized that by appearing on a nationwide television program he "would be doing a great service to the intellectual life, to teachers and to education in general, by increasing public respect for the work of the mind through my performances" (1959).

Van Doren's account of Van Doren versus Stempel. In this quiz show rigging drama, notice that Al Freedman is the *corruptor* and Van Doren and Herb Stempel are the *corruptees.* We can, however, locate substantial differences between the latter two in the *degree* and *kind* of corruption to which they succumbed. Van Doren's corruption is somewhat more surprising because, in principle, he had so much more to lose: He was forced to resign his instructorship at Columbia; he was fired from a profitable job as a cultural correspondent on the *Today* show; and his malfeasance disappointed his family, friends, and academic peers, not to mention his fans and admirers. In contrast, Stempel's employment as a Transit Authority employee was not imperiled by his admissions; he was able to complete his education on the GI Bill (Stempel was an ex-Marine), and he became what he had set out to become, a New York City schoolteacher. In addition, NBC executives offered him several jobs, which did not pan out. Interestingly, however, both men landed on their feet since, like Stempel, Van Doren completed his education—a Ph.D. in English at Columbia—and went on to work as an editor, ghostwriter, and, eventually, author at several respectable publishers, mainly the Encyclopedia Britannica and Praeger, and eventually settled into semi-retirement as an adjunct professor at the University of Connecticut at Torrington. Risk and post-scandal recovery aside, Van Doren collected the lion's share of the show's loot: $128,000 to Stempel's $50,000, not to mention vastly more than the lion's share of media and public attention, fame, adoration, and adulation. (Van Doren claims he never expected the acclaim—or as much money—and of course, *after* the scandal broke, that attention turned as sour as spoiled milk.) But Van Doren's corruption is most easily measured by the fact that, until the congressional investigation, he never intended to report the cheating; as we saw, he had already issued false statements to the press, committed perjury to a grand jury, and lied to a DA. He was dismayed by Stempel's exposure of the rigging by blabbing to the press; *he,* Charles Van Doren, scion of an American intellectual family, would not have done such a thing. In his eyes, going to the press was vulgar, unseemly, and exhibitionistic; it displayed a lack of character.

By imagizing his corrupters and Stempel as more eager than himself, and himself as the corruptee, Van Doren offers a kind of neutralization rationale that amounts to both an apology and a justification. His choice of words is subtle and yet persuasive. It forces an angle of vision on the reader that focuses the fault on NBC, generates empathy for his own wrongdoing, and throws a harsh, angular, Weegee-like spotlight on Stempel and his deeds, as if he had captured the hapless savant groping around in a dark room for tender, innocent victims. Van Doren's mission is two-fold. Rather, it is one two-part mission whose first objective is to portray Stempel in an unflattering light in order—and this is the interlocking second part of the mission—to depict himself as positively as possible. Nowhere does Van Doren sketch out any mutuality with his peer, co-conspirator, and fellow corruptee. The point is to make the contrast as sharp as possible; in his memoir, he and his acts appear in a more flattering light when contrasted with the harshness of Stempel's sleazy character and deeds. Van Doren depicts himself as a principled but flawed gentleman, and Stempel, a bumbling, ethically shoddy species of humanity.

By portraying Stempel's NBC-coached appearance and performance, Van Doren ratifies the man's untrustworthiness; by describing in detail what Stempel had to do to portray the "unsympathetic and unattractive" personality NBC had hired him to play, Van Doren shows us that Herb *is* an unsympathetic and unattractive personality. Charles's description *imparts* such qualities to Stempel that the man *becomes* a sweaty, vulgar lout—and duplicitous to boot for acting so. Quite the contrary, Van Doren's pose is not a pose at all. His job is to portray a contestant who is sympathetic and attractive—suave, urbane, knowledgeable, from an illustrious family, and professorial in an Ivy League sort of way—all qualities he *already* possessed. His act, if it could be said to be an act at all, was to play himself. His performance earned him a *Time* magazine cover (complete with the superimposed earphones he wore in the glass contestant booth), dates with movie starlets, and women clamoring at his door to meet him (2008, p. 64). Stempel's character is tainted by Van Doren's description while Van Doren's is exculpated; the counterpoint is startling and revealing. As Van Doren almost sheepishly admits, a critic at the time wrote that his "was a remarkable and seductive performance" (p. 64).

In 1958, after stories about the quiz show rigging began appearing in several New York newspapers, Van Doren had lunch with Al Freedman, the NBC producer who had first approached the bumbling pundit. Freedman mentioned that Dan Enright, an NBC executive, had said that Stempel was "crazy." Enright, said Freedman, knows damning things about Stempel, "psychiatric treatment, threats, all sorts of things" (p. 66). Because of the juxtaposition in the same column of type of the media revelations and Stempel's alleged psychiatric status, the reader is left to believe that there is some relationship between the two—that only a mentally unstable person would reveal to the world his participation in such a fraud. And yet it is ironic—given the fact that Stempel blew the whistle—that, says Van Doren, "Herb Stempel was the first to agree to the fix" (p. 68). Without Van Doren spelling it out, the reader is left to wonder about Stempel's hypocrisy. Equally telling, when Robert Redford was making *Quiz Show,* his 1994 motion picture depiction of the scandal, he sent Van Doren a contract to agree to serve as a consultant; Van Doren declined the deal, turning down a hundred thousand dollar fee, and Herb Stempel did not: "The contract lay on the table in the kitchen. I picked it up and tore it into pieces" (p. 69). The message is clear: Charles Van Doren is an ethical, high-minded man; Herb Stempel is not. We receive Stempel's side of the story from a popular literary magazine and, in an earlier version, buried in congressional testimony delivered over half a century ago (http://historymatters.gmu.edu/d/6565), so it is Van Doren, and not Stempel, who possesses both access to the educated reading public and the capacity to fashion a well-written, urbane account that the public deems plausible and valid. Hence, it is Van Doren's account, not Stempel's, that will be regarded as legitimate and definitive: In short, we take it as the truth. And his account is as close to exoneration as he is likely to receive. In it, he comes off as a decent, well-meaning, and honorable but fallible human being, who trusted the wrong people and succumbed to an emotionally understandable temptation—a jam in which virtually all of us could have found ourselves trapped.

Jim Bouton, "If We Explain We're Shooting Beaver, They'll Understand"

Jim Bouton was a Major League pitcher (1962–1970, 1978) who had one great and one good season (1963 and 1964) with the New York Yankees (a won-lost record of 21–7 and 18–13, respectively, and 2–1 in the World Series), but he hung on long after his pitching arm had deserted him. His lifetime career record was 62–63, with an ERA (earned run average) of 3.57. At the invitation of the sports writer Leonard Shecter, during the 1969 season, pitching with the soon-to-be defunct Seattle Pilots and later, the Houston Astros, Bouton took notes and, after the season was over, collaborated with Shecter in writing *Ball Four,* a record of his season's baseball and extracurricular activities, along with observations about the sport, its players, and life in general (1970). In 1978, years after the book was published, he appeared in five games with the Atlanta Braves. The book, insightful, ironic, and amusing, sold hundreds of thousands of copies in hardback and several million in paper and went into multiple editions, including *Ball Four Plus Ball Five* (1985) and *Ball Four: The Final Pitch* (2000). Bouton followed his baseball career with sports broadcasting, first with CBS and then with ABC, from which positions he was fired. He appeared as an actor in a Hollywood movie, *The Long Goodbye*

(1973), and co-developed and marketed "Big League Chew," a type of bubble gum that resembled chewing tobacco, which proved to be extremely profitable. But among people who worked with and wrote about him, Bouton continues to be a controversial figure.

As measured by the attention it has received, Jim Bouton's *Ball Four,* along with its subsequent reissues, is the most important baseball book—some say the most important sports book—ever written. Hundreds of newspapers and sports magazines reviewed it, and hundreds of sports figures have publicly commented on its author and his veracity. The book amassed a subsequent paper—and, later, electronic—trail that became an immense, turbulent sea of observation, opinion, and commentary, perhaps more vituperation than praise. *Ball Four* addresses human nature as much as baseball; it is about how baseball *expresses* human nature. Baseball is an allegory for life, Bouton says, and its players are neither better nor worse than the rest of us. Baseball stars are revered as heroes, even demigods, but even the best of us have feet of clay and one does the society no disservice for making that observation. After the revelations in *Ball Four,* Bouton tells us, sportswriters were unable to peddle the inoffensive "milk and cookies" image of baseball and its players that had then prevailed (1985, p. xiii).

But in the short run, telling the truth proved costly for the author, the midwife of this transition. Bouton became a "deviant," a "social leper," a "turncoat," a "traitor," and a "liar" (pp. 406–408). He violated the norm, "don't say anything bad about baseball" (p. 50). Someone hung a sign in the Milwaukee Brewers' and the Minnesota Twins' clubhouse that read, "What you say here, what you see here, what you do here, and what you hear here, let it stay here" (p. 219). In response, Bouton rhetorically asks, "If I were a C.I.A. man, could I write a book?" (p. 219). The answer is, of course not, no, you couldn't. But while the rules that apply to employees and former employees of the C.I.A. are contractual and legal, those applying to Major League Baseball are social and informal.

By today's standards, Bouton's sins seem small. At the time, 1970, the anti-"milk and cookies" message of *Ball Four* sounded positively revolutionary. Baseball owners' objections to Bouton's revelations centered on players' rights, his challenge to owners' authority, and his attempt to undermine their dominion determining players' salaries and the owners' entitlement to deny players the right to discuss their own salaries. The reader might be tempted to conclude that Bouton was on the side of the players and hence, they ought to endorse, not excoriate, his book, but *Ball Four* was mainly about public image, not free speech or economic rights. What players and other personnel objected to was that the book *made them look bad.* One or more players in the San Diego Padres organization, Bouton says, "burned the book and left the charred remains for me to find in the visitors' dugout" (p. xi). Pete Rose, then an infielder for the Cincinnati Reds (and barred from the Hall of Fame because of his involvement in gambling), stood on the top step of the visitors' dugout in Houston and screamed, "Fuck you, Shakespeare!" (p. xi). Bowie Kuhn announced that Bouton had done the game of baseball "a grave disservice" (p. x). Bouton tells us he has never been invited to Yankees Old Timers' Days, exhibition games when former players compete on the field with one another. "Understand, everybody gets invited back for Old Timers' Day no matter what kind of rotten person he was when he was playing. Muggers, drug addicts, rapists, child molesters, all are forgiven for Old Timers' Day. Except a certain author" (p. xi). In 1998, Bouton's son Michael, then a philosophy student at Hunter College, sent a letter to *The New York Times* describing the ballplayer's anguish over the death of his daughter Laurie the previous year. Michael begged the Yankees to honor Bouton on Father's Day, which management agreed to do, ending a nearly quarter-century exile.

From the point of view of image, Bouton sinned on multiple fronts. First, there was what he said about ballplayers' use of "greenies" or "pep pills," otherwise known as dextroamphetamine sulphate or Dexedrine, a type of amphetamine or "uppers." Bouton's sin was not merely revealing that baseball players illegally and routinely used amphetamine, and on a widespread basis; it was also the casual acceptance of the use of the drug in Major League Baseball that seemed surprising to the reader. A player (whom Bouton identifies) asks, "How fabulous are greenies?" Clearly the author shares baseball's acceptance of pep pills because his reply is, "The answer is very" (p. 81). When another player (whom he also names) pitched in his former ballpark, he received a standing ovation. In honor of the occasion, he swallowed three greenies. "They didn't do a bit of good" (p. 168). When one of his teammates receives a supply of five hundred greenies, Bouton responds, "They ought to last about a month" (p. 211). Bouton quotes a source to the effect that, at the time, more than half of Major League players took amphetamines, including nearly all of the Baltimore Orioles, most of the Tigers, and most of the players on the Seattle Pilots (which moved after one year to Milwaukee and was renamed the Brewers), Bouton's team (p. 212). A teammate (again, whom he identifies) flew into a rage after being called out on strikes. He stormed off the field, entered the clubhouse, kicked over the water cooler, and threw its metal cover onto the field. When asked what had gotten into him, he responds, "Just when I got called out on strikes, my greenie kicked in" (p. 221).

Then there was the beaver shooting. "Beaver shooting" refers to peeping at or ogling women to get a better look at their anatomy, usually up their skirt or down their cleavage. The activity could be done from the field or from a hotel window or roof, often with binoculars or, occasionally, a telescope.

Unlike taking greenies, beaver shooting has nothing to do with on-the-diamond performance—indeed, it seems singularly juvenile, almost masturbatory—but Bouton is remarkably candid about the participation of his peers, including himself, in this puerile activity. The Shoreham Hotel in Washington, he claims at the time (1969), was "the beaver-shooting capital of the world." A teammate (named) retorts, "You could stock a whole league" with those guys (p. 37). Shooting some particularly desirable beaver, says Bouton, brought respect and prestige to the enterprising Peeping Tom. He claims that, when Bouton first became a Yankee, Mickey Mantle himself often led "squads" of fifteen or so teammates on beaver shooting expeditions. Bouton confesses that one of his first big thrills he received as a Yankee "was joining about half the club on the roof of the Shoreham at two-thirty in the morning" on one such expedition. He says to himself, "So this is the big leagues" (pp. 38–39). When a Seattle teammate (also named) brought a pair of binoculars to the bullpen, peered into the stands, sharing the spy-glasses with his fellow relief pitchers. When someone said they'd better stop, the umpire might think they were stealing signs, Bouton replied, "No. If we explain we're shooting beaver, they'll understand." He added, "And they would. If there's a baseball universal, that's it" (p. 245).

Why did he stir up so much anger? Why was he regarded as a "deviant"? "There had to be some explanation for the intensity and longevity of baseball's collective anger toward me" (p. 407). He formulates his answer after "a behavioral scientist" (his second wife) explained it to him. In all groups, there are norms—"shared expectations of behavior. Any member who deviates from these norms calls into question the basic values of the group." And members of groups "don't like their basic values questioned" (p. 407). What is the norm Bouton violated? It is the secrecy or "no blabbing" rule: "What you say here, what you do here, let it stay here, when you leave here." He broke that rule, and that makes him a deviant, "sociologically speaking." For rules to exist, Bouton continues, deviant members must be punished. The more intimate and "primary" the group is, the more severe the punishment will be. And the less status a deviant member has, the less tolerant the group will be toward his or her normative violations (p. 407).

Being assigned a stigmatized or "deviant" status clearly demanded a response from the author. Bouton formulated a vocabulary that neutralized the stigma implied by the hostile, derogatory statements by his critics. (He was accused of spewing "lies" and "horseshit," was called "a real prick," was told he would "make a maggot throw up" and that he would "get a punch in the mouth.") His verbalizations neutralizing his transgressions are revealing.

First, Bouton says, he did not quote some of the most damaging statements players uttered in the clubhouse—namely, their racist and anti-Semitic remarks (p. 81). Second, he says, he didn't *hurt* anyone (p. 82). Third, there was nothing secret about what he was doing. Everyone knew that Bouton was writing a book (p. 86). Fourth, if a baseball player can't write a behind-the-scenes book about what he sees and hears, who can? No politician or political writer, no actor, no doctor, and, for that matter, no novelist could (p. 87). He did it for the money? Who doesn't? What's wrong with that? And, according to Bouton, when it comes to stories about incriminating *sexual* behavior, he never names names. Stories about beaver shooting? That doesn't count; it's not incriminating (p. 88). Nothing he wrote, he says, could result in a divorce action by a ballplayer's wife. In short, Bouton seems to be saying this: *I shouldn't have been regarded as a deviant for revealing the "inside baseball" behavior of players. Grow up! The sports world is changing and I was part of that change. I helped bring down the "cookies-and-milk" image of baseball, and perhaps that's all to the good. Isn't telling the truth a virtue? Apparently not. But I didn't do anything wrong; I'm not the deviant—you guys, yes, you, the guys I'm talking about, all of you who don't want to own up to what you did and who you are, you're in the wrong,* not me. *I'm opening up a closet and exposing deviance-tainted heroism to fresh air and sunshine. What the hell's wrong with that?* The *truth* is Jim Bouton's deviance disavowal: *The guys I told the truth about are hypocrites—they deserve to be condemned, not me. Hell, I performed a service to society: No more "milk and cookies."* For most readers, Bouton's justifications are persuasive; we "honor" or "buy" his account. The reader, perusing *Ball Four,* can almost hear a chorus of fellow readers cheering him on.

The Transgressive I, the Exculpatory Account

In her discussion of the sociological literature of accounts, Terri Orbuch (1997) addresses the issue of *why* people utter or write accounts justifying, explaining, excusing, or warranting their behavior. The earliest sociological literature on accounts argued that people attempt to expiate the condemnation audiences are likely to direct toward them for having committed untoward behavior (Sykes and Matza, 1957; Scott and Lyman, 1968; Hewitt and Stokes, 1975; Stokes and Hewitt, 1976). I draw on the literature that stresses self-exculpation as a motive for, or at least an accompaniment of, rendering accounts. The account is my oyster—it is what I am interested in here—elucidating it is my mission. To me, the behavior in question is the writing of the accounts themselves; they are data, as documents in the material world that demand sociological investigation and understanding. Accounts are *social constructions*; the sociologists who study them are interested in how they are put together and infused with meaning.

It seems almost self-evident that what we encounter, on the page, when we read a memoir is not "the writer" but *how the writer wishes to appear to others.* As Diane Bjorklund (1998) says, autobiographers "use vocabularies of the self in their attempts to impress readers that they are persons to be admired by contemporary standards. . . . They are trying to persuade their audience that they are a particular kind of self—a self worthy of dignity" (p. 13). It is also likely that autobiographers and memoir writers are influenced by a *status* factor: The higher their status within a collectivity, or the society generally, the more latitude they are permitted among their peers, the more seriously they can violate the norms without recrimination, the more confident they are in their dignity and status, and the less they have to "work" to neutralize the wrongdoing of their untoward actions. But what happens when there is a bump in the road, a pebble in the shoe, a pitch on the ship's deck—some untoward facts that nonetheless need explaining away, some inconvenient facts that detract from the narrator's dignity or worthiness? How does the actor-author address these inconvenient facts, interpret them, explain them, and, if need be, justify them? By asking this question, we shine a light on *the deviant account as a sociological document.* Clearly, the memoir writer is not our typical deviant actor, and not all persons who engage in condemnation-worthy behavior write memoirs—though many have. Hence, how our memoir writers address their supposed malfeasances is tied up in the writing process. Being literate, self-reflective, and insightful enables people with those qualities to write memoirs and present a more or less socially presentable image, barring those who do not possess them from from doing so. Moreover, publication represents a series of hurdles that allow relatively few writers to arrive at the finish line, printed copies of the book in hand; not all authors of written narratives that explicate deviance and its neutralizations are successful in getting their work published. All of this is true. But here I am interested in how memoir writers neutralize, justify, explain, or self-exculpate their wrongdoing or supposed wrongdoing *in* their published life narratives, *as* they present these verbalizations to the book reader. There are more efficient means of studying deviance neutralization than through memoir, but as for me, I have chosen the most engrossing, gratifying, and, I hope, illuminating route. I would like you, the reader, to embark on my mission with me.

2

Autobiography and Memoir

WHEN DID AUTONARRATION—the chronicling of one's own life stories, or memoir and autobiography—begin? The origin of such complex social practices and institutions is usually lost in the mists of time; moreover, *what the question means* is not as straightforward as it seems. "Telling one's life story"—the *meaning* of what that entails—is exquisitely bound up by historical time, society, culture, and social location; even the seemingly simple act of self-expression is a socially constructed product. But ancient historical materials that are *autobiography-like* do survive. (Of course, the antiquity of strictly *oral* narration of life stories cannot be known.) People in all literate eras have written diaries, journals, accounts, confessions, chronicles, family histories, personal histories, observations, commentaries, letters, "vitae," cautionary tales, reports, apologies, narratives, travels—writings that today we would call autobiographical in nature, though what is *included* in them varies by time and place. By contemporary lights, how focused on the details of the author's own life, and how true to literal autobiographical fact, does an account have to be to for it to be classified as a memoir or autobiography? How many particulars and how much reflection on that life earns a work the right to be referred to as *an* autobiography? How long does an autonarration have to be to qualify?

Late in the 1200s, Dante wrote commentaries on his own love sonnets and lyrics to Beatrice and collected them together as a book, *La Vita Nuova*; was that *an* autobiography? Most observers do not think so—too much poetry and commentary on it, not enough narrative details of a life.

The Travels of Marco Polo, set down in the early fourteenth century, was noteworthy mainly for the author's supposed reports of the societies he visited rather than for the life he led. As to length, in addition to several works on the history of the Jews in the Roman world, Flavius Josephus (37–100 C.E.) is also the author of his own twenty-five-thousand-word "autobiography" or "life"—a fragment, to be sure, but a tantalizing one. Leonor López de Córdoba (ca. 1362–1427) wrote her *Memórias* or "Autobiografia," in which she states, "All that is written here is true, for I saw it and it happened to me"—a powerful autobiographical statement—but the surviving fragment of the manuscript of this memoir is but a nine-page English translation.

Georg Misch, a German philosopher, traces hundreds of precursors to modern autobiography, including Egyptian tomb inscriptions, records of deeds of Babylonian and Assyrian rulers, first-person life narrative in "ancient Oriental tales," Greek autobiographical oration in court, Hellenistic political memoirs, and chronicles of military campaigns by Roman generals. None of these are personal or contain much in the way of self-reflection. The term "autobiography," Misch tells us, did not appear until the end of the 1700s, and "who coined it is unknown" (1950, p. 5). He emphasizes that the autonarration of one's life is contingent on certain cultural prerequisites, including the sensibility that each member of a society possesses a sense of uniqueness, an *identity* that sets everyone distinctly apart from everyone else, that each one of us is the seat of an individual consciousness. Moreover, he adds, the narrator must hold a conception of a life that is capable of stepping back, viewing that life as both subject and object, and narrate its ongoing developments to that point. What is necessary, he concludes, is "a man's need for self-revelation," which is so broad and comprehensive as to encompass a wide range of ancient expressions (p. 9).

For the most part, what the ancient world did not boast were the requisites of a social structure that could have produced and sustained the *volume* of our contemporary paradigmatic, book-length life stories: a large and diverse population, widespread literacy, commercialism, a huge wellspring of widely available disposable income, self-consciousness, and a democratic, populist ethic, generating the notion that each person is special. While brief autobiographical statements were not uncommon in the ancient world, what *was* uncommon was a flow of coherent, book-length discussions focused largely on one's life; that is, in societies around the world, and in the ancient and medieval West, autobiography was not an *established literary form.* In that respect, most informed observers believe, Augustine's *The Confessions* (ca. 400 C.E.) was unusual for its time, and unique among surviving documents.

Interestingly, Misch does not mention Chinese sources. Wu (1990) discusses the question of whether any early Chinese writings can be considered autobiographical; he concludes that it depends on one's definition. We have to consider several issues. First, as to POV, or point of view: For the most part, throughout most of China's history, "self-written biographies" were told in the third person; hence, the subject, though technically the author, wrote about him- or herself as if he or she were someone other than the author. Second, as to facticity: Many of these early self-written biographies were ironic, not a portrait but a pose, an attempt at cultivating an image that was often considerably at variance with reality. Third, as to genre: Chinese literature was rich in forms of writing that paralleled but differed from biography and autobiography, such as genealogical charts, clan records, commentaries on one's ancestors, poetry, anecdotes, self-written necrology, historiography, annals, travel writings, sayings, Buddhist testimonies, chronicles of spiritual development, Neo-Confucian exhortations, Taoist admonishments, imaginary trials, letters, and so on. Fourth, as to subjectivity: Until the twentieth century, Chinese autobiographies "recorded external events," but "seldom tried to probe inner stirrings or disclose complex motives" (Wu, 1990, p. xi). And last, as to length: Nearly all of these early autobiography-like writings were brief, though some were chapters buried within books. Nothing on the scale or detail of Augustine's *Confessions* existed in ancient China; no diary that introduced subjectivity or emotionality existed until the fifteenth century, and no spiritual autobiography was produced there until the sixteenth century.

Tacitus (55–117 C.E.) insists that numerous figures in the ancient Greek and Roman world recounted full, possibly book-length, accounts of their lives, but as with so much material that was produced in that era, these manuscripts have long since perished. The *Commentaries* of Caesar (written about 50 B.C.E.), sometimes mentioned as a candidate for the earliest memoir, is told in the third person and focuses entirely on the Roman military campaign against Gaul. In a like manner, Libanius (314–394 C.E.) penned a manuscript that some observers refer to as an "autobiography" (Misch, 1950, pp. 554–563), but it is made up mainly of a series of orations or rhetorical exercises. Instead, St. Augustine's *Confessions* is told in the first person, covers a major portion of the chronology of the author's life, and concerns a personal, spiritual struggle of a man to find God—an autonarration of specific events in a man's life that infuse this struggle with significance. Unarguably, Augustine's *The Confessions* constitutes the oldest surviving equivalent to the modern memoir (Hampl, 1999, pp. 166–183; Yagoda, 2009, p. 15). It is fair to say that Augustine virtually *invented* what we now refer to as autobiography.

St. Augustine of Hippo (358–430 C.E.) was born into a Latinized North African Berber family. His father, Patricius, was a pagan until his conversion shortly before his death; his mother, Monica, a Christian, exerted a strong influence on his spiritual development. Early on, Augustine took up Manichaeism, a Zoroastrian philosophy that featured an eternal struggle between good and evil. He describes his youth as wild, given to idleness, hedonism, and theft; he fell in with a circle of young men who were obsessed with sex, he himself having maintained a long-term relationship with a concubine, a union that produced an out-of-wedlock child. An outstanding student, Augustine taught rhetoric in Milan, where he met the renowned St. Ambrose. Realizing the limitations of his materialist philosophy, Augustine succumbed to Christianity and was baptized by Ambrose in 387 C.E. *The Confessions,* completed about 400 C.E., recounts the author's struggle to overcome a sinful past, his embarkation onto the path of righteousness, and the affirmation of his devotion to God.

The Confessions, which imparted to the medieval Christian era an unmistakable aura of faith and piety, not only is the earliest surviving book-length memoir. It also represents an outstanding example of an effort to narrate the transformation of a formerly transgressive life into a virtuous, pious one, laying out steps along a teleological pathway to righteousness; emphasize how far the author has come to arrive at his present circumstance; and, by way of contrast, accentuate said virtue and piousness. It is one of the most influential volumes ever published; the Questa Library lists over six thousand books on or about St. Augustine's *The Confessions.* Its central argument is based on *redemption* through a negation of a corrupted past. The "I" I was, Augustine explains to God (and the reader), is not the "I" (or the "me") I am now; I reject that former "I" as illegitimate. I have been transformed, transmogrified, as it were, and am now a different "I," which is my true and valid self. I have realized the error of my ways and have cast off that former, corrupt, inauthentic self and have become new and whole. I abase myself before you, my God, and beg you to accept who I truly am. I now "blush to remember" (400 C.E./1963, p. 50) who I was before—a wretch among wretches, loving the company of wretches. "I boiled over in my fornications," Augustine declares (p. 41), "I was on fire to take my fill of hell . . . unable to distinguish between the clear calm of love and the swirling mists of lust" (p. 40). In his defense, he pleads prior ignorance, and present enlightenment, and implores God to acknowledge this transformation. Augustine states that he "wallowed in the mud of the pit and in the darkness of falsehood" and God "stretched out" his hand "from on high and drew my soul out of that deep darkness" (pp. 66–67). He invokes the voice of a child who constantly repeated the words, "Take it and read it" (p. 182), which he interprets as a command to read the Gospels. Augustine's rhetoric effectively reenacts his conversion in the form of bodily experiences that enable the reader to recognize that the writer rejects his former ignorant self as spurious, evanescent, and illusory and affirms his present enlightened self as genuine and eternal. As we will see, the *transformation* narrative—from a wicked person to a good one, from an unenlightened soul to one who sees things as they truly are—is common in memoir generally and in the "deviance" genre especially.

Yagoda (2009, p. 33) argues that the oldest surviving post-Augustinian memoir is *The Story of My Misfortunes,* penned by Peter Abelard, a twelfth-century French monk. But we can locate earlier memoir-*like* documents. In 1000, Sei Shonagon, a court lady to the Japanese empress, wrote *Pillow Book,* a collection of thoughts, musings, observations, opinions, and descriptions of court happenings; it is not quite what our contemporaries refer to as a memoir and certainly not an autobiography. Circa 1090, one Abdullah ibn Buluggin, a Muslim Berber, wrote *Al-Tibyan,* which some commentators call a "memoir" (Brann, 2002, pp. 42–43), but it turns out to be a chronicle of the downfall of his family's dynasty in Grenada; it is more history than memoir. Hence, the three earliest book-length autonarrations, or memoirs—Augustine's, Abelard's, and Margery Kempe's *The Story of Margery Kempe,* written at the end of the fourteenth century—were spiritual autobiographies, detailing the author's affirmation of a belief in God. John Martin tells us that, as a historical subject, *the individual* was not discovered until the European Renaissance (1997). Hence, only with the efflorescence of the Renaissance (roughly 1350–1650) did secular autonarrations come to be recorded in substantial profusion, of which Benvenuto Cellini's egocentric, blustery *Autobiography* (written between 1558 and 1562) is undoubtedly the most well-known and notable specimen. The appearance of *The Confessions of Jean-Jacques Rousseau,* completed in 1770 and published in 1782, clearly demarcated the full flower of the Enlightenment—as indicated by the fact that it was a work, like Cellini's, that was "directed not to God or a priest" but to the author's "fellow man" (Yagoda, 2009, p. 59).

Memoir and Autobiography

What is memoir and what functions does it serve? How is it different from autobiography? Even approximations to contemporary definitions of these terms did not find common currency until the end of the twentieth century. Today, it is impossible to draw a hard, clean, sharp line between the two. Yagoda says that memoir "is more literary than literal" (2009, p. 229), as exemplified by the absence of photographs and an index; the first memoir to adopt its current form, he says, was Tobias Wolff's *This Boy's Life* (1990). Diane Bjorklund, a sociologist who conducted a study of the autobiography and the memoir, *Interpreting the Self,* threw up her hands when it came to making the distinction: "I find that a distinction between autobiography and memoir is difficult to sustain in close analysis. Memoirists focus on the external world, but they often discuss their thoughts and feelings as well" (1998, p. 212). The distinction is best drawn pragmatically rather than formally: Today, a book with "memoir" in its subtitle is likely to cover a topic slightly different from one designated as an "autobiography." In *Palimpsest,* Gore Vidal writes, memoir "is how one remembers one's own life, while an autobiography is history, requiring research, dates, facts double-checked" (1995, p. 5). This seems to me to be the distinction that is truest to the currently accepted use of these terms.

As the term is now used, a "memoir" is a first-hand biographical account, replete with observations and expressions of emotion, of an aspect or the whole of a life, written largely from personal knowledge or experiences. The term derives from the French word for memory, and hence, the memoir presumably heavily depends on recollections or remembrances of past events. Instead, an *autobiography* usually describes the narrative details of a life, either in whole or during a specific, prolonged period (such as "the autobiography of my youth"). Typically, as Vidal explains, an autobiography demands fact-checking, the marshaling of historical documents, dates, and the reconstruction of a narrative sequence. Both, however, mostly share the same POV: a first-person, author-centered voice. The first person singular "I" is always the most common pronoun in both genres. Both are "about the author," and in both, the author is usually the central subject matter of the book.

Consider the following passage: "I was born on 11 August 1910, the eldest child of Robert and Abigail (Adams) Homans, at 64 Beacon Street . . . in the Back Bay district of Boston." This is the better part of the opening sentence of an autobiography, *Coming to My Senses* (1984), by George Caspar Homans (1910–1989), a distinguished Harvard professor of sociology and the scion of a prominent Boston family whose forebears included bankers, physicians, literary figures, and officers serving in the Revolutionary War, not to mention a couple of presidents, the Adamses. The details of the book's first few pages supplies much of the who, what, when, and where traditionally included in the autobiography. They unmistakably set the author's life into an economic, social, and historical context. *Coming to My Senses* details the facts of the matter of Homans's life. Although the word "I" makes a frequent appearance, much of the book is told from a third-person perspective, and its recollection is overwhelmed by documentable fact. The substance and subtitle of the book clearly locate it within the genre of autobiography.

Contrastingly, consider the following passage: "Night falls along the streets of Dublin. Children laugh and play under the streetlights, mothers call from doorways, smells of cooking come at us all the way, through windows we see people around tables, eating. I'm tired and hungry and I want Dad to carry me but I know there's no use asking him now the way his face is tight and set. I let him hold my hand and I run to keep up with him till we reach the bus place where Mam is waiting with my brothers" (McCourt, 1996, p. 53). This passage, from *Angela's Ashes,* the huge best-seller by Frank McCourt (1930–2009) about a life of grinding poverty in Limerick, Ireland, in the 1930s, contains little in the way of hard, concrete fact: virtually no dates, summaries, or laying out of recorded documentation. Instead, the author conveys feelings and sensations—sights, smells, sounds, emotion. McCourt obeys the writer's admonition, "show, don't tell." *Angela's Ashes* is made up of recollections—memories—of the author's boyhood years. Clearly, the book is memoir rather than autobiography, a fact conveyed by its subtitle.

Still, Homans, the autobiographer, does offer the reader numerous reminiscences of his life, and not a few descriptions of his feelings. All that remains of his paternal grandmother, he says, "is the impression of a small, plump, rather silent woman dressed in black or grey silk, happy to have me just sitting on her lap" (1984, p. 3). Of his father, Homans writes, "I never felt emotionally close or intimate with him" (p. 29). The reader's impression of Homans, conveyed by the author himself, is, at the time of the writing of his autobiography, that of a smug, self-centered, self-satisfied, sardonic, somewhat arrogant older gentleman born into an elite, aristocratic family. The albeit scanty recollections and emotions aside, however, two things tell us that *Coming to My Senses* is an autobiography: (1) its accumulation of documentable factual detail and (2) its coverage of the entirety of a man's life—from ancestors and birth through to the approximate current time of publication.

McCourt's narrative, likewise, contains elements of both genres. But what counts is the *weight* and *accumulation* of memoiristic recollection rather than autobiographical fact. The reader is told in the very first two sentences the particulars of the tale: "My father and mother should have stayed in New York where they met and married and where I was born. Instead, they returned to Ireland when I was four, my brother, Malachy, three, the twins, Oliver and Eugene, barely one, and my sister, Margaret, dead and gone." But notice that the facts of the matter are couched in foreboding rather than straightforward reportage, and the paragraph that follows is drenched with a sense of the horror and squalor the reader is soon to encounter: "When I look back on my childhood I wonder how I survived at all. It was, of course, a miserable childhood: the happy childhood is hardly worth your while. Worse than the ordinary miserable childhood is the miserable Irish childhood, and worse yet is the miserable Irish Catholic childhood" (McCourt, 1996, p. 1). The objective facts conveyed in McCourt's book, while crucial, are subordinate to the narration of his emotions, feeling, recollections, and experiences.

At one time, autobiographies were reserved for famous, accomplished, or remarkable personages—for example, Benjamin Franklin, *The Autobiography of Benjamin Franklin* (1790); Frederick Douglass, *My Bondage and Freedom* (1855); Ulysses S. Grant, *Personal Memoirs* (1885); Charles Darwin, *The Autobiography of Charles Darwin* (1887); Booker T. Washington, *Up from Slavery* (1901); and Helen Keller, *The Story of My Life* (1903). In each case, the author was notable, famous, accomplished, or important, led a remarkable life, and could depict a life filled with remarkable events. The very inclusion of the author's name in the title would attract prospective readers to the book. In earlier centuries, due to a number of factors, including the precipitousness of an author's death, the fugitive nature of single-copy paper manuscripts—or, in one major case, the autobiography (entitled a "memoir") of John Addington Symonds, the public shame of homosexuality—not all autobiographies of famous people were published during the writer's lifetime. Still, a "big" life demanded a life story, and the bigness of the life swept a sizable audience into the bookstore, their money into the store's cash register, and their eyes onto the book's pages. Although these titles are narrations of the lives of well-known figures of centuries past, some lean more toward autobiography, others more in the direction of memoir. The famous and remarkable may write both memoir and autobiography, but most readers will find the autobiography of a quotidian life unappealing and unworthy of their time and attention.

If adroitly spun out, a memoir, unlike an autobiography, transcends fame and even accomplishment; it is the book more than the life that attracts the reader. A well-written memoir may *render* its writer noteworthy and accomplished. In the consideration of time, the *work* may become the autonarrator's most remarkable achievement, a ticket to renown and immortality. While the accomplishments of Peter Abelard (1000s–1100s), Margery Kempe (1400s), and John Bunyan (1600s), and even those of Benvenuto Cellini (1500s), Jean-Jacques Rousseau (1700s), and Jacques Casanova (1700s), may have been substantial, the significance of their memoirs towers above everything else they did. Said Casanova, "Worthy or not, my life is my subject and my subject is my life" (Sciolino, 2011, p. C5).

I do not make much of a distinction between these two genres, which in the Weberian ideal-type world we can discriminate but in the on-the-page real world are less sharply separable. The two are sufficiently similar for my purpose, which is this: to examine and investigate a work in which the author admits to having engaged in behavior of which he or she is aware some others in the society do not approve. To me, the crucial distinction is not between autobiography and memoir but between works that are substantially forthcoming and candid versus those that conceal significant intimate, incriminating, or embarrassing details.

Consider the autobiography of Eric Hobsbawm (born 1917). The author reveals virtually nothing of his inner life; it is a self-admittedly evasive work, unsatisfying to the observer who is interested in the historian's subjective and emotive landscape (2002): "This book is not written in the now very saleable confessional mode, partly because the only justification for such an ego-trip is genius—I am neither a St. Augustine nor a Rousseau." Moreover, the historian goes on, a living autobiographer cannot "tell the private truth about matters involving other living people without unjustifiably hurting the feelings of some of them. I have no reason for doing so. . . . I suspect that readers with a taste for biographers that lift bedclothes would find my own life disappointing" (p. xii). The fact is that Hobsbawm was a seducer of women whose career he could help advance—a significant and apposite fact in the life of an academic Marxist who claims to be on the side of the powerless and downtrodden. Moreover, our eminent historian says of his own autobiography that it is not written as a defense of the author's life. "If you do *not* want to understand the twentieth century, read the autobiographies of the self-justifiers, the counsels for their defense, and of the obverse, the repentant sinners" (p. xii). But as my book argues, self-justification is the tip of the deviance iceberg, and had Hobsbawm admitted to having committed any wrongdoing, he would willy-nilly have been caught up in this process himself. Memoir, Hobsbawm argues, is what is written "from within" (p. xiv)—and it is precisely that which he is unwilling to do. He acknowledges having written a formal, inoffensive, emotionally unrevealing life history. Hence, memoiristically speaking, there is no "*there* there." The crucial issue for us here is whether or not writers put their asses on the line, describe their unconventional or unpopular or unacceptable behavior or views, and face potentially critical readers, and if so, whether they attempt to overcome the possible blemish of opprobrium by displaying their best possible face? And if so, how? What is the particular manner of deviance neutralization each uses, and is it related to their specific type of normative violation? Such questions are not addressed in a memoir or autobiography that avoids sticky personal, moral, or emotional issues.

I follow Neal Shover (2012) in his tendency to regard all autobiography, memoir, life history, and even personal diaries as blending into one another, their similarities far more substantial than their differences. What counts is forthrightness—the willingness to admit to having engaged in acts that others find offensive, and the inclination to set matters right by examining the implications of such acts with respect to one's presentation of self to a potential audience, oneself included. "Maintaining a bright-line, formal distinction between autobiographies and life histories is rendered nearly impossible" inasmuch as "hybrids" are more common than pure cases. Initiative to write, complete, publish, launch, and publicize a life story is likely to come from anyone, the author included, and who shapes the narrative, likewise, is not the exclusive agency of any single actor in the drama of life writing. Collaborators may or may not provide guidance or form the final manuscript or product; direction may or may not come from others; editorial reworking of materials may be light or heavy-handed—no matter. As Shover—and I—employ the label, "life histories are documents or productions written or in other ways recorded and made available to others that consist largely or entirely of first-person narrative about all or much of the subject's life" (p. 12). *For certain purposes,* the differences between memoir and autobiography are of great significance; for our purpose, here, the similarities weigh most consequentially.

The Memoir Explosion

The memoir explosion cannot be dated with exactitude, but some observers have placed its emergence into the limelight in the mid-to-late 1990s. A special issue of *The New York Times Magazine* (May 12, 1996) proclaimed the arrival of "The Age of the Literary Memoir." The author James Atlas referred to the triumph of memoir as a sign of the genre's "democratic" character. Six weeks later, in *The New Yorker,* fiction editor Bill Buford noted a "highly discernible trend" toward "first-person narratives" (p. 11). And an editorial in the July 1996 issue of *Women's Review of Books* took note of "The Memoir Boom," particularly stressing that there had been an "avalanche" of women's memoirs in the 1990s (Miller, 1997, p. 981). At some point between the hardback publication of Mary Karr's *The Liar's Club* (1995) and Frank McCourt's *Angela's Ashes* (1996), critics took note of three dramatic changes in the world of memoir publishing: First, the number of titles substantially increased; second, women were more likely to be their authors; and third, the memoirs were more likely to be about transgressive or non-normative lives. How do their authors grapple with the implications of their own "deviant" actions or lives? I intend to make answering this question the primary mission of this book.

From the 1980s to the decade of the 1990s, the number of catalogue entries in the Library of Congress (LoC) with "autobiography" in the title increased by from nearly 1,700 to almost 3,000; in the first decade of the 2000s, the number jumped again, to 4,500. In the 1980s, only 27 percent of the titles of memoirs listed in the LoC's catalogue were written by women; in the 1990s and 2000s, it was 40 percent. The memoir landscape looked very different within the span of only a decade, from the 1990s to the first decade of the twenty-first century, and it remains so today. But the seeds of this metamorphosis were planted much earlier.

In one of the *ur*-expositions on memoir and autobiography, *When Memory Speaks* (1999), Jill Kerr Conway declares that, with the coming of the modern—and now, postmodern—age, fiction writers retreated into a non-narrative, sometimes fantastical, altogether self-consciously literary realm inherently unappealing to the general reader. As a result, the novel declined as a popular form of narrative entertainment, and the public increasingly took up biography, autobiography, and memoir as a mode of experiencing the lives of others. "We want to know how the world looks from inside another person's experience," Conway argues (p. 6). Because most serious fiction writers have, for the most part, abandoned that broader public—compare the earthiness and directness of Charles Dickens with the esoteric literary contortions of Thomas Pynchon—and abdicated the narration of the vicarious personal experience, memoir writers have stepped into this void, and have succeeded splendidly.

Conway goes on not only to explain the success of the genre but also to point out its current manifestations. In memoir, lives follow "archetypical life scripts" (p. 7) adapted from "the story of the epic hero in classical antiquity" (p. 7). The hero violates a taboo and is rejected by his comrades, but is able to triumph over a series of trials and tribulations, and returns to his people in acclaim and shining glory. However much the nature of the Holy Grail differed from one century to the next and from one writer to another, Conway tells us, the quest was always and everywhere the same. As we saw, in his *Confessions,* St. Augustine turns what we would regard as minor sins (having sex with a woman and stealing a neighbor's ripe pears) into a struggle to know God and tread along the path of righteousness. In Rousseau's *Confessions,* the author overcomes his small-minded opponents, achieving the right to proclaim the ascendancy of democratic humanism and secularism over inherited convention. In his posthumously published *Autobiography,* Benjamin Franklin (1790) triumphs over a humble beginning and affirms the virtue of discipline, thrift, and delayed gratification as the keys to worldly success, explicating the archetypical quest-narrative, American style.

It is a basic axiom that memoirs, as with all cultural products, reflect the societies at the time and place that they were written. Most knowledgeable readers agree that the most celebrated memoir of the eighteenth century was *The Confessions of Jean-Jacques Rousseau,* the Swiss-French philosopher and novelist who believed that humanity is by nature good but forced into corruption by organized society. Yagoda refers to this volume, written in 1770, as "the greatest memoir of all time" (2009, p. 58). Rousseau (1712–1778) read excerpts to audiences from the volume, detailing shameful episodes (masturbation, spanking fetishes, his theft of a ribbon from a household, causing the dismissal of another employee from her position) that created such a scandal—one attendee told the police they should stop the author's readings—that he decided to have it published only after his death. Its honesty and frankness, emphasis on "the inner life of the mind and emotions," attention to the author's childhood and youth, and recognition that "mundane matters . . . could be as earthshaking as a grand battle" (p. 62) foreshadowed the form and content of future life narratives. Still, Rousseau's innovations did not catch on immediately; the life writings of David Hume (1711–1776), Edward Gibbon (1737–1794), John Stuart Mill (1806–1873), and (in the United States) Benjamin Franklin (1706–1790) remained as stuffy and lacking in intimate personal detail and strong emotional expressiveness as such efforts had always been. As I mentioned above, the memoir of John Addington Symonds (1840–1893), a homosexual, was not published until after the author's death. Edmund Gosse (1849–1928), who reveals a difficult, constricted childhood and a break with his father and with religion, originally published his memoir anonymously. Clearly, Western culture struggled for a century or more to overcome the stubborn, ingrained influence of propriety. Eventually, however, Rousseau's frank and candid approach to telling life stories became common practice among memoirists; very likely, the twentieth- and twenty-first-century children of his *Confessions* include Frank McCourt's *Angela's Ashes* (1996), Mary Karr's *The Liar's Club* (1995), and Jeanette Walls's *The Glass Castle* (2005).

During a considerable stretch of time, roughly from the mid-1930s to the late 1950s, Americans found solace and positive feelings in formulaic, "light," "casual," or "normative" memoirs (Yagoda, 2009, pp. 191–204), which projected a fuzzy, heartwarming, feel-good aura. Consider the titles of a few of the popular memoirs (some of them "lightly fictionalized") that were widely read at the time: *Please Don't Eat the Daisies*; *The Egg and I*; *Cheaper by the Dozen*; *Life with Father*; *Life with Mother*; *See Here, Private Hargrove*; *Meet Me in St. Louis*; *I Remember Mama*; *Guestward Ho!*—most on this brief list becoming enormous best-sellers, some the basis of movies, a few even the template for bland, laugh-track television comedies. These books offered a contrast with some of the grim and troubling world events swirling through people's lives at the time—the Great Depression, a long period of unemployment, World War II, the Korean War, the looming threat of world communism—and offered "the shared sense that the United States was the best place on earth, capable of overcoming any setbacks and fixing any flaws" (p. 193). The popularity of "feel-good" memoirs over those that depicted the gritty reality that prevailed at the time demonstrates the ascendancy of culture over history.

Memoirs depicting the gritty, harsh, even brutal side of human life also appeared at the time, of course, and a few were successful, including *The Snake Pit,* by Mary Jane Ward (1946), which detailed the author's horrifying experiences in an insane asylum; *Fear Strikes Out,* by Jim Piersall (1955), narrating a baseball player's struggle with mental illness; and *Lady Sings the*

Blues, by Billie Holiday (1956), the story of the singer's painful, humiliating encounters with out-of-wedlock birth, rape, prostitution, drug abuse, and alcoholism. But such exceptions are deceptively persuasive, and for several reasons. Even in these misery memoirs, the protagonist ultimately triumphs over adversity. And books of this stripe were in the small minority; the sales of the feel-good books substantially overwhelmed theirs. Consider, too, the paradigmatic experience of Richard Wright (1908–1960), author of *Black Boy* (1945), an indictment of racism in the old South. Because the six angriest, most critical chapters in the manuscript too starkly clashed with the dominant image of America as a just, decent, and humane society, the Book-of-the-Month Club refused to carry the book until Wright agreed to delete them (Yagoda, 2009, pp. 204–205). It was not until 1993 that Harper Perennial published the book's original, unexpurgated version, subtitled *American Hunger.* The expurgated 1945 edition was 228 pages long; the unexpurgated version, with "restored text" and notes, runs to 419 pages.

The 1960s deservedly holds a reputation for being a turbulent, edgy era, full of protest, public denunciations of the status quo, and rebellion that threatened to explode into revolution; memoirs written at the time reflected that zeitgeist. And, as Yagoda says, African American memoir led the way. The most popular of them were Dick Gregory's *Nigger* (1964), Malcolm X's *The Autobiography of Malcolm X* (1964), Claude Brown's *Manchild in the Promised Land* (1965), Piri Thomas's *Down These Mean Streets* (1967), and Maya Angelou's *I Know Why the Caged Bird Sings* (1969), all of which remain in print to this day. The cries of outrage that issued from the pages of these volumes infused the society with a spirit of rebellion and social change. In short, the 1960s witnessed the dawning of a new sensibility, a radical break with this tradition: the promulgation of cultural relativism, modernism, even decadence, along with "a new type of autobiography, the story of the modern quest for meaning" (Conway, 1999, p. 10). Autonarrative exploded into a wild exhilaration of expressions and manifestations, and, along with them, a variety of missions, motives, and forms. African Americans, women, feminists, homosexuals, transsexuals, people who grew up suffering through the shame of extreme poverty, women who had sex with their fathers—these people and others began telling tales about themselves that radically departed from the classic autonarrative mold: first, the fact that their stories were told at all and, second, that their authors were allowed to depart from the tradition and cast their tales into whatever form they chose. We now have "a new kind of narrative authority for the young, for ethnic subcultures, for those of different sexual persuasions, for the handicapped, for victims of abuse," in short, "for anyone whose questions about life fall outside the central narrative of worldly success, or of moral and spiritual growth, or power and its exercise—once the main themes for autobiographical writing" (p. 152). The realm once more or less exclusively occupied by Dickens and his peers has now been taken up by narrators of their own lives, people telling their own tales—some artfully, some so offensively and badly as to serve notice to William Zinsser, editor of a book on "the art and craft of memoir" (1998), and Harvey Swados, a middle-brow Marxist novelist who once bemoaned the proliferation of paperback "trash" (Howard, 2005, p. 148), that something was amiss in the publishing trade. To the contrary, I see the efflorescence of non-literary writing as a positive development, representing the democratization of autobiography.

What is the appeal of autobiography and memoir? Autonarrative is appealing to the extent that it permits the reader to enter the author's time and place, to see the world behind the author's eyes, to vicariously live another life—to both *voyeuristically* and *experientially* live the life of another person. We transcend merely peeking through the keyhole and witnessing intimate details normally kept from our gaze. If the author is successful, we do that and more: We *become* the person we are reading about. We get swept up in the whirlpool of the cinematic imagination, feeling ourselves inside the author's skin, acting out the narrator's life story. Autobiography is successful to the extent that readers can imagine themselves experiencing the drama they read about; there is something of the soap opera about autonarrative. And while the occasional life story can be crafted into a work of literary value, we now live (and read) in an era in which, for the most part, we need not apply such a lofty literary standard to all memoir. Contemporary autonarrative represents an expression of populism and, almost willy-nilly, manifests itself in a great deal of bad writing. As a sociologist, I delight in this populist impulse, am not distressed by the genre's exemplars of artless scribbling, and intend to revel in this popularization by appreciating autobiography and memoir of every conceivable ilk, including those with virtually no literary value. Still, I insist, most of the authors whose work I look at here are fine writers, and several are truly first-rate.

By the 1970s, all the elements of contemporary memoir had been put in place: unconventionality, even deviance, pain and anguish, as well as joy and triumph, introspection and the flamboyant expression of emotion, some intimate detail, an effort to reach back into one's childhood as far as possible, concrete particulars rather than vague abstractions, and the expression of ambivalence rather than glowing platitudes about family members, loved ones, and revered figures.

Until the last century or two, revealing secrets about one's past was widely regarded as a kind of betrayal. But today, it seems, practically every well-known sports figure, entertainer, and politician taps out a version of his or her life, or commissions a ghost writer to do it. Five times as many book-length memoirs were published in 2008 as in 2004 (Yagoda, 2009, p. 7). It is difficult to intellectually and emotionally travel back in time and imagine living in an age when an ordinary, non-famous person writing a life story was considered self-indulgent and the work, essentially unpublishable. Almost certainly the majority of the avalanche of life stories that have been published since St. Augustine's *Confessions* appeared during the past half-century, and most of them by ordinary, non-famous authors.

Literal Facticity: Does It Matter?

"I did not tolerate any dealings in prostitution or narcotics," says Joe Bonanno, once the head of a powerful organized crime family. "I was against extortion as an arbitrary instrument of collecting money from people," he adds (1984, p. 130). Addictive drugs "hijack" the brain, says William Cope Moyers, a former crack and heroin abuser. He had an addiction the way some people get cancer. He took drugs to "blot out the pain," to "fill the hole" in his soul: *Why couldn't I stop taking drugs? Because I was an addict. I'm not responsible for taking drugs; my addiction was* (2006). When we read assertions in a memoir, our first reaction is to ask, "Are they true?" I agree that this is an important and relevant question for certain aspects the memoir, but it is not the *only* question we might ask. Others are these: Why did the author make these assertions? Is factual validity *crucial* to the issues we are interested in?

As a factual record, memoirs are often fictional creations rather than historical accounts. I do not mean that the broad outlines of their narrative are mostly false, though often they are. I mean that they are crafted in a fashion that is alien to the subject—which was the author during much of the period described. Rigoberta Menchú (1984), Binjamin Wilkomirski (1996), James Frey (2003), and Ismael Beah (2007) notwithstanding, life writers do not usually invent the facticity of the broader outlines of their narratives, but they do reconstruct the *meaning* of the past according to their current understanding of it. For our purposes, unless critics uncover counter-factual material that denies the factual validity of a given autobiography or memoir, we can take their facticity for granted. But what is more interesting for the student of the genre is the author's imposition of a coherent narrative flow and an accounting of his or her normative violations. In any case, with respect to literal factuality, memoir *defines the self*—who the writer is at a *contemporary* time and place; he or she almost certainly did not have such a conception at the time of the events under discussion. Hence, the fictional quality of memoir.

In what other ways does life narrative differ from fiction? Must an "account" be factually accurate and true? *How much* of a life writing has to be literally and concretely valid for us to honor it with the descriptive terms "memoir" and "autobiography"? The answers to these questions are not as straightforward as they might seem, as anyone who has attempted to write a life story or who has seriously and systematically read one can attest. To begin with, there is the matter of dialogue. Everyone recognizes that, short of tape-recording conversation or having perfect recall, reproducing spoken conversation word for word is impossible. Reconstructions of dialogue are just that—reconstructions. How faithful to the spoken word does the memoirist have to be? The consensus seems to be that it is sufficient to reproduce the *gist* of what was said, but it is also true that when a participant other than the author reads an approximation of a conversation to which he or she has contributed, he or she is likely to find it a jarring, disorienting experience. Hence, these inevitable questions: How much confidence can we have in the factuality of events, dialogue included, recounted in memoirs? And does this distinction between fact and fiction matter? Does the issue of facticity matter? And *to whom* does it matter? *In what context* does it matter?

Scholars found the memoir by Rigoberta Menchú (1984) inadequate with regard to literal factualness: The family feud the author describes actually "pitted her father against his in-laws" rather than Menchú's and a wealthy landowning family; one brother who Menchú said she saw starve to death was fictional; another who was supposedly burned alive by army troops in the presence of her family died elsewhere, under different circumstances, not when the family was present; Ms. Menchú's claim that she could not speak Spanish until she worked on the book is false—she received an education at a prestigious private Catholic boarding school. The anthropologist David Stoll and *The New York Times* interviewed over a hundred people and consulted archival material, concluding, in Stoll's words, that Ms. Menchú's book "cannot be the eyewitness account it purports to be" because she describes "experiences she never had herself" (Rohter, 1998, p. A8; Stoll, 1998). If the reader or the scholar takes Menchú's memoir as a detail-by-detail chronicle of eyewitness accounts, true, it is inadequate and fatally flawed. But some leftist politicos see the volume as generic testimony, a record of exploitation and oppression of the indigenous Guatemalan people by the Ladino elite, and in this sense, *I, Rigoberta Menchú* provides an effective activist rallying cry for political change. Most critics disagree; they feel Ms. Menchú's embellishments are beyond the pale, unwarranted fabrications, dishonest to history's chronology, narrative, and eventology.

In considering the authenticity of a memoir or memoir-like document, it is necessary for the reader and researcher to keep *eyes on the prize.* If the memoir links experience with feelings, then the reader wants to be reassured that, at the very least, the approximate events the author describes correspond with what really happened in the material world. If the author claims to be a Holocaust survivor when he is actually a Gentile who sat out the war in safety in Switzerland (Wilkomirski, 1996; Maechler, 2001), then clearly the book cannot be taken as anything but a bogus memoir and is of utility as only a specimen of falsehood; the assertion of victimhood is a lie and should not be regarded as otherwise. Yet lies are alluring to both the narrator and the reader and listener; hence, the *narrative* tradition is very different from the historical tradition, and so, narrative truth is different from historical truth (Spence, 1982). Certain narratives make a great story but are not literally and actually true, while others are dull as stories but are factually accurate. What we, as students of deviance accounts, want to know is, did the narratives authors present as factually true descriptions of what happened *actually* happen to them, more or less as they are told? And is the author being more or less honest in expressing his or her feelings about the events in question? This a *relevant* (but not the central) issue because the author of a bogus memoir is likely to self-justify deviance in a different way from the manner in which the author of a work with a high facticity value does. But clearly, supposed memoirs about the Holocaust placing the author into events that he or she did not experience are so far beyond the pale of veracity that they evidence little but fraud; they cannot be taken seriously as memoir.

Erving Goffman has famously said, "True accounts are often good, but false accounts are sometimes better" (1971, p. 112). By that he means that a story that "works" emotionally and dramatically, that achieves the intended response, may not be literally and strictly factually accurate. But stories may be "too good to be true"—that is, they work a little too well; they are too pat; they pull all the right strings; they push neurological and affective buttons a bit too predictably. They make sophisticated audiences suspicious, put them on warning: Perhaps this tale is not what the author is making it out to be. Good-sounding accounts may "acquire a bad name" *as they are being told* because they take us for granted by playing on time-worn clichés and platitudes (p. 113). Still, clichés often work for less sophisticated, less thoughtful audiences. But again, a memoir that "works" is the not the same thing as a narrative that literally "happened."

All of which raises these issues: Is lying in autonarrative a form of deviance? Should we expect the author whose lying has been discovered to use neutralizations to justify the lies? If so, what form would we predict they would take? Or do such authors stonewall, insisting that they have told the truth all along? Or do different people interpret "fact" and "fiction" in different ways, insisting that the essence of veracity is more important than the literal, transcriptional facts of events?

In ordinary, everyday interaction, people almost always feel betrayed when they are told a significant lie. Telling the truth is expected, especially among intimates, and especially where matters of importance hinge on the truth. Contrarily, memoir writers do not know most of their readers, and very little of what they say in their life stories determines the outcomes of their readers' lives. Still, critics and readers tend to raise an enormous fuss when a memoir writer makes major assertions that are found to be baldly false. But where do we draw the line between assertions of major importance and those that involve niggling details that do not matter? And at least as interesting, what does the author say in response to accusations of lying? In the case of responses to charges of bogusness, we should expect the author make use of deviance neutralizations, but, as I said, are they the same as those occasioned by factually true accounts of the author's deviant activities?

How do we know that a memoir writer's assertions are true? Many assertions in memoirs cannot be verified, entailing, as they often do, acts engaged in by only the writer, or the writer and deceased co-participants, or co-participants who cannot recall the events in question or who recall them only hazily. Interested critics and readers can determine the veracity of some other assertions, however, and may even challenge the very factual foundation on which the memoir that makes them rests. In principle, we can determine truthfulness by checking identities, bogus and real, news accounts, documents (such as arrest, hospital, school, and treatment center records), interviewing witnesses and participants, and even, occasionally, by reading journal entries and diaries. Verifying many significant memoiristic assertions can be a slippery and daunting—but not impossible—proposition. Memoir is much like history in this respect; for some events, people leave a trail of evidence the interpretation of which is challenging but often surmountable—but again, unlike autobiography, memoir is as much in the interpretation as in the narrative account. Bogus assertions, though interesting in themselves, are mainly of concern for what they reveal about the systematic processes of recall, interpretation, and misrepresenting the facts.

Some critics have objected to the outrage hurled at authors of bogus memoirs. In comparison with the lies told by politicians, Francine Prose argues (2008), the consequences of their dishonesty are minimal. After "Abu Ghraib and Guantanamo, real estate foreclosures, poverty, unemployment, the handling of Hurricane Katrina"—deceptions, falsehoods, blunders, and tragedies of "huge consequence"—the lies of Margaret Seltzer (a.k.a. Margaret Jones), a suburban white girl who claimed to be a half American Indian gang member (Jones, 2008), and James Frey (2003), a supposed addict and criminal, seem trivial stacked against those of George Bush, Dick Cheney, and Donald Rumsfeld. Should literary lies generate volcanoes of criticism while the far more consequential political lies pass relatively unremarked on? After all, of the bogus memoir, Prose says she is tempted to remark, "It's only a book"

(2008, p. 88). A strange assertion, she agrees, "coming from a writer." Ironically, the essay that follows Prose's in the September 2008 issue of *Harper's Magazine* is a review of Jay Parini's *Why Poetry Matters.* Strange indeed: If poetry matters—if the *truth* of poetry matters—then why not the truth, the literal truth, of memoir? We want our memoirs to be literally true—but within the narrative conventions we all accept, that is, that authors leave out the trivial and the inane, condense dialogue and stick to the relevant and important, and so on. Hardly anybody shrugs at lies and agrees, "It's only a book." *But we also want the stories we are told to be dramatic and interesting.* And herein lies the rub.

Prose's answer is that flummery is acceptable, but only if the author can turn the dross of lies into literary gold. If it's art, it's not flummery—or, to put the matter another way, by implication, all art is flummery; in the words of Pablo Picasso, "Art is the lie that tells the truth." Commenting on the fabricated memoir *Love and Consequences,* Prose says she is not interested in whether the author's name is Jones or Seltzer or whether the exploits she enunciated are true or false; what is important is the quality of the book's writing. "Sadly," Prose laments, "*Love and Consequences* is not a great novel. As fiction, it has the generic quality of those B-list celebrity bios. The little girl's abuse is discovered when blood runs down her leg at school. There's a violent gang initiation, the senseless deaths of appealing young people, a rock of maternal goodness, Big Mom, struggling to hold her biological and foster family together" (p. 89). But Prose wants it both ways: Lies in memoir are acceptable only if the author writes a work of great fiction, but reading *Love and Consequences—as literary memoir*—fails to impress because it is so trite and clichéd. And if *Love and Consequences* is fiction, why doesn't the author label it as such? Prose seems not to accept the fact that most readers recognize that attention to autobiographical facticity constrains the author in a way that fictional accounts do not—just as literary conceits place demands on the writer of fiction in a way that factually truthful life stories do not.

The rest of Prose's argument is strange. The "big" lies of politicians are never excused by noticing the "small" lies of writers; here, Prose is juggling grapefruits and grapes. All the "big" political misrepresentations Prose mentions have attracted vastly more criticism than the "small" lies of literary hoaxers. But books *do* matter (to writers, at any rate, and to their readers—they are, after all, a major component of our heritage and culture), and hence, in the circles in which Prose moves, the lies of writers *matter,* independent of the doings of politicians, and certainly a great deal. Moreover, politicians usually compound the lies they tell on the job by telling lies in memoiristic form; the memoirs of Richard Nixon, Henry Kissinger, Bill Clinton, Ronald Reagan, Lyndon Johnson, Dean Rusk, Alexander Haig, and Caspar Weinberger, while not literary hoaxes, provide enough raw material to keep an army of fact-checkers in business for a century. Adolf Hitler positioned *Mein Kampf*—a Niagara of lies—as a memoir, and hence, "only" a book, yet it had a catastrophically toxic impact on its era. What is interesting to sociologists is that not all literary lies dead-end in the same obliteration. But writers and politicians share at least one practice in common—the use of rhetoric—and the language that weaves webs of deceit can also provide justification for malfeasances, and for the very lies that *constitute* lying, itself a major genre of malfeasance.

Kristina Lundgren (2008) of *The Los Angeles Times* briefly summarizes some two dozen "memorable literary hoaxes," several of which were produced by authors with more than one fishy book to his or her (dis)credit. An enterprising observer can scoop up even more fish than these out of the murky waters of memoir fabrication. Of course, not all faked memoirs are *totally* fabricated. Ishmael Beah *was* a boy soldier in Sierra Leone (2007), but, as Shelley Gare, Peter Wilson, and David Nason, a team of Australian journalists, argue, the evidence suggests that Beah fought for two *months,* not two years (Sherman, 2008). And James Frey *was* a drug abuser who committed some crimes, but, as he himself has admitted (for instance, on CNN's *Larry King Live,* January 26, 2006), much of the rest of his story was exaggerated or fabricated. Hence the Beah and Frey memoirs are only *partial* fabrications. As we saw, Binjamin Wilkomirski (a.k.a. Bruno Grosjean, a.k.a. Bruno Dössekker), author of *Fragments* (1996), a tale of "a small boy who spent his childhood in the Nazi death camps" (to quote the book's flap copy), is not Jewish, and he lived in complete safety in Switzerland during World War II. He was not a Holocaust survivor, and consequently his tale is *totally* fabricated. Regardless of the artfulness of the tale, Wilkomirski is an out-and-out liar, and the student of Holocaust narratives will learn nothing from *Fragments* (except how a particular type of Holocaust mythology—lying about having been a victim of Nazi atrocities—is constructed). Somewhere in between these two extremes we can locate the story of Herman Rosenblat, a true childhood survivor of two concentration camps, who created a false, largely literary-romantic *frame* of a story of love and romance *around* the Holocaust inner core. His book was printed but withdrawn before publication, though a children's picture-book version of it was released (Friedman, 2008). And though a Holocaust survivor, his future wife did not, as a child, stand outside the encampment fence and throw him apples, as he claimed.

While inventing major events in an autobiography or memoir and palming them off to the reader as literally and historically accurate is likely to be regarded as a form of deviance, this is not the topic of our book. If an author had written *another* memoir about the bogus memoir, explaining why he or she did it and justifying or excusing the sleight of hand, that would qualify as relevant to the subject matter at hand. However, narrating events that never happened as if they had *is* relevant to our subject matter in a crucial way—in a sense, it is the lynchpin of the argument of this book. Hence, we are forced, willy-nilly, to lay down the reasons we need to raise and explore this thorny and ramifying topic.

Memoir writers teeter on a balance beam between two contradictory tendencies: depicting themselves and their lives as so decent and inoffensive that they risk alienating their readers through sheer boredom and stupefaction, and depicting themselves and their deeds as so fascinating, eccentric, fierce, terrible, malefic, scary, bizarre, or unusual that they risk alienating their readers through repugnance—or critical credulity. Some authors, fearful of the overly bland side of the balance beam, chronicle tales of transgression so venal and damning that they risk plunging sideways, head over heels into the jaws of audience condemnation. Some authors so ramp up the sensational side of their character and behavior that they inflate it with swagger, bluster, hyperbole, and braggadocio. The sins whose narration they want to peddle are not as serious as they claim. The self-designated murderer for the Mafia did not really kill anyone (he robbed a few candy stores when he was seventeen), and he was not in the Mafia (he was in a small street gang); the supposed call girl never exchanged sex for pay with Arab sheiks and Swiss bankers (instead, her boyfriends sometimes took her out for a dinner and a movie); the cat burglar did not steal expensive jewelry in Cannes (she occasionally shoplifted at Macy's); and, it turns out, the alleged mercenary did not slaughter a hundred villagers and help install an African despot, making off with millions in gold bullion (he made bets with his pals about who could shoot the most pigeons in the park with their BB guns).

In the "deviance memoir" genre, the temptation to tell taller, more exciting, and more *dramatically transgressive* tales is compelling. Such tales are more satisfying, and telling them sells more books. Perhaps, as with the message on the cigarette package, a bogus memoir should carry a warning label: "This book is a memoir. Most readers believe that memoirs are narration of true events that, for the most part, took place in the materially real world. In order to boost the sales of this book and increase its literary value (see Prose, 2008), the author has fictionalized major features of this narration to more closely correspond to the conventions of literature. Readers are warned that they should not take the facticity of this narrative at face value. Doing so may harm their literary health and sense of well-being."

A second motive drives the authors of a certain species of "deviance proclaiming" memoir: *selling redemption*. In a nutshell, the more serious and reprehensible the malfeasance, the more remarkable the narrator's redemption:

I sinned; I indulged in filthy practices; I saw the error of my ways; I managed to pull myself out of the muck and the slime; hence, I deserve the highest praise for my accomplishment. The caboose of this train adds a codicil to the formula: *My exemplar offers a lesson to others who are mired in said muck and slime, and hence, I will receive additional shining accolades for triumphing over the horrific and unfortunate life I used to live—and very possibly a great many lucrative speaking engagements.* St. Augustine's theft of a few of his neighbor's pears may seem a genteel iota of the recovered addict's vomit-caked shirt, urine-soiled pants, and near-fatal drug overdoses (Frey, 2003), but they are intended to convey the same message: Repent the error of your ways, abandon the poisonous fruits of sin. "I once was lost but now am found / Was blind but now I see." It is a perfect formula: You can have fun sinning, and when you stop, you can seem virtuous and righteous to the good and decent people of the world; you can earn a bundle on your story, and then, when you are perceived as a role model and your story is challenged by critics, your readers will rally around you and defend you and the veracity of the story. But to pull this off, you have to find the right formula, pull the right motivational strings, and verbalize your sins—both in your life story and, if you are caught, in lying *about* your life story—in just the right way.

On this issue, again, let's keep our eyes on the prize. What we are interested in is how authors rhetoricize their non-normative activities. Our concern is not ferreting out and exposing bogus memoirs, it is about our memoirists' accounting of their illicit activities. The accounting systems generated by authors who fabricate life events may differ from those that are constructed by the authors who actually lived through the events they narrated. This is not our central concern here, but to the extent that this is true, we might want to stay alert to the possibility of memoiristic fraud.

Conscious lying about one's past constitutes a minute fraction of all factual distortion in memoir and autobiography. It is memory, not fibbing, that imparts the funhouse mirror images of self-narrated accounts of our past. Most of us have a flawed notion of how memory works, imagining that events that took place years ago are lodged somewhere in our brains, whole and intact, as they happened, detail by detail, just waiting to be retrieved. Most of us have graphic, realistic memories of occurrences that never took place, and cannot recall significant particulars of those that did happen. There is a *mythic* element to memory, much like didactic folk-tales, that shapes memoirs and other recollections of our past which makes *all* autonarration, including eyewitness testimony, suspect as strictly factual accounts (Kotre, 1995; Loftus and Ketcham, 1991). I take such distortions for granted, but deviance memoir is not *exclusively* about factual accuracy. I assume that the rough outlines of the narratives we consider here are more or less accurate—

that Charles Van Doren agreed to a quiz show fix and that he originally lied about it to investigators, that Jim Bouton and other professional baseball players took amphetamines to juice themselves up for the games they played, that William Burroughs and Steve Geng actually took heroin, that Pete Hamill was a heavy drinker, that Roman Polanski did have sex with a thirteen-year-old girl (one Samantha Gailey), that Joe Bonanno was the head of an organized crime family, that Jack Henry Abbott was penally incarcerated for his crimes, and so on. Moreover, I am confident that these biographical facts enable us to explore issues of deviance disavowal. Once we grant the behavior to which our actors and authors admitted, what is interesting here is how they *rhetoricize* that behavior and position themselves as enactors of it. But if our authors did *not* engage in the deviant behavior they describe, we have to wonder whether we can learn anything from the self-exculpation arsenal they employ in their memoirs. What would be the point of studying deviance neutralization devices use by someone who lies about having committed transgressive behavior? Such an enterprise would be undertaken by a researcher interested in a phenomenon very different from the one we look at here. But lying about having engaged in deviance is *itself* a form of deviance, and examining the rhetoricization of that lie *would* be interesting and revealing for us.

James Frey, "I Honestly Have No Idea"

Clearly, then, serious lying in memoir—lying about whether one literally enacted the behavior one describes—is a form of deviance. Among the more well-known cases of the tendency to juggle drama and uplift as against literal truthfulness, consider the nearly universally familiar case of a writer who hugely overstated and sensationalized the gravity of his crimes, invented his participation in sins he did not commit, and rendered what peccadilloes he did commit loathsome rather than unconventional. Remarkably, this writer blundered into exactly the right formula to guarantee a stupendous success; the explanations he used struck the most harmonious chord among a band of devoted followers, who hived off the mainstream and continue to affirm his righteousness in the face of public humiliation and debasement. This man became a hero in his blogosphere, and, despite his lies and disgrace, his books continue to sell extravagantly well. He provides a shining example of the power of neutralizations, but not because of what he says about the deviant behavior he himself autonarrated—but because of his followers' justifications for his lying.

In April 2003, Doubleday/Random House released *A Million Little Pieces*, the memoir of the former alcoholic, drug addict, and dealer James Frey. Though a number of critics dissented from the majority, many reviews glowed with praise. Anchor Books found enough positive notices to plaster the back cover and first couple of pages of the paperback edition, released in May 2004, with an abundance of laudatory blurbs. *The San Francisco Chronicle* said, "James Frey's staggering recovery memoir could well be seen as the final word on the topic." *The Boston Globe* called it "the most lacerating tale of drug addiction since William S. Burroughs' *Junky*." Here's the blurb taken from *The New York Times Book Review*: "Frey's book sets itself apart. . . . [S]pare, deadpan language belies the horror of what he's describing—a meltdown dispatched in telegrams." *People* magazine gushed, "Anyone who has ever felt broken and wished for a better life will find inspiration in Frey's story." The novelist Pat Conroy hyperbolically blurbed *A Million Little Pieces* as "the *War and Peace* of addiction." Reviewers used adjectives such as "pulsating," "intense," "compelling," "fierce and honorable," "devastating," "staggering," "mesmerizing," "gripping," "heart-breaking, "gritty," "dark and honest," "engrossing," "mythic," "harrowing," "inspiring." The list is long and its adjectives pulsate with praise. But notice: The praise for the book is contingent on its factuality—that *these* things happened to *this* author. And most of the reviewers' praise centers on the foundational themes of honesty, emotional intensity, and misery. *A Million Little Pieces* was the second-best-selling book in the United States in 2005, surpassed by only *Harry Potter and the Half-Blood Prince.* What *Pieces* offered was redemption, inspiration, and a *very* dramatic story.

Not all reviewers agreed. In a BBC News broadcast (May 23, 2003), Germaine Greer tagged *A Million Little Pieces* as "the greatest load of crap . . . , novelistic hogwash." In the April 21, 2003, *New York Times,* Janet Maslin's review mocked the book by depicting it as formulaic, reducible to a twelve-step program, the last step of which is "Publish. Attract a lot of attention. You know the rest." In July 2003, *The Minneapolis Star-Tribune* ran a story by Deborah Caulfield Rybak challenging the veracity of the author's account of root-canal surgery sans anesthesia and being allowed on a commercial airline with a hole in his cheek, blood on his shirt, and clothes covered in "spit, snot, urine, vomit, and blood." In the months following the publication of the book, scattered readers posted mostly anonymous blogs questioning the truth of numerous details of *A Million Little Pieces,* emphasizing the questionable veracity of the root-canal procedure, Frey's bloody airplane flight, his account of his treatment at Hazelden, and whether the book's dialogue rang true. (Zeller, 2006, reproduces some of these contemporaneous blog reviews.)

Soon after the publication of the paperback edition of the book, the editors and writers at TheSmokingGun.com (TSG), a website usually devoted to posting celebrity mug shots, obtained Frey's arrest photo, taken following a 1992 drunk driving arrest in Granville, Ohio, location of the author's alma mater, Dennison University. But TSG also noticed that some pieces of the Frey puzzle were mysteriously missing, specifically the records of several of the author's arrests. It began checking the author's autobiographical claims against the documentary record. Frey had not been incarcerated for eighty-seven days, as he claimed (he had been held only a few hours at the Granville police station); he had not been "wanted in three states"; he had not plowed his car into or beaten up any of the police officers who tried to arrest him; and he had barely known the suicidal young woman he was supposedly going to meet after being released from jail. And Frey's description of his agonizing root-canal surgery, without benefit of anesthesia, electrified readers, but it prompted skepticism from others. It was one of the fulcrum events in the book, providing documentation of how tough and defiant he was, how capable of enduring pain at a level most of us cannot even imagine, how determined he was to have his teeth fixed and return to some semblance of normalcy. But did Frey actually endure all that pain? Did his dentist subject him to a torturous operation without alleviating his suffering? When Oprah "took him to the woodshed" and challenged him on it, he prevaricated. "I honestly have no idea," he responded to the interrogation the Queen of the Talk Show put him through.

The time line is important: in April 2003, the hardback edition is published; in May 2004, the paperback edition appears; on October 26, 2005, Frey makes a respectful appearance on *The Oprah Winfrey Show,* complete with testimonials from women who had been "saved" by his book. So far, the positives outweigh the negatives, and sales, hugely boosted by the *Winfrey* appearance, have zoomed into the millions. On January 8, 2006, TSG publishes its exposé, "The Man Who Conned Oprah"; on January 11, 2006, Frey appears on *Larry King Live* and even after admitting to having "embellished" parts of the book, he receives a supportive phone call from Oprah. But on January 26, he makes a dramatic appearance on Oprah in which the host "takes the author to the woodshed," confronting him about betraying her and millions of Americans. (But notice that, though Oprah and her entire staff were deeply moved by Frey's exaggerations, and she publicly humiliated him for deceiving her and her audience, a book by Frey that told the literal and banal truth *would never have attracted Oprah's attention* and would *not* have been a ticket to her show and hence to instant best-sellerdom.) Later on the same day that Oprah denounced Frey, *Larry King Live* discusses the matter, again broadcasting Winfrey berating the befuddled, stammering writer. And that night, on *Anderson Cooper 360 Degrees,* a discussion about Frey's mendacity is aired. Within the time span of less than twenty-four hours, the brew that the author of *A Million Little Pieces* drank had transmogrified from largely sweet to almost entirely bitter. And the *nature* of Frey's deviance mutated from being a truthful, brutally honest, and much-suffering ex-addict and ex-criminal to being a fraud, a liar, a deceiver, a betrayer. As developments would have it, in 2008, Winfrey "apologized" to Frey for publicly humiliating him on network television (Luscombe, 2009).

Presumably prompted by demands from Doubleday's publishers, Frey's "A Note to the Reader" was inserted on January 13, 2006, into the paperback edition. The author offers this bland, blameless, noncommittal statement: "My account has been questioned by the treatment facility, and they believe my memory may be flawed." This feeble apology, however, stands in stark contrast to the electronic defensive onslaught Frey, through his supporters, manages to launch. (Without knowing the inside story, a publishing-savvy observer is likely to detect the hand of public relations and publicity experts in rallying Frey's readers and supporters to the beleaguered author's side.) At http://bigjimindustries.com and www.james-frey.com, Frey asks his readers, "What's all the fuss about?" "Was he right to embellish his memoir?" "Was Oprah right to support then shun *A Million Little Pieces*?" "Does it matter anyway?" "Make up your own mind. Have your say. Join the debate."

Frey's *institutional* troops encourage support for the author from readers in a variety of ways. Frey himself posted a blog that reads, "Just want to thank everyone for reading my work, and for your support." At http://bigjimindustries.com, he even offers to take telephone messages ("Call James Frey's cell phone"). In the "News and Events" segment of www.james-frey.com, for the August 19, 2008, inauguration of Frey's novel, *Bright Shiny Morning*, Sophie Arnold, the sales and marketing manager of John Murray, Frey's U.K. publisher, we find the following message: "We wanted to put across a strong message to potential Frey readers—to make them see that this was something a bit different—a powerful work of fiction by the author of the controversial *A Million Little Pieces*. We wanted to say that James Frey is back, he's unrepentant, and he's got something rather exciting up his sleeve." Arnold revealed a gimmick that addressed the "lying and embellishing" charge. It is a bookmark with the following message: "NOTHING IN THIS BOOK SHOULD BE CONSIDERED ACCURATE OR RELIABLE." In other words, this is a novel, where there is no such thing as lying or enhancing the narrative. A second bookmark, Waterstone's, a U.K. bookstore chain, highlights a quote from *The Evening Standard* ("Frey really can write brilliantly. And if you don't think so, f—— you"), along with the website address and the injunction, "Find out more—have your say." At the novel's launching, which Frey attended, Polly Ho Yen, the store's publicity, sales, and marketing assistant, added, "Leaning against the barrier of the balcony, battling against the wind, James Frey spoke out. As a Frey fan myself, what he said was everything I wanted to hear—he was the hero I'd imagined, I was not disappointed. I'm sure you won't [be] either." Along with the launching of the book, the publisher launched a blog "about the creative processes involved and the different stages of the book." Here we have an interesting case of institutionally generated *surrogate* deviance disavowal. Clearly, the bookstore vetted the messages and posted only or mainly the positive ones.

In effect, then, Frey's readers act as stand-ins or mouthpieces for Frey's own position; the author uses *their* methods of neutralization to justify *his* deviant act—that is, fobbing off fictional events as biographically valid. Accused of lying and exaggerating, he *indirectly* expresses defiance in the face of withering attacks by his critics—by using his readers' voices in his websites and blogs. The messages are not so much an exchange of views as the expression of a fan club, aided and abetted by corporate sponsorship, that is, the author's publishers and their bookstore distributors. Frey's readers offer a variety of justifications for the author's blurring of the line between fiction and factually based memoir. Their neutralizations include the following justifications (all of these messages were posted during 2008 and can be found at www.james-frey.com):

1. Frey's enhancements rendered his accounts more interesting. "At the end of the day you wouldn't bother reading a memoir if it wasn't interesting. Essentially a reader wants a good story. Frey wrote a good yarn with really good descriptions which gripped a lot of people."
2. Memory of the past is hazy and subjective anyway, so everything is up for grabs. "People's memories of real events are always dodgy. . . . Plus as time goes by you remember and camp up the facts that you want to remember and forget others."
3. Good writing should not be pigeonholed into fact or fiction. "I loved *A Million Little Pieces* and [*My Friend*] *Leonard,* and I must admit I am not bothered about what is true and what is not in books—they are both fantastic pieces of writing, compelling and entertaining."
4. *A Million Little Pieces* is uplifting and helps people recover from drug abuse. "*A Million Little Pieces* probably changed lives for the better. If it helped one person, it is a worthwhile book. . . . Who really cares [about the embellishments] except Oprah?"
5. Frey's writing evokes an emotional response—the hallmark of good writing. "I read *My Friend Leonard.* I just could not put it down. I loved it. I was laughing, crying, and smiling all at once. I loved this book. Loved it. This book was about a struggle. I had heard of *A Million Little Pieces* [until now] but had not read it.

When James finds out that Lilly is dead, I felt overwhelmed. I cried. Then as he journeys through life and learns from Leonard, I fell in love with Leonard. He was so sweet, and I loved how well he took care of James. The ending came as a complete shock. I really felt for James. Losing Leonard would have been the end for me. . . . I cried solid for the last 10 pages. From the very beginning I was drawn into his book. That to me showed he is a gifted writer. . . . I actually just finished *A Million little Pieces* today, and I knew I needed to come onto your site and just tell you that I think you're absolutely brilliant."

6. Because James Frey is brilliant, he is not subject to the rules of ordinary writers. "I am absolutely in love with the writing brilliance that flows out of James Frey. . . . You are an amazing writer. Nothing more about past issues needs to be said other than that. You have succeeded in what you have set out to do, and I for one will be forever grateful to your work."

In short, Frey's supporters think that critics and intellectuals are making too much of a "fuss" about Frey's fudging and garnishing the facts, do not believe that his exaggerations represent a form of deviance, downplay the arguments made in TSG's report of January 8, 2006, feel that Oprah was unjustified in taking the writer "to the woodshed" and that he was justified in hyperbolizing the factual record, that "the truth" that is truly important is the emotional rather than the literally factual truth, that the reader can trust a memoir as long as it resonates with them emotionally, and that small, inessential exaggerations do *not* matter. What is important is that good writing grips the reader and tells a good story. In posting messages on his blog, Frey's supporters believe that the writer has nothing to justify or apologize for, and no neutralizations are necessary. Of course, *denying* that one needs to neutralize is *itself* a technique of neutralization.

In *How to Become a Scandal,* Kipnis (2010, pp. 152–191) analyzes the Frey imbroglio as a prime example of a scandal. But it is remarkable how resilient the yarn-spinning writer was. True, Doubleday dropped Frey from its list of authors, his agent, Sara Nelson, likewise dropped him from her list of clients, Warner Brothers canceled a projected movie deal of *A Million Little Pieces,* and Frey had to admit that, like *Pieces, My Friend Leonard,* his second book, was partially fictionalized—for instance, he was never incarcerated as he claimed he had been. Frey succeeded in justifying his sins to his supporters because they share the values on which those justifications are based: the irrelevance of rigid academic distinctions between literary genres; the critical power of the reader, not the academic or the intellectual; the supremacy of emotion over artificial verbal devices; the centrality of uplift and inspiration as criteria for the quality of one's prose; and, most of all, the location of the relevant community of evaluators of the quality of a work away from experts and with whoever likes it and is willing to say so. Neutralizing the deviance of a beloved party means having to address only the other members of this electronic community and ignore the mainstream. With the patronage of corporate sponsors to energize the dissemination of these justifications, the formula is complete. The James Frey incident embodies the principle that in a postmodern world, reversing the condemnation of wrongdoing distinctly and exquisitely depends on where the observer is standing.

And the *A Million Little Pieces* hyperbolizations hardly tainted Frey's career as a writer. As we saw, after Frey's initial appearance on Oprah, *Pieces* stormed *The New York Times* Best Sellers list and remained there for most of 2005; his second book, *My Friend Leonard* (2005), also made an appearance on that hallowed list. And currently, Frey heads Full Fathom Five, a "book packager" that hires young writers to "generate content" of fictional works for teenage readers and sells the "package" to publishers. These writers would be anonymous, they generally received no royalty (only a flat fee), and the editing of their work would be done by Frey without the authors' control or consent. Says Conrad Rippy, a publishing attorney, the arrangement constitutes a "collaboration agreement without there being any collaboration." It says to the writer, "You're going to write for me. I'm going to own it. I may or may not give you credit" (Mozes, 2010, p. 44). Currently twenty-eight writers work for Frey under this agreement. So far, one of the firm's books, *I Am Number Four,* has been translated into twenty-two languages and has become a best-seller in forty-four countries; more are in the hopper, possibly to achieve similar success. When explaining the deal to a prospective writer who felt uneasy about wasting her time on a project that might not pan out, Frey sat back in his Eames lounger and stated, "I have nothing to lose" (p. 43). Cynical exploitation? From a writer's point of view, yes, very much so. But this is an extremely resilient man, we realize, with a *huge* fan base. Many non-fiction writers have gotten away with far worse fudging and fiddling. Why the Frey imbroglio? He is no saint, we conclude, but most of us have bigger fish to fry—and so does he.

3

Autonarrating Transgression

THE DEVIANCE CONCEPT, born in the 1920s out of research on urban decay and disorganization, remained a mainstay of the sociological curriculum for decades. But by the 1970s, radicals and Marxists began questioning the concept's viability (Liazos, 1972; Taylor, Walton, and Young, 1973). By the 1990s to the early 2000s, the assault had become something of an avalanche, with some of these challenges, from a left-wing perspective, by inventing a genealogy of the field, arguing that the sociology of deviance had died (Sumner, 1994), while others, adopting a conservative, essentialistic, right-wing stance, asserted that the field had abandoned a moral center, made claims contrary to "natural law," sustains a toxic, taboo concept, and hence, had "died" (Hendershott, 2002), and still others, claiming that they had evidence to support the charge that attention to deviance had precipitously declined in recent years (Miller, Wright, and Dannels, 2001; Best, 2004).

Contrary to some of field's critics, any investigation of the "death" claim must include a tally of the number of courses on deviance in sociology departments, along with enrollments. I made an inquiry at a dozen and a half programs and found that between the late 1970s and the early 2000s, the number of departments offering the course had more than doubled and the total enrollments in these courses had more than tripled. I also checked the number of articles in the social science literature with "deviance" and "deviant" in the title and found that the peak decade was the 1980s; for book titles, the top decade was the 1970s. None of this adds up to the "death" or "dying" of the sociology of deviance. It is possible that the field is less vital, creative, and innovative than was true in the past and that it is less of a fixture in mainstream sociology (though an argument could be made for the increasing irrelevance of mainstream sociology for American society). I would maintain, however, that the potential of the deviance concept has yet to be fully tapped, and indications of its importance is all around us. Perhaps most important is the fact that the field of sociology generally has incorporated many of the most important insights of its subfield, deviance—a case of Robert K. Merton's "obliteration by incorporation" (1979). We see it in queer theory, postcolonial studies, the sociology of medicine, the study of social movements, criminology, social problems, mass communications, and in the study of moral panics. And above all, we see it in narrative studies, particularly in its investigation of deviance neutralization. *The sociology of deviance* may have declined as a field within sociology proper, but *deviance* is an eternal concept, an ineradicable feature of social life, and will always be worth studying from a social science perspective. After all, if the sociology of deviance dies, who's going to study what is one of the most fundamental processes in human life—what happens when a member of the society violates a consequential social norm? To assert that "deviance" is dead, dying, or declining (Miller, Wright, and Dannels, 2001) is asinine.

The "I" and the "Me"

George Herbert Mead, an American philosopher, social psychologist, and university professor, developed the distinction between the "I" and the "me." Though Mead published a substantial number of papers during his lifetime, he never developed a systematic treatise spelling out his central ideas; his most often-cited work, *Mind, Self, and Society,* was assembled after his death by former students who stitched together their lecture notes from his 1927 and 1930 courses on social psychology, along with manuscripts and notes Mead left behind (1934).

The self, argues Mead, is composed of both the "I" and the "me"—they are inseparable—but his "I" refers to the acting self, the "human organism at any moment, but especially at the points at which the organism is launching itself into action" (Blumer, 2004, p. 66). In contrast, the "me" is "that action viewed by the organism from the standpoint of a generalized other" (p. 66)—that is, the self-conscious knowledge of the many evaluating communities relevant to the actor's behavior. The actor is alive to "their attitudes, knows what they want and what the consequences of any act of his [or hers] will be, and he [or she] has assumed responsibility for the situation" (Mead, 1934, p. 175). In short, "it is the presence of those organized sets of attitudes that constitutes that 'me' to which he [or she] as an 'I' is responding" (p. 175). The "I" is the person's action "over against that social situation within his [or] her own conduct, and it gets into his [or her] experience only after he [or she] has carried out the act. Then he [or she] is aware of it" (p. 175). The "I" is uncertain, unpredictable, "never entirely calculable . . . always something different from what the situation itself calls for" (p. 178). Contrarily, the "me" represents "a definite organization of the community there in our own attitudes, and calling for a response" (p. 178). Mead theorized about how the individual navigated between the satisfaction-seeking, egotistical activism of the "I"—the natural, impulsive, assertive self—and the restraints placed by the cultured self, the controlling, civilized community voice of the "me." Along parallel lines, Sigmund Freud distinguished the "id," that part of the self that determined selfish, instinctive impulses, and the "superego," or the conscience, the collective voice of the censorious community.

By *engaging in deviance,* the actor veers more toward the egotistical "I," and in *fashioning the memoir,* the writer creates a more socialized and community-conscious self, veering more toward the "me." Actors who engage in all actions, including deviance, take account of their audiences, and, as Mead argues, in every action in which the individual engages, the "I" and the "me" are inseparable—in practice, although not in principle. Actions that the actor knows offend sectors of the generalized other—acts to which we conventionally refer as *deviance*—might be regarded as behavior regarded as *that which could or should have been otherwise,* which should not have been enacted, acts that by their very nature require a justification or explanation. Conversely, the memoir is specifically that justification or explanation itself, a product of reflection and contemplation, taking into consideration the objections of the generalized other, the various communities to which the actor—now author—pays fealty. The "I" acts in ways that the "me" disapproves of, and, in demanding an accounting for such actions, gets it—in the form of the memoir. Murder, adultery, swindling, chronic intoxication, caddish behavior, sexual promiscuity, prostitution, political rebellion and revolution—all have their forum by way of the autobiography or memoir, the actor's *spin* on his or her unconventional actions: You may disapprove of what I've done, but these are the circumstances contextualizing why I did it; once you read my account (the self-presented "me"), you may feel a little different about who *I* am.

Vocabularies of Motive

"Motives are words. . . . They stand for anticipated situational consequences of questioned conduct" (Mills, 1940, 1963, p. 441). The essay that put the deviance neutralization concept into motion was "Situated Actions and Vocabularies of Motive," by C. Wright Mills, published when the author was a graduate student. Mills's argument is that speech acts are interpreted by co-interactants in such a way that certain utterances are taken to imply specific motives. Verbalizations inform audiences where the actor stands in relation to the moral order. Actors make utterances that influence the way audiences interpret the motivation behind their acts and hence, the valuation of those acts. It is not merely the actor's behavior that counts but the way the actor *verbalizes* his or her behavior. Certain utterances soften violations of the norms; *couching* deviant acts in certain ways offers a reinterpretation of the seriousness of those violations (Ben-Yehuda, 1990, pp. 3, 5, 18, 27, 76).

It is appropriate that the first extant book-length memoir written was, as we've seen, Augustine's *Confessions.* Augustine apologizes for his sins while many later "apologias" defend or justify the behavior of the actor-author. The *Confessions* manifests a logic similar to a long line of "deviance" autonarration: "I did something of which some parties may disapprove. There were reasons for what I did, and, properly contextualized, examined in a certain light, and taking all the available evidence and extenuating circumstances into consideration, much of what I did can be understood and absolved." I argue that one of the driving forces of memoir is the author's attempted self-exculpation for the self-narrated behavior. Augustine seeks absolution from God; contemporary memoir writers seek a species of absolution from an array of parties and audiences, including their readers. Many authors do not consider what they describe as wrong, but virtually all perceive that one or more audiences do, and that these audiences would condemn them for expressing such bald, raw assertions of their putative sins. Though contemporary authors live in a postmodern world—different messages for different audiences—none is completely immune to the nagging voice of the faultfinder.

Even actors who might normally seem beyond the pale of respectable society (and have no need of approbations from respectable society) write memoirs that seek, if not absolution, then a kind of empathetic understanding for their would-be transgressions—that is, acts that *other parties* consider transgressions. In fact, they are likely, in the same memoir, to offer an apologia—a defense of their behavior—*and* proclaim their independence from conventional values and social circles. The "apologia" is *not* coterminous with the apology; it encompasses any and all defenses of self. Felicity Nussbaum (1987, p. 180) remarks on the "scandalous" memoir genre by eighteenth century courtesans and other "transgressive" and "unconventional" women, which "vindicates the apologist from blame, while in contradiction it attempts to escape the moral and social system that requires that very explanation." The eighteenth-century memoirist addressed "folks like me"—that is, the writer's peers—many of whom did not take kindly to the scandalous goings-on of courtesans, obligating her to issue an apologia, or a defense of some kind, as she simultaneously rejected their prissy ways and projected condemnation of her. The audience of the contemporary transgressive women's memoir is likely to be much like the writer in sophistication, education, and liberal values—and so, find transgressions fascinating and titillating—yet be in need of reassurance of the writer's decency by way of her self-vindication. Memoirs writers remain alert to the fact that some of their readers will not fully approve of what they do; practically all of them plant one foot in the deviant world and the other in conventionality—and hence, the need for absolution.

Is to Explain to Condone?

We have all heard the condemnatory verbs that describe the justification of wrongdoing—"rationalize," "excuse," "condone," "doctor," "finagle," "spin": the terms that express pardon for that which should be anathemized. Sophisticated as we all are, we might expect we would be immune to the bogus, blatherous self-vindications of the transgressor. It is important to distinguish between *understanding* terrible acts and maintaining a moral stance toward them. Simply because a wrongdoer justifies a harmful action he or she committed does not mean that we have to set aside our sense of right and wrong. But a warning may not be sufficient.

In looking at court decisions in two murder trials in South Africa, Colman deduces, "Anything that helps to explain the behavior of a defendant might reduce the perceived blameworthiness of that behavior" (1991, p. 1078). Experimental social psychologists have tested audience reactions to accounts supplied by deviant actors and found that when perpetrators offer explanations for their "evil and cruelty," audiences consider them less blameworthy than when no such accounts are supplied. These findings run counter to the social science and popular injunction, "to explain is *not* to forgive." Summarizing three experimental studies, Miller, Gordon, and Buddie (1999, p. 265) conclude that when wrongdoers—cheaters on exams, for example—explain their actions, subjects are more likely to excuse these actions than if they offer no explanations. Folkes and Whang (2003) extrapolate from three of their studies to infer that their subjects were more likely to condone illicit corporate behavior (which could result in harm to employees) if executives explained reasons for their actions, justified them, or apologized for them than if they denied them outright. Even when we know that self-exculpation (and self-serving) modes are likely to be forthcoming from sinners, such modus operandi, when used, tend to mitigate our condemnation of them. Empirically—in the material world—explaining *does* condone wrongdoing. Hence, when authors offer explanations for their behavior—the "Why I did it" accounts—they tend to constitute recitations that employ deviance neutralization.

Whether or not authors consciously intended to soften the reader's condemnation of them for blabbing in the memoir about their offensive behavior, the mere act of engaging in such narrations typically serves to do so.

The Presentation of Self

The autobiography and memoir stand in curious relation to Erving Goffman's "presentation of self." To begin with, in a published work, we are not in the realm of Goffman's "everyday life." To the contrary, the book represents a carefully crafted statement that is neither spontaneous nor evanescent. In publication, interactive, give-and-take sociability is absent, and it is not clear what the author wants from the reader except some admiration and respect—as well as a good word to boost sales. Turning the equation around, the reader does not present a direct "face" to the author—indeed, he or she can throw an author's book against the nearest wall in disgust, and none will be any the wiser. Editorial comments, reviews, the public reading are such formal settings that, at first blush, few of Goffman's insights in *The Presentation of Self in Everyday Life* (1959) seem to apply.

But a closer look quickly reveals the relevance of the concept of the presentation of self for the memoir. What should a "deviance" memoir, one that reveals the intimate details of one's life and the lives of one's intimates, look like? Such a memoir would read along the following lines: *Some of the things I've done, and that others have done with or to me, might surprise some of my readers. What I'm telling you is an honest, more or less unvarnished inside look at what goes on behind the scenes. I realize I'm implicating the people I've interacted with, some of whom I love, because some of them collaborated with me in my nefarious activities, or may have looked foolish by not knowing about them, or victimized me or others in some way. Still, I'm not a terrible person. Okay, I'll say it: Sometimes I engaged in activities some people might regard as objectionable, and simply revealing such acts is often regarded as objectionable. The unsavory or unpopular things I write about are or were an aspect of my life. But there were reasons why I did the things I did; either I would be punished for not doing them, or I got rewarded for doing them. Maybe they made my life more exciting or pleasurable or rewarding. Anyway, here's my story. I'm going to get some flak from some of my friends and readers for telling you this because it was kind of a secret. It's something my peers don't want you to know.*

Any social setting, says Erving Goffman, may profitably be studied "from the point of view of impression management. . . . Within the walls of a social establishment we find a team of performers who cooperate to present to an audience a given definition of the situation" (1959, p. 238). Performers throw up barriers that keep audiences from observing inconvenient facts. The "front region" is the social and physical arena in which performers enact impression management; audiences see what performers want them to see. In the "back region" or backstage, performers reveal information to one another they keep hidden from audiences, and they rehearse the fronts they present to audiences. Access to the back region "is controlled in order to prevent outsiders from seeing backstage and to prevent outsiders from coming into a performance that is not addressed to them" (p. 238).

Not infrequently, something goes wrong with the performance taking place in the front region and audiences are exposed to inconvenient backstage facts and discover the bogus nature of the performance. "Sometimes disruptions occur through unmeant gestures, faux pas, and scenes, thus discrediting or contradicting the definition of the situation that is being maintained" (Goffman, 1959, p. 239). Often, the disruption is temporary, and audiences collude in their own disillusionment by working to recover the performers' misleading definition of the situation. But sometimes, the "dialogue" between the two teams—performers and the audience—comes to an "embarrassed and confused halt; the situation may cease to be defined, previous positions may become no longer tenable, and participants may find themselves without a charted course of action" (p. 242).

Upon reflection, however, it seems clear that the autobiography may be seen as a kind of "performance" in which the author presents the self through the narration of his or her life. Information, or what is offered as information, is presented or withheld to enable the narrator to construct a plausibly positive self-image or at least tell an interesting story. But the work itself represents a kind of staging of a character, putting "techniques of impression management" (1959, p. 208) into play. Every memoir author has skeletons in the closet, "well-kept dark secrets" (pp. 141–144), the revelation of which are likely to produce embarrassment—not of a face-to-face variety, but something with which the author, upon self-reflection, has to live. As with first-hand interaction, the narrator may give off "tells" or slips that inadvertently reveal what the author wishes to remain hidden, though, unlike the discretion involved in quotidian, first-hand interaction, critics often relish in exposing a memoir author's failings.

What sorts of memoir "presentations of self" fail? Perhaps three types of failures stand out most prominently.

The first is the failure of not living up to the self as advertised, in presenting a bogus self—that is, being exposed as a fabricator of one's past. Depending on the nature and the degree of one's fabrications, the punishment is likely to be public humiliation and the withdrawal of a book from circulation, sometimes even before it has been published—but this is not always the case. At the end of 2007 and the beginning of 2008, after critics revealed that some assertions in Herman Rosenblat's *Angel at the Fence,* a feel-good, life-affirming tale of a Holocaust romance, were enhanced and invented, Penguin withdrew the book—already printed but not yet released—from publication, and the Lerner Publishing Group likewise recalled the children's book based on Rosenblat's tale (Friedman, 2008). *Love and Consequences* (2008) by Margaret Jones (a.k.a. Margaret Seltzer) was likewise exposed as fabricated, and as a result, Riverhead Books yanked it from the shelves and canceled further printings. (I managed to obtain a copy only hours before its disappearance from bookstores.) On the other hand, as we likewise saw, James Frey's humiliation for inventing particulars in *A Million Little Pieces* (2003) hurt neither the sales of that book nor his subsequent career as a writer. Clearly, though with the general public, Frey's failure to create a credible "performance" as a memoir writer is manifestly evident, he carries with him a sufficiently substantially specialty following such that he remains, in their eyes, a credible writer.

The second type of failed presentation of self is that of being unable to impress as a competent memoirist, in effect, to manifest oneself, through one's writing, as a bogus writer. Most autobiographies and memoirs published during and since the 1990s are not literary masterpieces (the same can be said of books in general, in any genre, produced during any era); a substantial number are not even competently written. As we saw in Chapter 2, critics have savaged memoir authors for their indulgence in the lurid details of their lives and, as a consequence, producing gratuitously badly written books. In celebrating such books—or at least taking them seriously enough to discuss them on an equal plane with the masterpieces—I risk the kind of gratuitously snotty review that another sociologist, Diane Bjorklund, received from James Olney (1999) in *American Literature* because her *Interpreting the Self* (1998) examined autobiography *as* sociological and cultural documents rather than as literature. Her critic seemed to be saying, "Hands off! This is our domain, not yours! No sociologists allowed!" I am with Bjorklund here: How autobiographers and memoirists "stage" a presentation of themselves as violators of presumably acceptable behavior constitutes the substance of this book, not their literary talent.

And the third failure, of prominent interest to us as students of deviance neutralization, is the failure to convince one's reader that one's account is acceptable. Audiences may not honor or "buy" one's explanation or justification or excuses for violating those rules all decent, civilized humans accept as valid. While we can regard techniques of neutralization as *the use of acceptable reasons for engaging in unacceptable behavior,* not all audiences find the reasons the actor offers equally acceptable or appropriate *for the behavior in question.* Richard Nixon's failure to properly apologize for his Watergate "dirty tricks" led to his being forced out of the presidency (Harrell, Ware, and

Linkugel, 1975). Bill Clinton's initial neutralization for the charge of dallying with a White House intern ("I did not have sexual relations with that woman") not only was implausible but also was shown to be false, and its falsity led to his impeachment, though not removal from office. Most contemporary audiences would find John Wesley Hardin's claim never to have shot a man—over a score of them—who did not deserve to die (Hardin, 1895/1961) unconvincing, though the passage of time has turned the bandit into something of a hero. Roman Polanski's many explanations for having sex with a thirteen-year-old (1985) are likely to sound like rationalizations; they still ring false, as they did three decades ago, which is one of the reasons he has not been admitted back into the United States. Likewise, Hemingway's flabby effort to excuse his adulteries (1964) does not convince the reader, as the critic Alfred Kazin explains (1964). In short, we should always read the term "deviance neutralization" as shorthand for *efforts* to neutralize behavior that audiences find potentially discreditable. As to whether and to what extent accounts are "honored" is a separate but crucial matter (Blumstein, 1974).

Here, we are interested in how our authors explain and contextualize their lives, in the vocabularies they use to give meaning to them and the rhetorical chronicles with which they build autobiographical houses. Most lives do not contain much narrative tension, a basic ingredient of fiction, and narrative tension is what readers thrive on, dip into a book to be gripped by, and yes, authors bend and stretch, fudge and fiddle with details and chronology to tighten up the plot of their memoirs to make them seem more gripping, to infuse more coherence into their narrative than existed in their lives. Almost certainly all or most of the authors of the memoirs we will look at here have done some of this. All students of memoir take these finagles and embellishments for granted, but as we saw, there are some liberties that are so extreme that few of us will tolerate them.

Accounts

Marvin Scott and Stanford Lyman provided us with a systematic discussion acknowledging the strong link between accounts and deviance (1968). They *define* an account as a "linguistic device employed whenever an action is subjected to valuative inquiry" (p. 46). If an activity "falls outside the domain of expectations," audiences anticipate, and hanker after, explications rendering what the actor did meaningful to one or more audiences. Of course, accounts are "situated" according to the statuses of interactants; particulars as to context or circumstances; and societies with respect to time, place, and subgroup. By "account," then, Scott and Lyman mean "a statement made by a social actor to explain unacceptable or untoward behavior" (p. 46). When we engage in expected or "routine, common-sense behavior in a cultural environment that recognizes behavior as such," no account need be forthcoming. In Scott and Lyman's scheme of things, accounts are chiefly "linguistic forms that are offered for untoward actions" (p. 47).

What counts in this picture is the account renderer's *audience*; the narrator anticipates a certain reaction or judgment from a given audience and adjusts the account accordingly. *For certain audiences,* the narrator's rendering of particular accounts is needless because the behavior is not regarded as a malfeasance (though the account might also have to acknowledge that some of the participants *do* regard the act as wrong). The offering of an account might be needless for a second reason as well: The narrator is likely to perceive that a given audience will refuse to acknowledge the legitimacy of the account. If a white person offers an "I didn't mean it" account to an audience of black people after uttering a racial slur, that is likely to sound feeble, self-serving, and implausible; that audience will not honor such an account, although offering *no* account is almost always less acceptable than offering a feeble one.

Scott and Lyman do not claim that their typology of accounts is exhaustive, but they do offer two more or less mutually exclusive principle types: excuses and justifications. *Excuses* are "socially approved vocabularies for mitigating or relieving responsibility when conduct is questioned." In the excuse, the actor admits that the conduct in question is "bad, wrong, or inappropriate but denies full responsibility" (p. 47). Like excuses, *justifications* "are socially approved vocabularies that neutralize an act or its consequences when one or both are called into question" (p. 51). But by contrast, the justification asserts the act's neutral or positive value in the face of the contrary. "Justifications recognize a general sense in which the act in question is impermissible, but claim that the particular occasion permits or requires the very act" (p. 51). Scott and Lyman do not discuss apologies, which seem to me to be neither excuses nor justifications.

Accounts are "acceptable utterances"—a type of speech act—intended to mitigate the negative impact of putatively untoward actions. The very rendering of the account is intended to assure audiences that their judgment has been brought into the picture. Rendering accounts is a bridge-building verbal action designed to preserve, insure, or repair the moral order. Audiences that honor a given account may be regarded as a kind of *speech community* (p. 61) that not only honors the validity and vocabulary of a given account but also accepts that the utterance is atonement for the moral breach. Thus, the statements "I had to do it" and "It was him or me" will be acceptable to certain audiences of violent criminals, but the very rendering of these statements represents, at the very least, a genuflection among others acknowledging that the teller has recognized their point of view. Such accounts may *not* be acceptable, however, in a courtroom setting.

Accounts are verbal processes whereby actors attempt to align a positive self-conception, largely within their own moral framework and that of their significant others, with actions that, superficially considered, seem to contradict that self-conception (Hewitt and Stokes, 1975; Stokes and Hewitt, 1976). We generally want others we care about to think well of us; hence, we explain why we did what we did (or what we are, or believe) by invoking a vocabulary that protects our more or less positive notions of ourselves from being discredited. Sometimes we are reduced to offering excuses, but they too are part of our armory of self-justification. Sometimes all we can offer are justifications that make us seem less bad than the anticipated criticism, but again, that too is a type of neutralization. We all do it: "It's not as bad as it looks"; "I was drunk"; "I didn't mean it"; "I couldn't help myself"; "It was an accident"; "I wasn't thinking"; "It just happened"; "I was joking"; "We were just fooling around"; "I can explain everything"; "One thing led to another." Each of these common verbal utterances condenses into a simple, stereotypical phrase encapsulating a type of neutralization device.

It is important to keep in mind that we are not merely interested in how vocabularies of motive and techniques of neutralization are devised, but whether and under what conditions they are *honored.* Do audiences "honor" or accept them? Are they plausible to others? To onlookers and bystanders, to victims, to like-minded friends and associates, to antagonists, to the sympathetic, the people "in the know"? Have persons who devised them learned how to render them more acceptable and plausible to audiences? The *reception* of such vocabularies will prove to be a major issue throughout our investigations.

Techniques of Neutralization: Theory or Concept?

In 1957, a positivist criminologist and a phenomenologist sociologist teamed up to "uncover the roots of juvenile delinquency" (Sykes and Matza, 1957, p. 667). They puzzled over the failure of the then recently devised explanation of Albert K. Cohen to adequately account for the emergence of juvenile delinquency (1955). The flaw in Cohen's theory, they believed, was manifest and fatal. Cohen theorized that youths who are unable to achieve values stressed by mainstream middle-class society turn those values on their head and develop a delinquent subculture specifically in opposition to conventional middle-class values and norms. In Cohen's theory, delinquent youth *wholeheartedly* embrace criminality. Sykes and Matza point out the remarkable paradox in the fact that the delinquent does *not* wholeheartedly embrace criminality, but instead endorses certain features of conventional morality. For instance, he respects the honest person, is "keen" to "detect hypocrisy" in self-proclaimed honest people, often develops "fierce attachments" to honorable individuals, such as "a humble, pious mother or a forgiving, upright priest," and typically draws a sharp line between deserving and undeserving victims (p. 665). In short, the delinquent has one foot in conventional morality and one in delinquency. Sykes and Matza hold that the delinquent shares too many conventional values to explain his behavior through the process of "learning moral imperatives, values or attitudes standing in direct contradiction to those of the dominant society" (p. 667). These authors are not entirely clear, however, about exactly *what* delinquents "neutralize." In certain passages, they seem to neutralize the *condemnation of deviance*; in others, they neutralize *mainstream norms*. No matter—both come down to the same thing: Freed from either, the juvenile is able to engage in delinquency.

But the paradox remains: How is it possible, Sykes and Matza ask, for delinquents to engage in delinquency when conventionality maintains a strong hold on them? These authors' explanation of deviance among juveniles holds that young people do not engage in delinquency because they learn moral imperatives that contradict those of conventional society; they do so because they learn neutralization devices that allow them to *justify* engaging in illegal behavior. The authors offer an array of justifications, including the *denial of responsibility* ("It wasn't my fault"), the *denial of injury* ("No harm, no foul"), the *denial of the victim* ("He deserved it"), a *condemnation of the condemners* ("The system is unfair"), and an *appeal to higher loyalties* ("I couldn't let my buddies down").

"Techniques of Neutralization" is one of the most often-cited academic articles in the annals of sociology: It is the eighth most frequently cited article ever published in *The American Sociological Review,* the highest-impact journal in the field. Moreover, the article's impact has steadily grown since its publication, "with no sign yet that its peak has yet been reached" (Jacobs, 2005, p. 3). It has stimulated thousands of research projects, studies, theses, dissertations, and other academic articles. There is a *huge* literature on neutralization in criminology, delinquency research, and the sociology of deviance. In 2005, Maruna and Copes devoted a hundred-page article in the journal *Crime and Justice* to a review of a small sampling of the neutralization literature. It turns out that deviance neutralizations have been used to justify virtually any untoward actions we might imagine, from engaging in murdering people for pay (Levi, 1981) and being a racist (Berbrier, 1999) to shoplifting (Cromwell and Thurman, 2003) and missing college classes (Kalab, 1987)—practically as many modes of neutralization as there are types of deviance. The literature continues to grow apace; it is possible we could fill an entire volume simply with the *references* to neutralization publications. What have we learned from this immense literature?

Sykes and Matza's "techniques of neutralization" is both a theory and a concept. Its *theory,* or explanation, argues that as a result of neutralizing the stigma or imputed deviance of certain behavior, youthful actors are freed to engage in delinquency, crime, and deviance; neutralizations "precede" and "make deviant behavior possible" (p. 666). In contrast, the *concept* argues that neutralization is a common accompaniment or consequence of enacting behavior the society, or sectors of the society, regard as non-normative. Many sociologists regard the *theory* as fatally flawed—hardly any analysts today believe that Sykes and Matza have managed to "uncover the roots of juvenile delinquency" (1957, p. 664)—and we will see why momentarily. But as a *concept,* deviance neutralization remains a robust and enduring contribution to the literature, one substantially generalizable even beyond the broad territory of delinquency, crime, and deviance; it applies to the everyday lives of perfectly ordinary, mainstream actors. It is a fixture of all social interaction, everyday life, one of the many bonds that hold societies and their social structures together. Hence, we have to grapple with deviance neutralization's paradoxical legacy: its failure as a theory and its success as a concept.

As an explanation of crime and delinquency, deviance neutralization suffers from its positivistic and etiological thesis. Sykes and Matza's theory postulates techniques of neutralization as a *cause* of untoward behavior: First comes the neutralization and then, as a consequence, comes the behavior. Maruna and Copes (2005) conclude that "neutralization theory has received only mixed empirical support" because, as they argue, criminology has understood it "as a theory of criminal etiology," as an explanation for the cause of criminal behavior (2005, p. 221). In contrast, they argue, the field should look to the perspective for an understanding of "persistence in or desistance from criminal behavior" (p. 221). Neutralizing does not necessarily *cause* people to engage in deviance and crime, but once the actor engages in them, such modes of reasoning may permit them to *continue* engaging in them.

To me, it seems almost self-evident that being able to justify one's actions cannot be a sufficient, necessary, or adequate explanation for the *cause* of criminal behavior. (Moreover, this "explanation" begs the question, merely pushing the issue of etiology back one step further. At the very least, the criminologist who adopts this almost absurd position would have to explain *how* and *why* one was able to justify one's actions.) To my way of thinking, justifications are more likely to *follow* or at least *accompany* than to *precede* or *cause* a criminal act. Using neutralization as an explanation of persistence, likewise, seems incomplete since, again, one would have to explain how someone came to acquire such a roster of justifications.

This book does not concern itself with either of these endeavors. Here, my focus is on deviance neutralization per se; what many scholars and researchers have taken as a possible cause of crime I look at, in this volume, as *the phenomenon itself.* It is my butterfly. (Or oyster, if the reader prefers that metaphor.) I look at it, try to understand it, note its brilliance—or dullness—size, coloration, pattern, shape, habitats. As a sociologist and criminologist, I am not uninterested in the causes of crime—but that is not my mission here. This book's goal is not centered on the "Why did they do it?" question, it is focused on how people answer, explain, or justify "doing it" *once they've done it.* I address verbalizations as *facts in themselves* and leave the causal question to others. It is almost certain that the neutralization of the deviance of the behavior in which justifiers engage takes place either *in the course of* or *after* the behavior, not before. And it is likely that these justifications lie at hand to be picked up and used as the occasion demands. But my concern is entirely wrapped up in the vocabularies people use in explaining and justifying what they know or sense will be regarded by some audiences as wrongdoing. More specifically, I am interested in how *memoirists* come to justify the supposed wrongdoings they describe in the context of an autobiographical narrative of their lives or a portion or aspect of their lives. I take writing a memoir as a variation of naturalistic, everyday behavior, but with interesting differences worth exploring. Instead of the "Why do they do it?" question, I am interested in "How do they explain or justify what they are doing or what they did?" As Donald Cressey, a criminologist, said, "Listening to people tell you why they did it does not give you explanations of why they did it. When you ask people why they commit crime, they make sounds. I call them verbalizations. These are data. You study them" (quoted in Laub, 1983, p. 139). I regard neutralization devices less as causes of deviant behavior than as after-the-fact explanations, justifications, defenses, or "rationalizations" of that behavior. Deviant acts come before justifications, not the other way around. As a supposed explanation for the deviant behavior itself, "techniques of neutralization theory" falls within the domain of positivist criminology; as an exploration of how people account for their untoward behavior, it is mainly the domain of the social constructionist. I assume enactors of deviance and criminal behavior are, in some ways, different from persons who adhere to the conventional norms and laws, and that the weaker emotive and cognitive hold those norms and laws have on them is part of the reason why they stray, but I do not see their ability to neutralize as the key to this explanation.

More than a few commentators have also couched the techniques of neutralization concept in either-or terms: *Either* enactors of untoward behavior have the same values as the rest of us—in which case they engage in techniques of neutralization—*or* they have values that differ from those of the rest of us, in which case they do not *have to* engage in neutralizations. To my way of thinking, this is a false dichotomy, a narrowly logical cause-and-effect argument and an unproductive way of looking at normative violations. Even people who hold values and beliefs that are very different from the majority engage in neutralizations. Their justifications do not necessarily arise from the discomfort they feel as a result of having violated their own sense of what is right. For nearly *all* miscreant behavior, the enactor has values and beliefs that are different from the majority. Almost *every* imaginable action, deviant and otherwise, attracts people who hold values and beliefs different from those who do not enact that action: people who believe that UFOs are extraterrestrial aircraft versus those who do not, theists versus atheists, people who consume pornography versus those who do not, voters versus non-voters, heterosexuals versus homosexuals, liberals versus conservatives, evolutionists versus creationists. Yet when we are called upon to account for our actions or beliefs we know or sense lie away from the moral straight and narrow, we tend to employ neutralization devices. Our neutralization devices are likely to be directed to our significant others, not the society at large, and those "others" may not like what we do—or may not like our writing a memoir about what we do, even if they do not disapprove of it as much as the society at large.

To summarize, it is difficult to imagine anyone thinking that learning or endorsing *the ability to neutralize transgressions* causes crime. In fact, it is the other way around: *Engaging in crime leads to using techniques of neutralization.* Miscreants may vary from the mainstream in their respect to neutralize crime, but the magnitude of the relationship is such that most or nearly all people who engage in criminal and other deviant behavior are *called upon* to account for themselves and their actions, and they typically come up with neutralizations in response to such an expectation, from a grab-bag of items ready at hand, from the society at large, or their subcultural group, or from their imagination, their inventiveness, from the simple impulse to render their character more or less respectable. Virtually anyone can—and does—verbally neutralize behavior that others find offensive or unacceptable. It is the nature of these verbalizations that is interesting—how specific behaviors shape their form, configuration, and patterning. This is the mission of this book; I believe that attempting to determine whether and to what extent such verbalizations *cause* deviance and crime is an illusory, quixotic, and barren quest from the get-go, but I do believe that such verbalizations are worth a close investigation.

To Whom Are Self-Exculpations Addressed?

The most telling feature of deviance neutralization is its interactional quality. Self-exculpation is not activated simply because "norms" are violated, such as the Ten Commandments' "thou shalt not" norms. For the most part, actors do not employ exculpatory verbalizations because they break abstract rules, they do so because they have disappointed, hurt, or betrayed specific parties or "audiences" in their lives—or, in their minds, they *will* do so. In the special case of the memoir writer, in addition to such parties, the narrator has an additional audience in mind: the reader. Even St. Augustine invokes three parties whom he has betrayed with the wrongdoings he committed in his young life. He invokes his pious Christian mother, with tears streaming down her cheeks, who "saw the death" in which he lay, and you, he explains to his Lord, heard her "weeping for my perdition," answered her prayers. He invokes the wisdom of his teacher, St. Ambrose: He was "so kind as to discuss things with me, expose my mistakes, to unteach me what was bad, and to teach me what was good," yet he was wise enough to recognize that he, Augustine, was not yet "fit to be taught" and needed instead to discover the error of his ways by "wallowing in the mud of the pit and in the darkness of falsehood." But it is God whom Augustine most betrayed by his countless sinning. He addresses God hundreds of times throughout his confessions ("Hear me, God"), from whom he seeks compassion and redemption. He says, in one way or another, over and over again, "In your eyes what could be more disgusting than I was" (1963, pp. 37, 66–68). "*Have mercy upon me,*" Augustine supplicates God, "*for I have sinned against Thee*" (p. 71). But in addition to his mother, St. Ambrose, and God, St. Augustine addresses his readers. At the very end of his *Confessions,* after praising God's eternal powers and gifts, he raises this crucial question: "*How can one man teach another man to understand this?*" (my emphasis). His audience clearly encompasses all men (and women). In order to teach other men to revere God, he must narrate the sinfulness of his life and how he redeemed himself, and to do so, he must employ devices that God—and man—honor; this is the central purpose of *The Confessions of St. Augustine* (p. 350).

In effect, in their accounts, in one way or another, memoir writers are asking specific parties or audiences to "forgive" them for their sins—or at least satisfy themselves that the parties they address understand what they did—although their requests assume a multitude of forms and shapes, infinitely more varied than the holy sage of Carthage could have imagined.

Autonarrating deviant behavior shares in the same dilemma that describing a life dissimilar to that of the reader does: Reading it both repels and attracts; the details of the writer's involvement in acts widely considered wrong are both alienating and fascinating. The tendency toward an author's use of self-exculpation—specifically, strategies of deviance neutralization—entails "eating" one's cake and "having" it, too. Personally strange and alien though robbery or murder are to the typical reader, the common ground authors lay down and onto which they invite readers to step is the contrivance of explaining their motives for transgressions in vocabularies that resonate with their audience. Augustine, though addressing God, knew his readers were likely to share the same template of temptation, guilt, a sense of revulsion, and the desperate need for redemption. However unsullied by commercialism the artist-memoirist might feel, he or she always puts pen to paper—or fingers to keyboard—with an audience in mind. That audience might be small and similar to the writer in crucial ways, or large, heterogeneous, and mostly different, but they do so *to the extent that* their readers are likely to feel that they, the author, offers a rationale or defense for wrongdoing that their audience can appreciate. And to this extent, likewise, he or she extends to readers a means by which readers can identify with the author, feel that they share a mutual understanding—an intersection of humanity, so to speak—and hence, feel that reading his or her book is enriching and rewarding. When successful, self-exculpation works through mechanisms that invoke commonality between the writer and the reader—essentially no different from detailing the mutualities of biography the author assumes readers share with him or her.

Our objective is the analysis of deviance neutralization, true, but our venue is the memoir. Hence, we have to consider the audience to whom the author directs his or her narration, along with neutralizing the deviance of his or her acts. To repeat, all motivational accounting systems are interactional affairs, and neutralizers are influenced in their accounts by their anticipated audiences. The writer makes a pact with the reader; instead, the delinquent makes a pact with his fellow delinquents, and this is a very different sort of pact. Topalli (2005) argues that this process works even for delinquents, although their verbalizations are directed to *other* delinquents, a small network of local hoods. In contrast, writers picture tens or hundreds of thousands of readers guided by specific sensibilities that they themselves partly share. As I said, the author of the memoir may differ in crucial respects from the reader. But during the writing of the memoir, the author has to have lived a sufficient number of years to have accumulated enough acts to write about, and time enough to marinate and reflect on, and write about, the nature and implications of the act and its victimization, if any took place, and what they all imply for the actor's shared humanity with the reader. No such process takes place with the delinquent or criminal. The writer-reader bond implies a measure of shared values that encourage narrators of deviant behavior to express remorse for wrongdoing and neutralize its blemish. Hence, the delinquent who expresses a certain vocabulary of motives with his fellow delinquents in mind as a real or potential audience shares similarities with yet differs markedly from the memoir writer, whose audience is made up largely of colleagues and prospective readers.

In Sum: Neutralizing Deviance

In a very real sense, our authors are trying to answer the "Who am I?" and the "Am I not a decent person?" questions. Their neutralization rationales are *not* mere rhetorical or tactical strategies to get powerful actors off the hook after the fact. Our authors attempt to establish that, in spite of their flaws or supposed flaws, they are good, decent human beings worthy of dignity and respect. Deviance neutralization grows out of the rich soil of the social interactionist's approach to human behavior. We cannot understand behavior without understanding reactions to it, both positive and negative. How significant others view us and what we do powerfully influence how we see ourselves and our own behavior. It is difficult to maintain a self-image that sharply conflicts with that of a consensus of significant others. The self is reflexive, and this reflexivity shapes what we say and do. We tend to behave in such a way that our acts verify our self-image. When we do things that challenge or subvert that identity we tend to feel emotionally uncomfortable and cognitively in a bind, and attempt to explain away, account for, or reconcile our participation in them—or alter our behavior. Most of us are uncomfortable with a negative self-image. Few people enjoy despising themselves. And to maintain a positive self-image, we are likely to gravitate toward others who agree with us and enable us to do so. Moreover, we have to offer an account of our past behavior—whether we feel it is wrong or not—to peers we like and respect that reconcile our current decency with its moral shakiness.

These three propositions—the self is reflexive, our identity tends to strive toward consistency, and we tend to strive for a positive self-image—pose a distinct problem for the study of deviance: How do we come to do things that are widely condemned? More specifically, when we *contemplate* engaging in such acts, how do we convince ourselves that it's acceptable to engage in them? And how do we address the charges by conventional audiences that we've *done* something wrong?

The most commonsensical explanation, one that many of us are likely to come up with, is that the actor charged with deviance *denies* the charge. Denial is common in face-to-face social interaction and offenders often use it as a neutralization device. For instance, research shows that a substantial number of convicted child molesters deny having had sexual contact with minors (McCaghy, 1967). As we saw, President Bill Clinton initially denied sexual contact with a White House intern ("I did not have sexual relations with that woman"), a denial that broke down when evidence poured in about the case. But denial is less common in memoirs than other techniques when others and ourselves are critical to the point of not buying our story. In fact, all the other techniques of neutralization stress the *interpretation* of known malfeasances, not their very enactment. Since authors writing their life histories can control the story, by simply failing to mention secret deviant acts they committed, in effect, they have denied their misdeeds. However, when an act is as pivotal and as widely known as Clinton's indiscretions, this option is not available. Again, denial, whether overt or covert, rarely works; it's the interpretation that counts—the "spin" on what was done—and it's interpretation that must carry the burden of neutralization.

Many actors *exceptionalize* their potential or actual deviant behavior. That is, they agree with the general principle that such acts are wrong but insist that the acts they engaged in do not *belong* to that general class of acts. For instance, Donald Cressey studied a sample of convicted embezzlers (1953), many of whom insisted that they endorse the laws against violating financial trust, but what *they* did was not embezzlement. They developed "vocabularies of adjustment" that argue that they were "borrowing," "not really stealing." "I was caught in an unfavorable cash flow," they would insist, maintaining a self-image that as honest and law-abiding. These were conventional men (all were men) who could not tolerate a self-image of a thief; in their eyes, they were not deviants or criminals.

Likewise, many actors who engage in non-normative behavior *excuse* their actions. They admit having engaged in wrongful behavior; they condemn the general category of behavior and *under normal circumstances* condemn what they did as well. But what they went through were *not* normal circumstances, they insist. Blame is deflected onto circumstances, not themselves, their motives, or their character. Lofland refers to such a mechanism as "special justification" (pp. 88–93). We can locate three subtypes of excusing: *deserving victims, lack of personal control,* and *transcending commitments.* As we saw, Sykes and Matza (1957) call these "denial of the victim," "denial of responsibility," and "appeal to higher loyalties." The actor adopts a kind of "billiard ball" notion of his or her actions: *He hit me first. I was drunk and didn't know what I was doing. I couldn't let my buddies down.* Excusing one's behavior comes perilously close to rendering it conventional—to oneself, at any rate—while the deniers and the exceptionalizers draw a bright, sharp line between their character and the act they engage in and alienate themselves from the contamination of the stigma of deviance. By way of contrast, excusers have one foot in the world of deviance by admitting that, seen in a certain light, what they did *could* be deemed as deviant. *All right, under normal circumstances, what I did was wrong,* they admit, *but I couldn't help it; I was forced into it; I didn't have full control over myself; I'm not responsible for what I did—I can't be blamed for it.* As we look into the manner in which our actors neutralize the supposed negativity of their actions, it becomes increasingly clear that none of them would refer to what they say about it as an *excuse.* From where they sit, and to an empathetic observer, only some of Sykes and Matza's "excuses" qualify for the term. In fact, properly understood, what they refer to as "appeals to higher loyalties" and "transcending commitments" should be called *justifications.* This qualification is especially crucial in the case of politically oriented neutralizations.

These three mechanisms—denial, exceptionalizing, and excusing—have one important quality in common: They all reflect some degree of allegiance to conventional values or conventional others who do or would or might condemn the actor. They also show that someone can do something that he or she does not support morally or ideologically and that values and actions are not necessarily consistent with one another. We often feel ambivalent about what we do because we are caught in a double bind: Both alternatives in a situation may be unacceptable. Most importantly is the fact that we possess enormous powers of explaining, justifying, accounting for, conceptualizing, inventing, creating, and infusing our behavior and our motives with meaning.

Normalization is distinctly different from denial, exceptionalization, and excusing. It is a rationale that renders or defines as "normal" and acceptable that which is widely regarded as "abnormal" or unacceptable. As Augustine says, "No thief will submit to being robbed by another" (p. 45), a self-evidently true statement, but *many* practitioners of non-normative behavior want to live in a world in which their condemned activity is acceptable. Such neutralizers feel that their chosen behavior has gotten a "bum rap" from conventional society. The behavior should not be regarded as wrong, and the society should not punish or condemn it. It is morally neutral or positive in value, and the stigma or deviance attributed to it by others is illegitimate; normalization is a type of deviance neutralization that renders the activity acceptable.

The interested observer can locate two subtypes of normalization, one that downgrades the putatively negative qualities others attribute to it and the second that emphasizes its positives. When a pimp says that sex for pay is not that different from a housewife being supported by her husband, he is downplaying the negatives of his profession by conventionalizing it within the context of conventional marriage. By saying that the conventional husband "slaves" away to support a self-indulgent, free-spending wife, while he, the pimp, convinces women to work to support him, he is emphasizing the negatives of the conventional marriage as against the positives of his job (Milner and Milner, 1972). With the growth of gay liberation in the 1970s, many homosexuals began to assert that "gay is good" or even that "gay is better than straight." The practitioners of many behaviors that mainstream society regards as worthy of condemnation regard mainstream social control as illegitimate.

The apology is a major form of deviance disavowal (Tavuchis, 1991). In Erving Goffman's words, the apology "is a gesture through which an individual splits himself [or herself] into two parts, the part that is guilty of an offense and the part that disassociates itself from the delict and affirms a belief in the offended rule" (1971, p. 113). The apology *seems* straightforward: "Something happens; something is said or done that is interpreted and judged offensive, improper, or harmful. An apology is called for, someone apologizes, the apology (let us assume) is accepted, the offender is forgiven, and life goes on *as if* nothing had happened. Although some tension may remain—we are, after all, creatures endowed with the faculty of memory—for all practical purposes, the social slate is wiped clean. So commonplace, frequent, widespread, taken for granted, and yet so mysterious, is this occurrence" (Tavuchis, 1991, p. 4). The apology differs from the other neutralization techniques and fits into the following template: *I did it, I was wrong, and there's no excuse for it, but I'm still a decent, honorable human being, and I deserve to be treated with respect. Condemn me if you wish, but my mistake shouldn't stigmatize me forever.* Whatever else it might be, the apology represents an attempt to neutralize the stain of deviance, or stigma, in the eyes of some or certain audiences. Apologies work to the extent that the neutralizer projects sincerity to the wronged party, promises reparations of an acceptable kind, and genuinely appears to repent the enactment of the sin that prompted the act in the first place (Lazare, 2004). But sociology's conception of deviance neutralization is much broader than this, since it includes verbalizations for behavior the enactor does not feel is wrong, yet such actions call forth the appropriate warrants. Who cares? Apparently we all do.

4
Criminal Behavior

CRIME MEMOIRS provide an abundance of insight into the author's interpretations, motives, and feelings about illegal behavior; in turn, the writer's imagized audience provides a spur to those interpretations. When Jack Henry Abbott tells us about his abuse at the hands of the criminal justice system, he hears a coterie of leftists and other critics of the criminal justice system encouraging him and digs deeper into his treasure trove of stories of atrocities visited upon his rebellious spirit and all-too-human flesh. Joseph Bonanno, Eddie Bunker, and even Jordan Belfort—all had their followers, supporters, admirers from near and far. But they also had detractors from the larger community, which is why we have to factor in the matter of "to whom" deviance neutralizations are addressed. Some of their explications and judgments elicit approval from like-minded peers while some of them elicit condemnation from socially and culturally dissimilar communities and social circles. While in principle all are equal before and subject to the law, not all wholeheartedly agree with the law, at least not in all its particulars or in all instances. All laws make exceptions under certain circumstances, and many criminals attempt to verbally invent, and squeeze between, cracks in the law, magnifying the exceptions, the special circumstances, the contingencies, and qualifications. "There are reasons why I did what I did," they say. "It's not as wrong as it seems." "Anyway, I shouldn't have gotten all this prison time; I'm being unfairly targeted." As a perusal of "deviance" memoirs demonstrates, the capacity of humans to self-exculpate is almost infinite, although the forms this mental enterprise takes tends to be both patterned and idiosyncratic. Crime memoirs teach us not to be too literal about the facticity of the author's narrative and to focus on what makes them sociologically noteworthy: They depict the writer as a far more decent person than a police rap sheet does.

Memoir writers are not representative of the categories of the people whose behavior they write about, and the behaviors about which they write are likewise not representative of the total universe of such offenses. For instance, most white collar crime is not exciting; it usually involves diddles and fiddles, book-juggling and figure-finagling, cutting corners, making technically illicit transactions, purposely incorrectly adding up columns of numbers, then pocketing fairly small sums of money. The Bernie Madoffs of the world—the corporate swindlers whose schemes filched millions or billions—are wildly exceptional, far from the rule. White collar criminals tend to be drab little people with a narrow vision and commonplace goals rather than colorful, flamboyant, romantic economic swashbucklers. Still, the most popular and widely read memoirs by white collar offenders describe crimes that are more exciting and noteworthy than the run-of-the-mill variety that constitute the bulk of such felonies—most of which would make for extremely dull reading. Films centering on white collar crimes tend to be exciting *because* they are atypical and depart from the quotidian representatives that take place in the material world—consider *Wall Street* (1987), *Rogue Trader* (1999), *Boiler Room* (2000), *Catch Me If You Can* (2002), *The Hoax* (2006), and *Duplicity* (2009). *The Wolf of Wall Street* (2013) on the exploits of Jordan Belfort, one of this chapter's cases, was also made into a movie. It is also unrepresentative of more typical, run-of-the-mill white collar crimes.

As a kind of template of the less exciting white collar story, consider the memoir by Jerome Mayne, *Diary of a White Collar Criminal* (2010). Self-published, it recites the tale of a real estate broker working with low-income, usually first-time buyers. These were, he says, "loans from hell" (p. 17). Somehow, unwittingly, he claims, Mayne made several transactions that were illegal. In one, he failed to record that a buyer had switched jobs in the middle of a contract settlement. In another, a colleague sold a house to someone before she had taken possession—a "legal loophole," he said (p. 19). In a third, an associate slipped him a hundred dollars for doing a good job on a loan application. In another, he was given "a wad of cash" consisting of five hundred dollars and a bottle of Sapphire gin (p. 25). Once, he was the loan officer for the borrower who bought a house he owned, enabling him to make a profit on the sale. The book is rife with descriptions of small offenses such as these, yet Mayne gets arrested, convicted, and slapped with a two-year sentence to a federal penitentiary (whose location he is allowed to choose) still wondering what he did wrong.

"I think back and try to figure out what I could have seen; what could I have done differently?" In the end, however, he realizes that "there were so many things in the ensuing months that were huge red flags, that I ignored or justified" (p. 120). After serving less than half of his sentence, the author is released to a half-way house, then put on parole. He is now an inspirational speaker for professional associations to alert their members to avoid the mistakes he made. He is also a comic, a musician, and an improvisation performer. Reformed, yes—a white collar criminal no longer. A different career, certainly, one in which he can no longer fiddle and diddle the books. Still, the reader wonders, if what is legal and illegal is so difficult to discern, why was it that Jerome Mayne was caught and prosecuted while most other fiduciary fiddlers, diddlers, and jugglers are not? Such are the mysteries of legal and normative transgressions; it is one of the things that make them eternally fascinating.

White collar crime typically sharply contrasts with conventional street crime in that its offenders almost invariably discount the outright criminality of their acts, yearn to "set the record straight," insist that what they did entailed "mistakes, technical violations," and who they are were "victims of treachery, persecution, or official ineptitude" (Mayne, 2010, p. 18).

Most of the "common" criminal behavior that attracts arrest and prosecution consists of clear-cut crimes, those that need virtually no interpretation, that everyone agrees should be against the law. Joe Bonanno was the head of an organized crime Family whose members were convicted of illegal actions ranging from gambling and the distribution of illicit narcotics to murder. Jack Henry Abbott engaged in check forging, assault, bank robbery, and murder and spent more than half his life behind bars before being released as a result of the support of influential admirers of his writing; after his release, he murdered another man. Several years following his reincarceration, he committed suicide. Eddie Bunker was an armed robber, an extortionist, a check forger, and a drug dealer. And Jordan Belfort was convicted of securities fraud and money laundering.

Joe Bonanno, "This Is How I Earned My Living"

In the pre-dawn hours of January 20, 2011, over eight hundred federal, state, and local law enforcement agents swooped down on and arrested 125 reputed organized crime figures in New York, New Jersey, and Rhode Island, nearly three dozen of them "made" members of New York's five crime families—specifically the Colombo and Gambino clan leadership. The mob has been "remarkably resilient," said an F.B.I. agent, charging that the characterization of organized crime as a thing of the past is "a myth." The arrestees were, Attorney General Eric Holder stated at a press conference later on the day of the arrests, "among the most dangerous criminals in our country" (Rashbaum, 2011, p. A21). The operation was, said Holder, the "largest mob roundup in F.B.I. history," and the crimes that officials charged them with included extortion, racketeering, assault, arson, illicit drug sales, loan-sharking, money laundering, and murder (p. A21).

In spite of the code of *omertà* (or silence), numerous organized crime figures and their relatives have published memoirs and autobiographies about mob enterprises (www.sonofscarface.com/reading-mobmembers.html), including Joseph Bonanno ("Joe Bananas"); his son, Bill; his daughter-in-law, Rosalie; Vincent Charles Teresa; Jimmy Fratiano; Henry Hill, the subject of Nicholas Pileggi's book *Wiseguy*, which Martin Scorsese made into the film *Goodfellas* (1990); Chris Capone, Al's grandson; Albert DeMeo, son of a Gambino family killer; Michael Franzese, a former Colombo family member; and Louis Ferrante, a former Gambino family member. The fact is, the public *loves* stories about the Mafia ("Cosa Nostra," or "our thing"), as the *Godfather* films (1971, 1974, 1990) attest. (Mafia figures also deny that "the Mafia" exists; Bonanno calls it "our Tradition.") Wise guys make a sharp distinction between criminally implicating their associates, especially in government testimony, which calls for death or a disappearance into the witness protection program, and narrating their own legal and already known-about illegal activities in a book. Bonanno says nothing he has ever said sent an associate to prison.

Joseph Bonanno sets up *A Man of Honor* (1984) in epic terms. The volume is divided into six books, numbered with Roman numerals, portentously entitled "The Odyssey," "The Castellammarese War," "The Commission," "Between Hammer and Anvil," "My Golden Years," and "The Grand Inquisition." The Sicilians, explains Bonanno, have a "genius for survival" without which they would have "long ago lost their identity." It was that genius that made it possible to "endure subjugation and to survive" (1984, p. 13). Prevented from ruling their own land by a succession of conquerors and plunderers, Sicilians withdrew into their own families, developed their own dialects, customs, codes, folk laws, sense of justice, and rules of conduct. It became a subculture that prevailed alongside that of their rulers, from the Greeks through the Romans, the French Bourbons, to the Italians. The "man of honor" remained true to the ancient traditions, took care of his family and the people to whom he was loyal, and carried himself in a manly fashion. He was *mafioso* without necessarily belonging to the Mafia. True? Early on in the book, Bonanno narrates a story about a respectable young Sicilian woman who was being "manhandled" by a French solider, whose boyfriend saves her, and her honor, and kills the soldier. "Scholars now consider parts of the story to be legend or folklore," notes Bonanno. "That may be true, but so what? The important element of the story is not its factual veracity, but the Sicilian spirit which it exemplifies" (p. 22). Reading between the lines, the reader begins to suspect that the same principle may animate the supposedly factual stories the author narrates as memoir. In other words, in the stories of his life, Joe may be offering us as much legend as literally true life history. "Don't worry about whether these anecdotes are true," he seems to be saying, "they tell a great story and have a strong moral."

The passage of the Volstead Act, which ushered in Prohibition, made the manufacture, distribution, and sale of alcohol illegal; it was the dying twitch of a rural, Protestant America struggling to prevent the inevitable social change sweeping the country. But Prohibition also provided a golden opportunity for immigrants to earn a great deal of money. When they were young men, two friends invited Bonanno to join them in running a small still located in the basement of a New York City apartment building. The brother of one of his partners owned a truck with which they made deliveries, and another brother had contacts with politicians and the police so that there would be no government interference in their operation. "When I first got into bootlegging I thought it was too good to be true. I didn't consider it wrong. It seemed fairly safe in that the police didn't bother you. There was plenty of business for everyone. The profits were tremendous. And let's face it, especially for a young man, it was a lot of fun" (1984, p. 46). Unfortunately, one of Bonanno's partners fell asleep in the basement next to the still. Alcohol spilled onto the floor under the burner and set his partner on fire; he died that night, which put Joseph out of the distillery business.

But before long, a mobster named Salvatore Maranzano—soon to be inducted into the Mafia, an aspiration shared by Bonanno—and offered him the job of checking on whiskey stills in Pennsylvania. And if the job also entailed engaging in a shoot-out or threatening to rearrange the leg-bones of a snitch, well, one has to do what is required. His position entailed obedience to his superiors, silence about his illicit activities, curbing his lust toward the wives and relatives of friends and associates, being accountable for his actions, and standing at the ready to bear arms to protect the Family's interests (p. 59). "Because of my heritage, I took all this for granted. I knew the ground rules even before they were explained to me" (p. 59).

Bonanno is careful to point out that some Family members had illicit businesses, such as bookmaking or numbers, which he found perfectly acceptable, while he considered some other illegal activities unacceptable according to his code. He did not tolerate dealings in prostitution or narcotics, he tells us. Likewise, he claims, he was opposed to extortion "as an arbitrary instrument of collecting money from people. Perhaps other Families didn't adhere to my strict guidelines, but this was my way. . . . In the main," he explains, "I was a venture capitalist. This is how I earned my money; this is how I earned my living" (1984, p. 133). Bonanno puts many readers on his side with his assertion that prostitution and the sale of narcotics are "dirty" businesses which he banned from his operation. However, well-informed observers (Maas, [1968] 2003; Zeigler, 1970; Moldea, 1983; Raab, 2005) have conducted considerable research and report that for years the Bonanno Family held a controlling interest in the heroin trade; it sold roughly two-thirds of the heroin that moved into and out of New York. And two of Bonanno's underbosses were convicted of narcotics trafficking. In addition, they say, prostitution was one of his family's economic mainstays. In other words, Joe is not telling us the whole truth about the nature of his Family's business. Clearly, *denial* is Joseph Bonanno's principal deviance neutralization device here; however, he does it with a great deal of charm.

Violence? "In discussing the role of violence in my world I don't expect outsiders to condone or approve of the rules by which we lived. I would only ask the outsider to appreciate the context of our lives. The first step is to recognize that traditionally a Sicilian has a personal sense of justice. If a man of honor is wronged it is up to him to redress that wrong personally. He does not go to the judicial machinery of the state" (1984, p. 135). When thieves burglarized the home of a Family member, the word went out, and "justice was done." One Sunday, in a neighborhood church, thieves stole the crown and jewelry of the Madonna; the word was passed around, the finery was restored, and justice was served. The reader can only imagine what happened to the thieves. Admitting that retribution was served on the thieves for stealing religious relics, but avoiding detailing what he and his colleagues did to them, is a wise and persuasive device to win readers over to his side. The fact is, a Bonanno-owned funeral home was reputed to bury customers in double coffins, one compartment for the client, the second one for their gangland victims (Raab, 2005). Clearly, the Family did much more than "rearrange the leg-bones" of wrongdoers.

"Gambling, like moneylending," explains Bonanno, "is one of those human activities that defy government intervention, no matter how well-meaning. That should have been obvious during Prohibition when the government tried to ban the selling of liquor. People . . . found a way to buy their liquor. . . . Bootleggers simply filled a demand. . . . The same can be said for gambling. . . . If you remove the current private individuals who provide illicit gambling services . . . , other individuals will take their place, because there will always be customers" (1984, p. 202). Of course, the same is true of narcotics, but Bonanno does not say that, since, as we have seen, he claims he has no truck with the drug business. His own tradition, he claims, shuns narcotics peddling, extortion, and kidnapping; we consider these "unmanly activities" (p. 257), he tells the reader. Again, Mr. Bonanno's veracity has been called into question by numerous well-informed observers. We "didn't consider ourselves criminals," Joe asserts. In fact, "we considered our code of ethics stricter and fairer than any we encountered in America" (p. 208). Sadly, he laments, the Tradition he and his Family followed "deteriorated until it lost its connotation of honor and became instead a byword for gangsterism" (p. 208). He saw his Tradition "die away completely and a distantly related mutation take its place" (p. 209). His book, he feels, justifies and explains his behavior and exculpates his sins. He is, after all, "a man of honor." Bonanno's memoir stretches the notion of deviance neutralization almost beyond the point of recognition, yet he does it with a kind of old-world charm, grace, and panache; I felt, while reading it, that I was listening to stories told by one of my Sicilian great-uncles.

Edward Bunker, "What Else Could I Do?"

Bunker's memoir expresses contradictory, conflicting, even paradoxical sentiments about his experiences as a criminal and a convict, as well as his life in free society. *Education of a Felon* (2000) harbors three principal themes. The first is Bunker's advocacy of the convict code and consequently his attitude of *moral superiority* over the ordinary man, particularly if that man is a law-abiding citizen. Second, the virtues Bunker extols and supposedly possesses are *manly* virtues, which is the key to his writing. And the third theme is Bunker's *ambivalence* about his life of crime and his prison experience.

Eddie Bunker was born in Los Angeles. His mother, a sometime chorus girl and dancer in Busby Berkeley productions, was neglectful and unloving. His father, an occasional stagehand, an alcoholic who was sometimes violent, descended into premature senility. An aunt, who could have taken him in, was a religious fanatic.

Eddie grew up almost feral; his parents and caretakers left him to fend for himself at an early age. During his preteen years, he was sent him to a succession of foster homes, boarding schools, and military academies. His formal education stopped in the seventh grade. He soon began running away and committing crimes on a routine basis. As a teenager, Bunker was committed to a number of reform schools. After a pattern of compulsive recidivism, he was sent, at the age of seventeen, to San Quentin—the youngest convict there at the time—where he resided for four and a half brutal years.

Following his release in his early twenties, unable to find work, he continued to commit crime: armed robbery, car theft, drug trafficking, extortion, forgery, and other felonies too numerous to detail. After spending nearly twenty years behind bars, Bunker was released for good in 1975, when he was in his early forties.

Eddie Bunker was a voracious reader, having discovered early on that while they were prison inmates, Cervantes wrote most of *Don Quixote* and Dostoyevsky wrote most of *Crime and Punishment.* In his late teens, he read an article by Caryl Chessman, a fellow convict, which appeared in an issue of *Argosy,* a major-circulation men's magazine. Bunker figured that if Chessman could write and publish, he could, too. After writing four unpublished novels in prison, he managed to attract an agent's attention with his fifth, *No Beast So Fierce,* which appeared in 1973; in 1978, it was made into a film entitled *Straight Time,* starring Dustin Hoffman. As it did for Abbott, what obtained Bunker's release from prison was the talent that influential authors recognized through this book. Eventually, he published three other novels, *Animal Factory* (1977), also made into a movie (2000), *Little Boy Blue* (1981), and *Dog Eat Dog* (1996)—as well as his memoir, *Education of a Felon,* published in 2000. He also coauthored several screenplays, including *Runaway Train* (1985), which was nominated for an Academy Award. And he acted in twenty-three films, including Quentin Tarantino's *Reservoir Dogs* (1991), in which he played a character named Mr. Blue. (The British edition of his autobiography was entitled *Mr. Blue: Memoirs of a Renegade.*) His last acting role was in the remake of *The Longest Yard* (2005). In 1979, after his release, he married his counselor; in 1994, when Bunker was sixty and his wife was forty, they had a son. In July 2007, at the age of seventy-one, Edward Bunker died in Burbank, California, from complications stemming from diabetes.

How does Bunker neutralize the stigma of his criminality? How does he express or "imagize" his superiority over the average man? What are his special, distinctly honorable qualities, and how does he advance his case for them? Bunker is anything if not immodest. There are times when he brags, he crows, he puffs out his chest.

Bunker asserts that his special qualities began from the very moment of his conception. He was conceived, he says in his first paragraph, during an earthquake in Southern California and born during a torrential deluge, "with palm trees and houses floating down" the canyons of Los Angeles (2000, p. 1). The reader infers that anyone conceived and born under such unusual circumstances must be exceptional.

In another place, he claims he was tested by Duke University and found to have ESP (p. 46). As an aside, the Rhine Research Center, which tests for ESP, had not been affiliated with Duke for decades, but the invocation of the prestige of Duke University is noteworthy, coming from someone so desirous of excoriating conventional society and conventional hierarchies.

At another point, Bunker claims he was tested against the graduating class of Harvard University and found to be in the top 5 percent in intellectual ability of Harvard graduates, plus, he says, he "had skills they never dreamed about" (p. 147), again putting forth assertions that invoke conventional prestige.

Throughout his memoir, Bunker takes his acts of rebellion against the system, against the law, against The Man—against whoever is in charge—as a badge of pride, a sign of moral superiority. At one point, Bunker contrasts the extreme brutality of the guards' attacks on him with the stoicism he expresses to his fellow inmates about these attacks, and he asks us to consider the brutality of these attacks and valorize his account. After one particularly brutal beating—during which, it should be noted, he stabbed a guard in the hand—an inmate looks at his "bruised and battered face."

"Looks like they fucked you up," says the inmate. "Yeah, they danced on me a little," he replies, playing down the incident. "It's no big thing." But of course in telling us it is "no big thing," he asks for our respect in being able to take such brutal punishment, then he emphasizes the brutality of the punishment, and then asks us again for our respect for being so modest—a seeming contradiction.

Commenting on his belittling of the guards' attack he says, "The stoicism valued in the underworld was . . . a part of me. Never snivel" (p. 35). Being what's called a "stand-up con" has high value in the inmate community, and he puts himself forward as an exemplar of that value, as verified by what the other convicts say to him. But he still wants you to know how brutal the guards were to him.

His narration of his attack on an inmate expresses that same attention to upholding convict values—don't complain; don't whine; don't snivel; do what you have to do to survive; assert your rights. A prisoner named Billy Cook, condemned to death for the murder of seven people, among them women and children, makes a pass at Bunker, who at the time was a teenager. "He's a sicko," says D'Arcy, another inmate, an armed robber (2000, p. 39), expressing convict values (armed robbery, good; killing innocent women and children, bad). Bunker knows he is going to have to attack Cook, otherwise he is going to become his bitch. He fashions a cutting instrument out of a toothbrush and a razor blade. "You've got guts, youngster," says Cicerone, a mob figure whom Bunker respects (p. 40)—again, the expression of which tells us what dominant inmate values are.

One literary modus operandi Bunker uses to authenticate his rebellion against authority is to adopt the generalized righteous convict voice in the guise of the words of specific inmates whose representativeness he establishes. They are Mafia figures, mob guys, gangsters, armed robbers, safecrackers, car thieves, bookmakers. They are most decidedly *not* rapists, child molesters, or killers of women and children—who are *inauthentic* convict voices. In harnessing these strategies to his narrative, he simultaneously neutralizes the stigma the reader might attribute to him as a result of admitting such behavior.

Another literary strategy Bunker uses is to ask the reader rhetorical questions whose answers are preordained and to issue statements the reader is willy-nilly forced to agree with.

The Cook incident illustrates this second strategy well. When Cook is taking a shower, Bunker rushes in and engages in a preemptive strike, slicing open his tormenter's chest and abdomen. "What else could I do?" Bunker asks rhetorically. The choice among cowardice, ratting on an inmate, and standing up and being a man, is clear to Bunker—as it would be to any stand-up con. Though his attack earned him a beating from the guards and landed him in isolation, in the dark, for five days, he nonetheless says to himself, "I could take a beating with the rest of them. I thought of Billy Cook crying like a bitch as I kicked his ass. 'He won't fuck with me no more'" (2000, p. 43). Was it against the rules? Absolutely. Was it worth it? You betcha.

After a bank robbery, Bunker feels depressed about the bleakness of his life options. But then he asks himself precisely the same question: "What else could I do? Give myself up. Yeah. Right," he answers sarcastically (p. 219). However limited, his choices were clear: *Under the conditions I faced, anyone would have done the same thing, although not everyone would have triumphed as I did.*

When he considers his belligerent response to being cheated on a drug deal, Bunker says to himself, "There was no way back without putting my tail between my legs. At least I had behaved so I could look in the mirror. Mine was a macho world, with . . . rules that belonged in the Code of Chivalry" (p. 143). His questions and statements imply that if the reader *had not* done what Bunker did, *he, the reader, would* have put his tail between his legs, he would *not* have been able to look himself in the mirror. This strategy asks the reader to *think* as Eddie did, *feel* the way he did, and in his mind, *act* as he did. If you were a real man, Bunker implies, you could not have done otherwise, either. And in so doing, the reader is forced to judge Eddie Bunker not in harsh, condemnatory terms, but through an aura of respect and admiration. He takes a vice and turns it into a virtue.

Bunker's expression of ambivalence toward the ruthless world of crime and the hellish world of the prison is even more interesting and complex than his sense of moral superiority in upholding the righteous convict code. But his ambivalence theme is also less emphatically expressed than the first theme—that is, his sense of moral superiority.

When Bunker was released from San Quentin, he admits, he should have gone straight. He was helped by a wealthy, idealistic woman, Louise Wallis, the wife of the Hollywood producer Hal Wallis, who got him an apartment, some tailor-made suits, and (most important) a typewriter. "How could I fail?" he asks himself. "How could I let her down? She had made the dream real for me" (p. 149).

Bunker's problem is that he possessed *manly flaws* (Liebow, 1967, pp. 116–126). He could not adjust to the conventional world and avoid prison, he says, *because he was too much of a man.* He wanted the rich, abundant promise that illicit behavior had to offer, and not the sawdust taste that law-abiding life gives us: "The lure of bright lights, fast cars, and sweet-smelling young women with long legs was too much for me. . . . [Every] day outside prison was swollen to bursting with possibilities for adventure" (Bunker, 2000, p. 150). Says Eddie, standing on the balcony of his Sunset Boulevard apartment, high on marijuana, listening to Ella Fitzgerald, a gorgeous girlfriend in his bed, "The whole world was spread at my feet. I was king of all I surveyed."

Again, this is a rhetorical statement. He is asking his readers, at least his male readers, to put themselves in his shoes—in fact, in his bed; contemplate the fact that if they are law-abiding, they are somewhat wanting in the masculinity department, because they passed up the rich opportunities that the criminal world has to offer. He wants his male readers to admit that he, Eddie Bunker, is more of a man than his readers because he has taken full advantage of crime's abundant cornucopia. "I was more concerned with . . . having as much fun and as many adventures as I could find" (p. 171), he says. Admit it, Eddie seems to be saying to the male reader, if you were honest with yourself, and if you had the balls, you would have done the same thing I did. What man could stigmatize or deviantize him? he indirectly asks. The reader—the male reader at any rate—would have done the same thing if he had had the opportunity. Condemn me? he asks. I should be honored.

Bunker had a dog-eat-dog vision of convict life, in fact, of lower-class street life as well; one of his novels, as I said, is entitled *Dog Eat Dog.* He emphasizes throughout his memoir that he thrived in this Hobbesian atmosphere in which the ordinary man who normally lives in conventional, law-abiding society would have perished. He survived San Quentin, he says—he "graduated from a nickel" (that is, a five-year sentence) "in the House of Dracula"—and *we* didn't. "Surviving five years in San Quentin will do wonders for self-confidence" (2000, p. 175), he says: You *don't preach to* me *about the morality of crime.* I've *paid my dues*; you *haven't. That makes me a better man than you.*

But Bunker's rebellion, his honesty, and his yearning for adventure also have their down side. Still, this side is distinctly deemphasized.

He is squatting behind some bushes in a cold California rain after escaping from prison, after being chased from his apartment by two detectives, and he is thinking: "I'd once gotten a sort of thrill at playing fugitive, but on this particular dawn, I was a wet, miserable wanted man" (p. 214).

When Bunker gets a work detail to clean out part of the prison yard, he is looking around, thinking that eighteen years before he was standing in exactly the same spot; "if I had known I would stand here 18 years later, I would have killed myself" (p. 271), he says, a sad commentary on his view of the life he had fashioned for himself.

Bunker's ambivalence emerges most strongly in the Afterword, which brings events up to the time just before the publication of his memoir—that is, the late 1990s. He is in Paris, acting in a small French film, when he asks a man for directions to the set. "I know you," the man says, in French-accented English. It turns out he recognized Bunker from his role in *Reservoir Dogs,* and moreover, he had read his three by then published books. "I found it hard to believe that someone would recognize me on a Paris sidewalk, six thousand miles from home, someone who had read all of my books. . . . Who would have imagined such [a] thing from my first 40 years of life? It may not have equaled the metamorphosis of St. Augustine, but it certainly was unexpected" (p. 296). But then he is forced to say, "Whatever happened, happened. . . . I changed as my circumstances changed" (p. 297). Commenting on the weak sales of his third book, he ruminates on the possibility of returning to a life of crime.

As delicious as the delights of being free were, and as sweet the savor of the life of a semi-successful writer, the allure of crime for him never completely receded. Bunker was a success as a writer *because* he had been a criminal, a felon, a fierce and relentless outlaw. He drew his material as a writer entirely from his lawlessness. Take away those experiences and you take away the writer. He aged out of crime simply because he grew old and found something else to do. His cachet, his very identity—not only as a writer but also as a man and a human being—are saturated, even *coterminous,* with his criminality. His status as an outlaw was a point of pride with him; he would not, he *could* not, have extricated the crimes from his life any more than his masculinity. Carefully read, Bunker's memoir screams out one central message: *I don't regret a thing!* And in this enterprise, he wants the reader on his side, admiring rather than condemning him. Bunker's memoir goes beyond self-justification; it is an act of self-glorification.

Jack Henry Abbott, "If You Behave like a Man, You Are Doomed"

In 1977, while working on *The Executioner's Song,* a "true life novel" about the life of the convicted and executed murderer Gary Gilmore, Norman Mailer received a series of letters from a convict named Jack Henry Abbott. The letters focused on Abbott's prison experience and his reactions to them. That

Mailer would be impressed by these letters was almost a foregone conclusion. Abbott wrote with a passion and fury with which Mailer had attempted, with uneven success, to energize his own work. Earlier, Mailer had eloquently written about what he referred to as "existential violence"—the beauty of acting with a righteous fury in a society that attempts to crush the human will. Once he heaped (albeit qualified) praise on three adolescents who murdered a candy store owner, arguing that they displayed not only virility but also creativity and moral courage (1959, p. 347). Violence, Mailer argued, is an act bursting with energy and vitality, a catharsis that prepares for growth. In *An American Dream* (1965), the protagonist, Steven Rojack, a war hero, engages in sexual intercourse with his wife, a socialite who mocks and taunts him; murders her; then anally sodomizes her maid. Two years before the publication of this novel, at a raucous party, Mailer's wife, Adele Morales, had taunted and belittled his sexual prowess, and he stabbed her with a pen-knife. (She survived and brought no charges against him.) Mailer likened crime and violence to a religious experience. In his introduction to Abbott's book, he insisted that not only the worst of young men were sent to prison but also the best, "the proudest, the bravest, the most daring, the most enterprising, and the most undefeated of the poor."

For more than a century, writers, readers, and much of the general public in Western society have used prison as a literary metaphor; in the United States, Billy the Kid, Butch Cassidy, Bonnie and Clyde, Al Capone, Jesse James, and John Dillinger have been fashioned into heroes (Franklin, 1989; Kooistra, 1989). No surprise, then, that American literary figures generally and Norman Mailer specifically should have been attracted to the writings of Jack Henry Abbott. How engaging to hear or read about underdogs struggling against an oppressive establishment! And if they break a few heads along the way, so much the better!

Abbott was born on an army base in Michigan; his mother was a prostitute. When he was nine, authorities sent him to a juvenile detention center, and at age twelve, to reform school. At eighteen, he burglarized a shoe store and stole some checks, which he made out to himself. Convicted of check kiting, he was sent to a penitentiary where, three years into a five-year sentence, he stabbed and killed a fellow inmate and was given a three- to twenty-year term. In 1971, he escaped; committed armed robbery; and was caught, convicted, and sentenced to nineteen years. During a fifteen-year stretch, Abbott had lived as a free man for only nine and a half weeks; during a twenty-year period, he had spent a total of fourteen years in solitary confinement. His prison record in five institutions shows multiple infractions and violent incidents. Abbott once leaped from the witness stand of a courtroom and began throttling a witness, who had said something he did not like. In another episode, inexplicably, while a prison physician was stitching up his arm after he was slashed by another inmate, Abbott stabbed the doctor in the nose with a sharpened ballpoint pen.

After reading and having been profoundly impressed by Abbott's prison letters, Mailer contacted some of his friends in the literary establishment, including the editor of *The New York Review of Books,* Robert Silver, and Jason Epstein, a major Random House editor. *The Review* published several of Abbott's letters, and Random House collected them into a book (1981). These writings, along with the endorsements from Mailer and other literary figures, persuaded prison authorities to authorize early release in 1981. Mailer told the Utah Board of Corrections that Abbott has "the makings of a powerful and important American writer." Abbie Hoffman likened Abbott to unjustly imprisoned political prisoners such as Jacobo Timerman and Alexander Solzhenitsyn (Kakutani, 1981, p. 1). Not all observers found the book as impressive. Lionel Abel, a critic for *Commentary* magazine, regarded *In the Belly of the Beast* "without interest" and Abbott, a writer possessed of "few literary gifts. His book is, in fact, a fraud on the public. . . . There is no continuing narrative here, and no lyricism of either language or event" (1981, p. 65).

Whether of literary value or not, Abbott's book, a synthesis of memoir and personal essay, created an enormous stir in New York literary circles. Abbott's ruminations on the criminal justice system, especially as it touched on the life of one inmate in particular—himself—constituted the spine of the brief volume. The revelations, as rendered by the author, were news to many of its readers, and its insights were searing, troubling, off-kilter, and provocative. Men and women of conscience were forced to rethink their own passivity in the face of such injustices that Abbott uncurtained. He was, he says, a "state-raised convict." He was sent to prison so early, and he had been there so long, that he forgot how he got there in the first place; he hardly recalled what it was like to be on the outside—perhaps being free was "exactly identical" to living in heaven (Abbott, 1981, p. 3). He wanted to convey the sensation to the non-incarcerated reader of being a long-term convict, of being imprisoned since childhood, the daily routine, the indignities and humiliations, the *rage* he feels when contemplating and experiencing the injustices.

The feeling of being forced to "sit beside a stinking, stupid wino every morning at breakfast." To have "some loud fool in his infinite ignorance" come up to him and slur, "Gimme a cigarette, man!" Abbott says he just looks into his eyes and he would "want to kill his ass there in front of God and everyone" (p. 5). Guards demand that he subject himself to a strip-search. When he refuses, they knock him to the floor. Repeatedly. He complains of cramps; the guards rush into his cell and attack him, beating him to the floor. His hands and ankles are handcuffed, his back suspended in air. He is left like that all night. Once, falsely accused of planning to escape, the guards choke him almost to the point of strangulation—at which point, they remove their hands from his throat, now blotted with blue bruises. Imagine thousands of such indignities and intrusions into your life, Abbott tells the reader, "every hour and minute of every day, and you can grasp the source of this paranoia, this anger that could consume me at any moment if I lost control" (p. 5).

"We were sent to prison to be broken," Abbott tells the reader (p. 153). In defiance, he turns his mind "to steel." Only in this way can the inmate "be equal to the hardships that surround him" (p. 41). America is "the most unjust and oppressive country in the whole world," Abbott declares, "and I'm not going to go into lawyerlike details and comparisons. . . . I am totally convinced—and I do *not* believe I would have suffered greater injustices in *any* country in the world than I have here for a lifetime" (p. 108). He adds, "If I'm wrong, show me," which contradicts his statement about not wanting to "go into lawyerlike details and comparisons"—no matter. A segment of the population is incarcerated because they are poor and because they refuse to act as agents of the police and betray their friends, Abbott argues.

The central message of *In the Belly of the Beast* is this: *I'm not the deviant. The American prison complex is a monstrously and grossly unfair system of social control. It treats inmates as subhumans and, having been subjected to such treatment, prisoners* become *subhuman. American social control is monstrous in its execution and monstrous in its consequences. I'm not to blame, nor is any other prisoner; we don't deserve to be labeled deviants, though, ironically, we* become *deviants as a result of the way we are treated.* It is a process that, long ago, Robert Merton dubbed "unanticipated consequences" (1957, pp. 60ff.) or "the self-fulfilling prophecy" (pp. 421–436). Or perhaps the consequences, Abbott ruminates, are not so "unanticipated." Perhaps the prison system was always *intended* to turn out monsters. What lunatic would turn ordinary men into monsters? Only those sadistic or insensitive enough to be indifferent to the authentic prisoner's voice (*his* voice, the voice of Jack Henry Abbott—it is a classic neutralization device) "condemning the condemners" (Sykes and Matza, 1957), more accurately, "condemning the oppressors." It is not a form of "normalization" because it argues that once you are poisoned by the prison system, you are no longer "normal."

Six weeks after his release from prison, while dining with two young women at the Binibon restaurant in New York City, Abbott asked a waiter, twenty-two-year-old Richard Adan, a Cuban-born aspiring actor and playwright, where the Binibon's restrooms were located. Adan explained that the only toilet was off the kitchen and, since the Binibon had no accident insurance for customers, only employees could walk through the kitchen. This restriction on his freedom struck Abbott as infuriating, and he challenged Adan to step outside. After a brief exchange of words, Abbott thrust a knife between Adan's ribs into his heart, killing him instantly (Farber, 1981a, 1981b). Abbott quickly made himself a fugitive and was apprehended working on a Louisiana oil field seven weeks later, convicted of first-degree manslaughter, and sentenced to a fifteen-year-to-life term. One of the most telling, albeit accidental, developments in the Jack Henry Abbott saga is that the stabbing and death of Richard Adan took place in the early morning of July 18. Nearly simultaneously, the next day, July 19, their editors unaware of the killing, *The New York Times Book Review* published a review of *In the Belly of the Beast,* written by Terrence Des Pres, a university professor, which stated that the book was "awesome, brilliant, perversely ingenuous; its impact is indelible, and as an articulation of penal nightmare it is completely compelling" (1981, p. 14).

The literary figures who had supported Abbott were stunned, shocked, traumatized by the murder (Abbott was sentenced to manslaughter); they expressed a kind of betrayal. Aside from a few platitudes, Mailer, otherwise so eloquent on any subject that confronted him, seemed incapable of formulating a detailed, coherent response to this tragic set of events. At a press conference held soon after Abbott's arrest, Mailer, probably intoxicated, seemed belligerent, defensive, arrogant, and self-righteous, terminating the conference after he and a reporter began shouting obscenities at one another. On his part, Abbott claimed that the killing had been the result of a "misunderstanding."

Michiko Kakutani, in a major review of the Jack Henry Abbott saga in *The New York Times Book Review* (1981), wrote that Mailer and his friends had suffered from a confusion between metaphor and reality. They were deluded into thinking that talent could act as a redemptive force, that the act of writing "can somehow transform a violent man into a philosopher of violence" (p. 1). Mailer had spent years "nurturing a theory of violence, only to find out that if an individual lives by such principles, the consequences can be terrible indeed" (p. 38). Said Joyce Carol Oates, a novelist, certain circles of upper-middle-class intellectuals are able to romanticize criminals such as Abbott because they are unacquainted with them (Kakutani, 1981, p. 36). They see violence as a metaphor for a struggle against a repressive bourgeois society without bothering to understand its real-life motivations and consequences. They want literary and metaphorical violence, not real violence—clean, sanitary, purely ideological violence with all the politically correct accouterments; they want violence with all the warts removed.

Of all the literary figures who came into contact with Abbott, perhaps it was Jerzy Kosinski who saw him in the most clear-headed and perceptive fashion. Kosinski began a correspondence with Abbott while the latter was in prison, but the relationship ended with sour recrimination and even hatred on both sides, judging from the letters. Kosinski, who had undergone more than his share of brutal, horrifying experiences, wrote to Abbott, prophetically, years before the stabbing of Richard Adan, to the effect that Abbott seemed to believe that, since he was hurt as a child, he had the right "to hurt and kill and molest and torture others in the name of that once-felt pain and rage." Though he broke off all correspondence with Abbott, and still recognized him as a violent man, Kosinski nonetheless joined in the dinner honoring and welcoming him into the literary establishment. "By toasting him," Kosinski guiltily explained after the killing, "I endorsed his philosophy. . . . I blame myself for becoming a part of 'radical chic.' I went to welcome a writer, to celebrate his intellectual birth. But instead, I should have been welcoming a just-freed prisoner . . . , a man from another planet who needed to know how to control [his] negative emotions" (Kakutani, 1981, p. 38).

In 2002, prison guards found Abbott in his cell hanging from a bed sheet, an apparent suicide. He left a note, which the authorities refused to disclose. Mailer issued a statement on the Abbott suicide (*The New York Times,* February 11, 2002): "I never knew a man who had a worse life. What made it doubly awful is that he brought a deadly tragedy down on a young man [Richard Adan] full of promise and left a bomb crater of lost possibilities for many including most especially himself."

Jordan Belfort, *"$12.5 Million! In Three Minutes!"*

What really caused the subprime mortgage market to go wild was Wall Street buying these [subprime] mortgages, pulling them up in the CDO's [collateralized debt obligations] and then selling them around the world. And to do that required a few things to happen. It actually required an ethical compromise on every single level, from the home owner on Main Street who went and bought the home he knew he couldn't afford because he didn't have to put any money down and get a cheap payment for a couple of years. . . . To the real estate broker that sold the house and turned the other way. To the real estate appraiser who bumped up the appraisal, to the mortgage broker that showed them how to lie in the mortgage applications, to the underwriters who looked the other way and pretended it was all OK. To the bankers on Wall Street that packaged all this stuff up. To the people of the credit rating industry that stamped it Triple-A and sold it around the world. You ended up with—excuse my expression—a heaping pile of cow shit that was sold as if it were Triple-A. Because at each level, everyone turned their head the other way to make some money, to have some benefit.

—Jordan Belfort, interview on *ABC News* [Australia], August 20, 2009

In the early 1990s, Jordan Belfort—dubbed "the Wolf of Wall Street"—founded Stratton Oakmont, a stock market brokerage firm, which at its height employed over a thousand traders; at the time, Belfort earned a million dollars a week. In 1998, Belfort was indicted by the F.B.I. for securities fraud and money laundering. His offense was running what is commonly referred to as a "pump and dump" boiler room operation—manipulating or running up the price of stocks to artificially high prices and then selling them at their peak, earning huge profits, leaving stockholders in the lurch, holding what had become worthless or extremely low-value stocks. According to Belfort, his firm operated very much like a cult. Belfort hired young, hungry brokers, for the most part, "educationally challenged dream-seekers," without a college education but with wildly unrealistic aspirations. Their obligations were to swear loyalty to him, cold-call potential customers, and read his sales-pitch over the phone (Wells, 2007). For his crimes, Belfort spent twenty-two months in a federal penitentiary; he is currently a public speaker on the topic of business ethics. Clearly, what he did went vastly beyond simply earning a great deal of money. What was the nature of his crimes? His book, *The Wolf of Wall Street* (2007), became a best-seller and was translated into eighteen languages. A film directed by Martin Scorsese and starring Leonardo DiCaprio is currently in production and will be released in 2013. What makes the man's life interesting is not his riches alone; he is interesting because he did something seriously wrong.

At one point, Belfort began mentally totaling up how much he was going to make on a shoe company, Steve Madden Shoes, whose stock he was selling, and how much he would earn on many similar such transactions. "To make all that money and not commit a crime!" he marvels to himself (2007, pp. 94–95). Inspired, he gave a speech to likewise inspire his brokers. He called their attention to the phone on their desks. That phone, he said, is "like a loaded M16 without a trained Marine to pull the trigger." Never take no for an answer, never hang up until a client "either buys or dies," and make a sale on every single phone call (p. 96). The phone on your desk "is a license to print money. . . . That phone equals money" (p. 96). *You have money problems?* he asks rhetorically. *You're behind on your credit card bills? Good, then pick up the phone and start dialing!* He tells his brokers that they should do "whatever it takes to succeed"—sell lots of inflated stock, make lots of money, and become rich (p. 98). He tells them if they do as he says, within a few hours they will be thanking him "a thousand times over" when their clients begin making money. After the speech, he walks off the stage to the thunderous cheering of his ecstatic employees, who begin following his advice by immediately picking up their phones and "ripping their clients' eyeballs out" (p. 98).

In 1993, inflating weak or low-value stock by over-purchasing it, selling it at an artificially high price, then dumping it on the market was still legal. Instead of the National Association of Securities Dealers (NASD) allowing a natural balance between buyers and sellers to dictate at what price a stock should open, they allowed the lead underwriter—himself—to set the price (2007, p. 100). But during 1994 and 1995, the Securities and Exchange Commission (SEC) passed a series of laws criminalizing such operations, and suddenly Belfort was a historical anachronism, yet he continued his shady practices well past the time when it was appropriate. His traders (whom he refers to as his "ratholes") were instructed to buy a stock at the initial price he had set and sell them at a prearranged price. And if they were questioned about the deal, they were expected to follow his protocol—which was to shut up and "lie through their teeth" when questioned by a federal investigator. Meanwhile, as he had worked out the scheme, Wall Street, following his frenzied lead, would have driven the stock up several times higher than its IPO (initial public offering), so that when Belfort divested himself of the stock, he would clear a tidy sum of multiple millions of dollars (p. 100). He managed to swing this scam several times a week so that within a couple of years, his net worth was a hundred million dollars.

Jordan led a lifestyle to match his swollen profits. He owned a helicopter, which he flew himself, and several Gulfstream jets; a 167-foot motor yacht; and a twenty-four room mansion in a nearly exclusively blue-blooded WASP North Shore Long Island community (Belfort is Jewish) with a guardhouse manned twenty-four hours a day by two armed bodyguards (both of whom are named Rocco) and supported a "bizarre menagerie" of ten additional staff. He owned $50,000 bed sheets made of white Chinese silk; a $12,000 silk comforter; a $120,000 Edward Fields carpet; $500 bath towels; an $18,000 Bulgari watch; $2,400 black crocodile cowboy boots; and a superstretch Lincoln limousine with a bed, a bar, a TV, and a VHS player—a "$90,000 bordello on wheels." He had a beautiful wife named Nadine, who once did Miller Lite beer commercials and who spent $70,000 a month, $1,000 each on her Manolo Blahniks and $400 for each bottle of shampoo, and he had a child who slept in a $60,000 custom-made Bellini bed over which hung a $9,000 mobile that played Disney songs. He also supported an ex-wife, to the tune of a lump sum of several million dollars and $50,000 a month in maintenance.

As profligate as his spending and as lavish as his lifestyle were, there was also an edge to his indulgences that included a wide swath of illegal behavior. Across the cover of his first book, in red script, we see the message, "I Partied like a Rock Star, Lived like a King." He engaged the services of a very expensive call girl with puffy lips and "loamy loins" who, on at least one occasion, inserted a candle in his anus in an unsuccessful attempt to help him achieve an erection (p. 16). He also took twenty Quaaludes a day and snorted enough cocaine to wire up the population of Guatemala. And his employees? At his brokerage firm, virtually every drug ever concocted by chemists filled the pockets of his stockbrokers (p. 31). During their mid-afternoon coffee breaks, these employees would leave their office and "get laid by a happy hit squad of prostitutes" (p. 49). Remarkably enough, one out of ten Strattonites was a woman, and they, and the men, were having sex "under desks, in bathroom stalls, in coat closets, in the underground parking garage, and, of course, the building's glass elevator." Eventually, to rein in all this wanton, profligate, hedonistic behavior, he tells the reader, the firm passed out a memorandum declaring the building "a Fuck Free Zone between the hours of eight a.m. and seven p.m. . . . But, alas, no one took it seriously" (p. 52).

All of his "made perfect sense. Everyone was young and beautiful and they were seizing the moment." This corporate mantra "vibrated in the overactive pleasure centers of all thousand of their barely postadolescent brains. And who could argue with success?" he asks rhetorically. The amount of money they made was truly astonishing. A stockbroker just starting out with him was expected to make a quarter of a million in his first year. By the end of the year, he was expected to clear a million or more or he would become "a complete fucking laughingstock." Those were only the minimums; a major seller earned three times that. "It was nothing short of a good old-fashioned gold rush" (pp. 52–53). If you were just beginning your career and had not acquired the toys appropriate to your peers' lifestyle, you borrowed money so that you could. Kids "only recently acquainted with a razor blade were going out and buying mansions." On weekends, some of them threw wild parties that were so decadent, Belfort stated, that they were "invariably broken up by the police" (p. 53). Strattonite girls danced topless; "strippers and hookers were honored guests"; couples would have sex out in the open, in full view of everyone else, eager to give everyone an entertaining show (p. 53).

No doubt hyperbole plays a major role in Belfort's prose, but his swagger barely conceals the man's desperation to win his readers' respect and admiration. We stagger around, seeking the wellspring, the origin of all this extravagant behavior—including the author's florid verbalizations. Who is to blame? What is the cause? And in tracing out what went on all around him, is Belfort justifying deviance and neutralizing stigma?

What's wrong with any of this? Belfort asks. His underlings, he says, "were drunk on youth, fueled by greed, and higher than kites. And day by day the gravy train grew longer" (p. 53). *Everyone* seemed to profit by the riotous flow of cash—the real estate agents, the mortgage brokers, the interior decorators, the landscapers, the exotic car dealers (Porsches, Mercedes, or Ferraris required), the maître d's at the local hot restaurants, the ticket scalpers, the jewelers and watchmakers, clothiers and shoemakers and florists and haircutters and pet groomers—not to mention the hookers and drug dealers who delivered their services in the boardroom (p. 54).

In Belfort's mind, what redeems him to his reader? How does he position himself vis-à-vis wrongdoing? To what extent was he conscious of his multitudinous violations of the law? Does he ask for our forgiveness? Does he attempt to justify himself?

Stratton Oakmont received a huge jolt of energy when, one day, Wall Street announced that the firm it had touted, Steve Madden Shoes, had become the most actively traded stock in America. Upon hearing this news, Belfort told himself, "Stratton had all the power. . . . In fact, Stratton Oakmont *was* the power," and, as Stratton's leader, he "sat atop its pinnacle" (2007, p. 102). The stock's surge, what it represented, and the enormous profits that it generated intoxicated Belfort. He fingered the Quaaludes in his pocket to make sure they would be there when he wanted them; "the drug-god had been kind" (p. 104). He began mentally scanning the firm's afternoon "depravity," which was shaving the head of a young, blonde sales assistant dressed in a bikini, who would be paid ten thousand dollars cash in exchange for getting a breast augmentation to a D-cup. He weighed which depravity was worse—the head-shaving or hiring a midget so that the staff could toss him around the boardroom. "How else was a man to measure his success if not by playing out every one of his adolescent fantasies, regardless of how bizarre it might be?" (p. 104). *It's all for morale,* he told himself. He toted up the plusses and minuses on a moral balance sheet, conjuring up some act of kindness or generosity in which he might engage further down the road to compensate. On the other hand, he ponders, "we might just be depraved maniacs—a self-contained society that had spiraled completely out of control. We Strattonites thrived on acts of depravity. We counted on them, in fact; I mean, we needed them to survive!" (p. 105).

Notice what Belfort is doing. He is invoking the collective will here, even though he is the head of the company whose members are out of control. He is encouraging that very behavior that he recognizes is depraved. All of us were, he admits, "unadulterated adrenaline junkies" (p. 105). He recalls a twenty-one-year-old employee having sex in the glass elevator with a seventeen-year-old sales assistant, who was "blond, beautiful, and wildly promiscuous. At first I was shocked," he admits, but he soon recognized the young man's sales ability, as well as the fact that the young woman was "a real team player": Within a week, she had administered oral sex to all eight of the managers of the firm, one of whom she eventually married. In the firm, normal behavior was in poor taste, akin to being a "killjoy or something" (p. 106). "In a way, wasn't the concept of depravity relative?" he rhetorically asks his readers (p. 106). *After all, didn't the ancient Romans feed some of their slaves to the lions and demand that the others feed them grapes? I'm not to blame,* Belfort seems to be telling us. *I was part of an entire mini-civilization that was corrupt, depraved, and degenerate. I was no more responsible for the climate at the firm than the assistant who gave blow jobs—less because she took the initiative; I just went along with what everyone else was doing.*

Meanwhile, the money laundering and market manipulation continued unabated. Belfort receives a call from an agent at the SEC asking questions about the firm's financial practices; before long, he realizes, he is under investigation. In response, he devises a cash-out scheme that has Stratton Oakmont paying him a million dollars a month for fifteen years—a lifetime total of $180 million (p. 270). The architect of the finagle is the firm's accountant, nicknamed "the Chef" for his fondness for cooking the books. At his country club, Belfort places a phone call to a private investigator he has hired who tells him that he is the target of a full-scale SEC money laundering investigation; the investigator is checking out an allegation that Jordan has twenty million dollars in a Swiss bank. In the middle of the conversation, he realizes that he has become stoned on Quaaludes he swallowed half an hour before—a delayed reaction. He loses the power of speech and collapses to the floor, then decides to drive home, doing twenty miles an hour. Thinking he had arrived at his house safely, he climbs into his bed and falls asleep, only to be awakened by two local police officers, who inform him that he had seven different automobile accidents on his way home, breaking the arm of a woman and totaling his Mercedes. They cuff and arrest him and take him to the station. He tests positive for seven drugs, including cocaine and methaqualone; he is then transported to Nassau County central booking. Jordan Belfort is in real trouble.

Within months, he learns that one of the principals in his firm has been indicted for money laundering, as was his Swiss banker; both are sitting in a Miami jail, held without bail. He begins contemplating his prison outfit. He speaks with his chief Swiss book-cooker, "Master Forger," who tells him the Swiss police have records of his accounts there.

In December 1996, the NASD revoked the membership of Stratton Oakmont for stock manipulation and various sales practice violations. Legally, it was closed down, out of business—kaput. Belfort still owned shares of Steve Madden Shoes, and he was still paid when he introduced an IPO to the market, but he was no longer able to trade on the stock market. And he was still dropping Quaaludes and snorting cocaine. He attempts to deviance-neutralize his wild and illicit machinations by blaming them on the drugs (p. 392)—an intriguing dovetailing of two deviancies into one. But throughout the book, he has claimed that it is the extreme stress that market trading generates that makes such drugs necessary; moreover, he insisted at several places that for the adrenaline junkie, the stock market and drug use are very much the same experience—the rush of trading is virtually meaningless without accompanying it with the chemical high. He even uses the same words and phrases:

"I was hooked," he declares when he first observed trading (2007, p. 7). When he was a newbie, an old hand told him these wise words: "I promise you that cocaine can definitely help you get through the day around here" (p. 9). Belfort began riding a stock market wave—a bull before the crash—a heady, exuberant, ecstatic, out-of-control era, one of the wildest rides in Wall Street history. And the voice—both recaptured, of his amoral, ironic self at the time, in the 1990s, and reconstructed, from his wiser, more sober life in the 2000s—"allowed me to rationalize what stood in the way of living a life of unbridled hedonism" (p. 10). No, Jordan Belfort could not have excised drugs from his life in the '90s, and yes, he was destined to engage in illegal, unethical trading practices to earn the piles of money he felt was his due. Trade legitimately? Not possible. He was not that kind of animal. This stigma neutralization does not convince the reader because it is out of character—for Jordan Belfort, for the mini-civilization in which he worked, for the temper of the times, the crowd that was attracted to him, and the activities in which his milieu perforce engaged. Jordan's claim that it was the drugs that made him do it is self-delusional. It contradicts everything he has said before.

The months that followed Stratton Oakmont's demise unraveled with gasping speed. One evening, Jordan's wife, Nadine, invites several couples to their mansion for dinner. The men repair to the den to snort cocaine and watch TV, the women, to a separate room to chat and sip wine. Jordan and his pals devote the earlier portion of the postprandial festivities to snorting *powder* cocaine and the later portion to ingesting *rock* cocaine. At some point during the evening, stoned on the powder, he decides to make the segue, but he cannot find the bag of expensive, nearly 100 percent pure rock and becomes obsessive in pursuit. Is it under the cushions of the couch? He grabs a butcher knife and slashes several very expensive couches and a very expensive carpet in his frenzied pursuit of the elusive bag. Jordan is wrestled to the floor by one of his staff, a large, muscular former bar bouncer, who sits on him to calm him down. The evening's festivities come to an end, but Jordan's amok, berserker behavior has barely gotten started.

The next day, Jordan drives off on an errand and smashes his Mercedes into a stone pillar at the edge of his estate. He returns to the den and resumes snorting cocaine. He imagines a talking head on the TV admonishing him for ignoring his addiction; enraged, he hurls a Remington statue of a cowboy riding a bucking bronco at the face, and the TV shatters into hundreds of shards, covering the floor. He returns to his desk and resumes snorting. He passes out, his face falling into the mound of coke in front of him. His wife enters the room, Jordan lifts his head, sees Nadine's horrified face, and asks what's wrong. His face is covered with powder, and his nose is bleeding. "Oh, my God! What are you doing?" Nadine asks (2007, p. 428). They have an argument, and she leaves the room, distraught. He comes to the conclusion that the drawback of sniffing coke is that it causes nosebleeds; deciding to *cook* some, he rushes to the kitchen and begins grabbing implements and ingredients, but he nods off and causes an explosion. He returns to his study and falls asleep.

In the morning, Nadine appears before him, her bags packed; she says she is leaving him and going to live with her mother. They argue about custody of their two young children; it is clear that she intends to leave them there for the time being and then take them with her later. Jordan yanks the bags out of her hands and begins yanking the clothes out of her suitcases and hurls them into the fireplace and sets them on fire. Then he shakes out the contents of her jewelry boxes into the flame. As Jordan watches the blaze, Nadine runs outside, jumps into her Range Rover, and drives away.

Jordan arranges his mélange of a dozen kinds of drugs into bags, piles, and vials on his desk and admires their beauty. "How many men could take all these drugs and not overdose? None! Only the Wolf could," he pridefully exclaims (p. 433). The next day, Nadine returns and they begin arguing about custody of the children. Jordan runs downstairs and grabs Chandler, their young daughter; Jordan and Nadine struggle, and Jordan kicks Nadine down a flight of stairs. Jordan runs outside with Chandler; she is frightened. He forces her into the back seat of the car, and she plasters her face and hands against the window, screaming. Jordan drives away but immediately crashes into a stone pillar. In minutes, he hears police sirens and sees two cop cars. He is handcuffed and led away to the station. He pleads not guilty and is released.

There is a limo waiting for him outside the courthouse, and his two Roccos step out; one hands him his trusty Louis Vuitton bag full of dope, with fifty thousand dollars in cash. His lawyer informs him that his Learjet is waiting for him at the airport. He is confused and asks where he is going, and his lawyer tells him that they are flying to Florida. Jordan has no idea why he is being flown there but learns that his wife has taken out an order of protection against him and that he will be arrested if he steps onto his property. *Oh, well,* he tells himself. *I'll probably kill her if I see her, so maybe it's for the best.* And he finally tells himself that perhaps a few days in the sun might actually do him some good.

But in Florida, at a strip club, he gobbles the contents of a vial of morphine pills, an employee yanks some of them out of his mouth, and then he passes out. Jordan Belfort has overdosed on an unknown quantity of fifteen-milligram morphine sulfate tablets. He spends some time in the psychiatric ward of the Delray Medical Center, where a psychiatrist tells him, "You are . . . a *sick* person, Jordan; you're sick with a disease . . . that's no different from cancer or diabetes" (p. 456). He is transferred to the Talbot Marsh Recovery

Campus, a drug treatment facility in Atlanta, where, one day soon after intake, inexplicably, he experiences a profound and life-altering epiphany: "Just like that, in that very instant, the compulsion left me. I was done. No more drugs. I knew it. Enough was enough. I no longer felt the urge. Why, I would never know. All I knew was that I would never touch them again. Something had clicked inside my brain. Some sort of switch had been flipped and I just fucking knew it" (pp. 468–469).

Soon after returning home, while pulling into his driveway with Chandler in the passenger seat, Jordan notices a car parked outside his property, a gray, four-door sedan. The man inside asks him what address they are at; Jordan tells him and, afraid that the man is a kidnapper, begins to speed off. "It's okay, Jordan. We're not here to hurt you. Please don't pull away" (p. 513). Jordan stops his car. "What do you want?" he asks. "We're from the F.B.I.," the man responds (p. 514). Inside, after Chandler goes to her room, a female agent cuffs Jordan and announces that he is under arrest for securities fraud and money laundering, as well as for a host of other charges (p. 515). Within twenty minutes, twenty security agents swarm into the house, with "full regalia"—guns, vests, and lots of extra ammo.

Nearly all his associates are indicted, and most of them serve prison time; a few get probation, and two are declared not guilty. After Jordan's arrest, the judge sets bail at ten million dollars. On the courthouse steps, his faithful wife, Nadine, informs Jordan that she is divorcing him. It is five years from Belfort's indictment to imprisonment—twenty-two months in a federal prison camp. Do not expect Jordan to explicate a theory of social control. A wrinkle in the law permitted him to become almost unimaginably rich; when the loophole was closed, he violated the law as long as he could and was caught. He did not engage in an illegal enterprise to make a political statement, overturn the system, or exact fairness from it; he did it to become rich.

Accounting for Crime

All enactors of behavior that some audiences regard as wrongdoing must consider the question of what manner of neutralizations work to placate those audiences: *What can I say to make them feel better about me and what I did?* Likewise, certain vocabularies, certain neutralization techniques, pour forth from specific wrongdoers; others are likely to fall flat, both as they are welling up in the chest of the wrongdoer and as such words encounter the consciousness and emotional field of the victim, the observer, nonsympathetic audiences, skeptics, and critics—not to mention his or her peers. Friends and like-minded fellows in thought, deed, style, and emotion may draw forth verbal utterances that sound and *feel* better than "I *like* it."

They will growl: *I* buy *it. You hadda do what you hadda do. It was you or him, right? Am I right?* What do deviant actors say on the page? And of the many things that they are likely to say, what palliates their diverse audiences most? And what among the sins we discuss here is likely to produce a connection with one or another neutralization device?

Though "crime" is a legal—and therefore constructed—category, for a substantial sector of the public, it is ineluctably an essentialistic, concrete reality. In some neighborhoods, residents live in daily fear of assault, muggings, rape, and robbery. To them crime is not an abstraction but a hard-core presence that cannot be defined away by the terminological niceties that left-wing intellectuals, in their theoretically rich but relatively crime-free reserves, are free to dissect and soliloquize about. To repeat St. Augustine's line, "No thief will submit to being robbed by another" (p. 45)—in other words, no matter how hard predatory criminals may try to justify their crimes, *they* would not want the same crimes they commit against others to be committed against *them.* The Jack Abbotts and Eddie Bunkers who plead that to survive they had no choice but to resort to victimizing others will receive no sympathy from their victims and fellow citizens for their choice of neutralizations. Abbott's initial audience was made up of left-wing intellectuals with a strong underdog bias, Norman Mailer—no surprise here—his very first reader, and later, the subscribers to *The New York Review of Books.* Abbott's charge that "incarceration made me do it" (1981, p. 11) is likely to fall on deaf ears among wide swaths of American society, from conservatives and evangelicals to hard-working lunch-pail stiffs, who feel that a man like Abbott, however polluted he became as a result of the indignity and degradation of prison life, should never have been released. Perhaps the greatest irony of Norman Mailer's life—this intellectual and would-be tough guy who claimed to stand side-by-side with the underdog—is that upon the occasion of Mailer's death, in his obituaries, in the summation of his life, the subject turned to the terrible mistake he had made with Jack Henry Abbott. Most of *The New York Times* posts focused on Abbott, not Mailer, and on his blunder, not his attempt to do good. Abbott, says one, "should never have been paroled." Norman Mailer is now "answering" for the death of Richard Adan, the man Abbott stabbed. "Mailer is no different from the intellectual bleeding hearts who are trying to ban execution of even the most murderous, bloodthirsty villains in jails," reads another.

Joe Bonanno was an old-world, old-fashioned, traditional guy, a gentleman. He wrote his memoir, told his stories, and put into play his self-exculpations for people like him, his community, the people he grew up with, those who respected him; he—and no doubt his coauthor, Sergio Lalli—also revealed just enough of himself, on both sides of the ledger, to attract even larger audiences. In his public presentation, Bonanno was not trying to rock the boat. If he committed crimes that he, his peers, or the public at large, considered heinous, he did not narrate them. To him, certain crimes are unseemly and unmanly, even if he had to commit them, and, if they are unseemly and unmanly, they must not be spoken or written about. "You gotta do what you gotta do" seems to be his watchword throughout *A Man of Honor* and, no doubt, through his life as well. Joe is not a whiner or a complainer. The image he projects is that of a benevolent uncle, very much at the opposite end of the spectrum from Jack Henry Abbott. And he is also very much unlike Jordan Belfort, whose motto seems to have been, "If you've got it, flaunt it." Joe Bonanno does not deny having been a mob figure or committing an extensive roster of criminal acts, and he does not make excuses for what he did. He does not deny responsibility for the actions he narrates—no "billiard ball" he—but he does minimize the victimization of the people in his milieu. And his milieu is crucial here: What was considered a crime in the Anglo-American community, or according to state or federal statute, was acceptable, common practice among Italian Americans in the first half of the twentieth century. "What is seen as extortion from the outsider is viewed as self-protection by the insider" (1984, p. 61). Obedience to one's superiors "was one of the duties of a Family member. Silence was another cardinal duty. One had to learn to keep a secret and not betray one's friends" (p. 59). Joe Bonanno's verbalizations make use of classic neutralization Sykes and Matza called *transcending commitments*—an "appeal to higher loyalties," including "I couldn't let my buddies down." What is conventionally regarded as right becomes unacceptable; what is wrong is redefined as right. In order to do a good thing (among us, in our culture), it is necessary to violate the law. Bonanno takes full responsibility for his acts, but he does not accept the legitimacy or the righteousness of the law.

And the use of his neutralizations is as much collective as individual. He is not exonerating himself so much as his community, his ethnic traditions, his background, his culture, his friends and fellow goombas (his ethnic peers, Sicilian Americans). In other words, Bonanno's crime and his neutralization fit together like jigsaw puzzle pieces; *his exoneration grows out of his crime.* He is exonerated, in his eyes, because in committing his crimes, he simply followed ethnic and historical tradition. The federal government called them crimes, his community called them necessities of life. "Prevented from participating in the rule of their own land, Sicilians withdrew all the more into their own families" (p. 13)—and the mob, the Mafia, organized crime was only of a number of such "families." "In discussing the role of violence in my world I don't expect outsiders to condone or approve of the rules by which we lived. I would only ask the outsider to appreciate the context of our lives" (p. 135). The Sicilian "has a personal sense of justice" that demands that he address wrongs against him personally and not seek the "judicial machinery of the state." In order for this to work, everyone "must understand what is wrong and what is right" (p. 135). I engaged in acts the American law considered wrong but Sicilian tradition considered acceptable, even necessary; I am narrating my story, taking myself off the moral hook, neutralizing the wrong of my act by means of my traditional Sicilian background. It is the perfect device: My honored tradition demanded that I do what I did, and my honored tradition was the reason why I did what I did and why what I did is not wrong—that is, *from the perspective of my honored tradition.* It is the classic case of the snake swallowing itself; accepting certain premises as true and inviolate, there is no way of refuting the logic. Bonanno comes very close to normalizing and legitimating certain kinds of criminal behavior—that is, proclaiming that much of what he has done that the state regards as illegal is so commonplace and acceptable within his community that it is de facto legal. He regards organized crime as a business much like any other business, though with a somewhat more flexible modus operandi. But notice: He can do this only if he denies or ignores his more heinous illegal activities.

Jack Henry Abbott likewise offers a vocabulary of motives that dovetails his crimes, some of them at any rate, with his self-exoneration. Abbott's transcending commitments, however, are not to a living, judging community and subculture, but to his own personal code of ethics. Like Bonanno, he does not invoke a lack of personal control and never sees himself as a human "billiard ball." Forced to live in an inhuman environment, Abbott engages in inhuman actions. His actions are forceful, manly, necessary, and above all *justified* under the circumstances. He is not the deviant; he is living under perverse, abnormal conditions. You call me a monster? Prison is a monstrous institution and it perpetrates monstrous acts upon otherwise normal inmates who, as a result, become monsters. Interestingly enough, a few years after his reincarceration, Abbott co-authored a play in which he depicts Richard Adan, the waiter whom he stabbed, as acting in a gruff and rude fashion, and himself as the perfect gentleman (Abbott, with Zack, 1987)—again, he was forced to do what he had to do, and Adan was a deserving victim. His crimes were acts of survival, and his justification rests on a synthesis of necessity and defense of his honor. Just as Bonanno's self-exonerations are atypical of those a street criminal might use (after all, very few of them are "men of honor"), Abbott's are explained by means of the unusual resort to honor—his own. But the verbalization was unsuccessful; the book containing his play was a failure, and virtually no one, not even Normal Mailer, honored his account.

To many observers and social critics at the time of his release, Abbott's claim to martyrdom seemed extremely convincing. Abbott exonerated himself by citing *deserving victims* and *transcending commitments.* He would not refer to either of these as an "excuse" or an apology, but as a justification. And after the publication of his articles in the left-wing *New York Review of Books,* and after the publication of *In the Belly of the Beast,* Abbott's exculpation was endorsed by a coterie of like-minded devotees who accepted his justifications, his explanations, and his exoneration—all of which collapsed with one expert thrust of his knife into the heart of a young waiter and aspiring actor. Mailer helped Abbott package and sell his self-exculpations to a small, leftist, convict-chic crowd, but his subsequent actions demonstrated how thin and self-serving they were. After that tragic event, Norman Mailer, his bully-boy supporter who had himself stabbed his wife, Adele, became something of an object of ridicule, and Abbott a fugitive, then, once again, a convict, a discredited writer, a naked rationalizer, and, eventually, a suicide. The Jack Henry Abbott saga should remind us as to the degree to which vocabularies of motives and deviance neutralization devices are socially and personally constructed—considered valid by some audiences but not others, honored under certain circumstances but not others, and accepted by key, respected figures who may themselves prove to be as brittle as glass. In the end, Abbott's neutralizations devices collapsed like a house of cards.

Eddie Bunker was a more typical criminal than Jack Abbott, but like Abbott, he regarded himself as mentally and morally superior to the ordinary man and considered his rebellion against the powers that be as a manifestation of his manliness. Both authors sidestepped the implications of the old convict joke, "If you're so smart, how come you got your ass in prison?" For both, the contradiction between the strength of their masculine will and the need to explain away their limited options is irreconcilable. Neither apologized or made excuses, both condemned their condemners and the conditions that resulted in their incarceration, but both regarded their criminal behavior as inevitable. Anyone who has read convict memoirs recognizes these as familiar themes.

Superficially considered, Jordan Belfort, the self-appointed "wolf" of Wall Street, shares very little with Bonanno, Abbott, and Bunker aside from engaging in illegal acts and a term in prison. His vocabulary of motives—"why I did it"—indicates an outsized ego and reckless ambition, as well as the impulse to play outside the rules. Belfort's actions clearly illustrate Robert K. Merton's theory of anomie (1957): If legitimate pathways to a much touted goal are blocked, the resourceful will seek, and act upon, illegal ones. But, one might object, initially Belfort became immensely successful earning money on Wall Street *legally*; why seek illegal means? It's simple: Jordan looked around and saw greater success than his. *Relatively speaking,* he was a small fry. He wanted a Ferrari, not an Acura—not one car but a fleet of them—he wanted a house in Little Neck, not in Forest Hills; a luxurious yacht, not a cabin cruiser; diamonds, emeralds, sapphires for his wife, not costume jewelry and silver and turquoise. And the list was endless, the sky was the limit—actually, there *was* no limit. Why stop at rum and pot? Coke got you so much higher, so much mellower—so much, well, *cooler.* More stoned. More *there.* Piles of it. Piles so high and wide your face can fall into it. And when you get too wired, why, Quaaludes will bring you back to the here and now. And the *only* way Jordan could get the things he wanted was by cutting corners, skirting the law, being bolder and more daring than his peers. And gaining the respect of his peers and running the show got under Jordan's skin—*he wanted it all!* And he got it, all of it. Innovation, in Merton's terminology: He figured ways to get what he wanted—*illegal* ways. And he got caught. And he served time. Bonanno, Abbott, Bunker were brothers under the skin—they just thought smaller and played rougher. And, like them, he wants us to understand *why* he did what he did.

So, yes, of course, types of accounts are related to types of misbehavior. Though crime is crime—and virtually every violator knows what the law is, what is legal, and where the line is crossed—the fact is, not all crimes are prosecuted with the same vigor. Almost by definition, engaging in crime entails cutting corners, getting something you want illegally because you cannot get it through conventional means. But engaging in street crime generates justifications that sound a little different from engaging in white collar crime or organized crime. Floating a vocabulary to the public about mugging a little old lady for the twenty dollars in her purse will always be a tough sell, even among street toughs, but the generic "You had to do what you had to do" always gets nods in certain social circles. Not all miscreants can say the same thing. And to legitimate your argument, to "sell" a life of crime as necessary behavior, it helps to give it up, then write about it—in a dramatic way, perhaps somewhat wistfully, but as an activity in which one no longer engages. This is how the game of memoir is played; this is how one convinces readers that one's account makes sense.

5

Substance Abuse

OF ALL THE POPULAR "deviance" memoir genres, perhaps alcoholism elicits the least justificatory and the most redemptionist stance. Few alcoholics proclaim that they wish to remain compulsive, destructive drunks; nearly all, by the time they pen their life stories, have stopped their heavy drinking, most have stopped drinking altogether, and the great majority write that abstinence served as a salvation or redemption for which they are grateful. And the memoirs they produce bear testament to heavy alcohol consumption's destructive power: ruined marriages; wrecked careers; alienation from friends, family, and children; suicide attempts; car crashes and accidents of every conceivable description; bad sex; blackouts; unrecalled misadventures subsequently embarrassingly narrated by others; episodes entailing a loss of consciousness—these and countless other damaging consequences are litanized as if they constituted a catechism. But most memoirs of such undesirable events and conditions also recall the sense of adventure, friendship, conviviality, joviality, and warm spirits that drinking evokes, but the bad nearly always outweighs the good, both in frequency and in magnitude.

Epidemiologists find that the heavy use of alcohol is statistically co-occurrent with risky, deviant behaviors, such as driving under the influence; having an accident while driving; committing crimes; engaging in violence; becoming a victim of crime and violence; engaging in sex with multiple partners, unprotected sex, or sex with strangers; abusing illicit drugs; and committing suicide. This generalization is true whether we compare drinkers with non-drinkers, more intoxicated states with less, or degrees of magnitude of intoxication during drinking occasions. This is true everywhere in the world, though the strength of the association varies by society, culture, and locale. Not only is heavy alcohol consumption a form of deviance; it is also likely to lead to a range of other deviant behaviors, both in strictly cause-and-effect terms—through disinhibition and discoordination—and through the influence of drinking companions, whose behavior, including the willingness to engage in drunkenness, is more likely to be unconventional than that of non-drinkers.

These statistical relationships readily translate into the experiential realm and hence become woven into memoiristic narrative. Given that heavy drinking is related to significantly harmful consequences, it often becomes the fulcrum of the tale that recovered drinkers tell: *I drank, I suffered, I made others suffer, I experienced an epiphanic event, I realized the error of my ways, I stopped drinking, and now I'm a different person—I've transformed and redeemed myself.* Most such narratives are triumphalist or "feel good" accounts. Pete Hamill succumbed to the allure of drinking, suffered because of it and, in turn, left suffering in his wake, then sobered up, and, as a consequence, enlarged and enhanced his life.

Consider one of the most famous of all "drunkalogues" of all time: *John Barleycorn* by Jack London, published in 1913. *My drinking was the fault of my need to be convivial,* he says, *to be in the company of like-minded men, to share in their companionship and their rituals, to compete with them in drinking contests and generosity.* "At every turn in the world in which I lived," London tells us, "John Barleycorn beckoned. There was no escaping him. All paths led to him" (1913, pp. 10–11). *I don't particularly like alcohol,* London tells us, *but I like being with brave, hearty, "chesty" men, and I like to talk man-talk with them.* "Drink was the badge of manhood. . . . Men . . . congregated in saloons, the poorman's clubs, and they were the only clubs to which I had access. I could get acquainted in saloons. I could go into saloons and talk with any man" (pp. 28, 72). What is wrong with that? Life is an adventure, and talking about one's adventures is one of life's sweet masculine pleasures. "I drank because the men I was with drank, because my nature was such that I could not permit myself to be any less of a man than other men at their favorite pastimes" (pp. 97–98). Drinking alcohol serves functions that using other substances or engaging in any other activities does not; it relieves stress, assuages exhaustion, provides a mask for courage, soothes nagging doubts and insecurities, and lifts depression. Alcohol is a vehicle; it is also an instrument for other things. True, the insights it imparts are insidious, shocking, cynical, and gloomy—but you pay for what you get. *Am I depraved, an evil person because I drink?* London asks himself. *Of course not. I do what other men do, live the life of a manly man, and comport myself as any stouthearted, bold, and fearless man must.* Drinking is part of being manly, an essential component of the world of men; to be abstemious in that world is to be unmanly. "*Glass in hand!*" London declares. "There is magic in that phrase" (p. 207): *Hence, I drink, and heavily, and I should not be blamed or stigmatized for it—nor should any man.*

Alcoholism and drug addiction share significant features—both are "substance abuse"—but they differ as well. They differ in the sense that moderate alcohol consumption is not a form of deviance; it does not attract generic social condemnation, while any use of the illicit drugs, marijuana possibly excepted, does. But the two share the quality that, at the extreme end, both are addictions, both result in an inability to perform conventional social roles, both are condemned—and both attract memoir-writing. The drug use/drug abuse/drug addiction memoir remains one of the most popular of the autonarration genre. As with alcoholism stories, most offer a tale of redemption and rehabilitation, though the authors of a few defy the tradition and report largely positive experiences and announce that the author intends to continue using his or her drug of choice, thank you very much.

The most basic facts about drug use are these: Most drug use is more pleasurable than painful, most triers of nearly all drugs do not go on to use regularly, and most regular users do not go on to become dependent or addicted—though the proportions differ from one substance to another. Catastrophic effects—a drug overdose, for instance—tend to be atypical, though for some substances (heroin, for instance), they take place in substantial enough numbers to warn everyone away from even experimental use. Of course, heavy alcohol consumption can likewise cause death, and does, to the tune of roughly seventy thousand to a hundred thousand Americans a year. For other substances, like marijuana, overdoses are virtually nonexistent. But an account of the more or less benign and more or less experimental consumption of a psychoactive substance is not particularly interesting and cannot serve as the basis of an exciting memoir. Accounts about dabbling in drugs and finding the experience pleasing are about as exciting as watching a plant grow; hence, books narrating such experiences range from rare to virtually absent in the memoir literature. In contrast, destruction, degradation, redemption, and rehabilitation memoirs are exciting and dramatic—they function as morality tales; they are uplifting; they draw the reader in. In such tales, though, we see the tiny tip of an enormous iceberg, which is probably as it should be, but as a result, readers may be misled as to how representative this tip is. Still, many users and abusers are unable to control their drug consumption and end up destroying their lives; feeding a ruinous habit; leeching off their friends and relatives; and experiencing a round-robin of arrest, treatment, rehabilitation, and relapse. Those who survive and stay clean have a story to tell, and many of them have told it.

Perhaps the first book-length substance abuse memoir was *Confessions of an English Opium-Eater,* by Thomas De Quincey, a renowned British writer—the author's most notable work and the most outstanding drug memoir written in the nineteenth century. Originally published as an anonymous two-part essay in *The London Magazine* (the author never delivered the promised third, and final, part), the book, which appeared a year later (1821), subsequently underwent several editions. It proved a sensation and has never gone out of print. Normally, the author explains, he who experiences "infirmity and misery" keeps it to himself. De Quincey is willing to breach that rule of modesty because he feels no guilt about his actions: first, because his motives for use were honorable and, second, because he was able to untwist "the accursed chain which fettered" him—that is, he overcame his addiction to opium. De Quincey's justification for telling his tale is disingenuous in that, though analgesia was his initial reason for self-administering the drug, his motive for continued use was quite different, and when he wrote *Confessions,* he was still drug-dependent and remained so for a span of four decades (Lindop, 1993, pp. 249–250, 390).

In his slim volume, De Quincey openly addresses his readers for the purpose of disarming their critical faculties, to forestall their judgment that he has engaged in deviant, reprehensible behavior by become dependent on opium. In fact, in its entirety, *Confessions* may be regarded as something of a deviance-neutralization contrivance. "This is the point of my narrative, on which," he explains, "as respects my own self-justification, the whole of what follows may be said to hinge" (De Quincey, 1995, p. 46). He refers to the reader's "good opinion" of him, which may be in jeopardy by learning of his indulgent habit. At one point, he explains, "I began to take opium daily. *I could not have done otherwise*" (my emphasis). "I cannot face misery," he admits, "and I am little capable of encountering present pain" (p. 47). Let no man "expect to frighten me," he challenges, "by a few hard words into embarking any part of it upon desperate adventures of morality" (p. 48). His medical justification, along with his torment during withdrawal, offer justifiable reason for us, his readers, to respect him and lay aside our condemnation of him as a self-indulgent slave of a psychoactive drug. Likewise, our view of him is altered by virtue of the fact that he frequently boasted to his friends that he had conquered the opium habit, only to relapse soon after.

Early on, he raises the "Why?" question in the following fashion: "How came any reasonable being to subject himself to such a yoke of misery, volunteer to incur a captivity so servile, and knowingly to fetter himself to such a seven-fold chain?" (De Quincey, 1995, p. 4). The author denies having taken up the practice "purely for the sake of creating an artificial state of pleasurable excitation" (p. 5). True, he admits, pleasure provided one motive in a stew of others, but the author's need to take opium—more specifically, laudanum, a tincture of opium, which was drunk, not eaten—began for medical reasons. He began taking the drug daily, he says, for the purpose of "mitigating pain in the severest degree," which itself was caused, he states, as a result of bouts of "extremities of hunger," which he suffered as a young man (p. 6). *Confessions of an English Opium-Eater* is a remarkable and dazzling display of virtuosity in deviance neutralization.

Pete Hamill, "This Is What Men Do"

Pete Hamill describes a scene in which Billy, his father, and several uncles, big men with "sour smells clinging to their jackets," wearing hats, smoking cigarettes, singing, and laughing loudly, drink beer out of "tall glasses and giant brown bottles." For a long time, he tells us, he sat on the floor and watched what he calls this "magic show." The night the Japanese navy bombed Pearl Harbor, his father went out, got drunk, came home, and sat down hard at the kitchen table, knocking over a glass of beer. Ordered to bed, Pete later peered into the kitchen and saw his father sprawled, face down, his arms stretched out across the table, fast asleep (1994, p. 9).

The elder Hamill frequented a dozen neighborhood saloons, one of them named Gallagher's. There, he and his cronies talked, smoked, sang, and drank beer and whiskey. Billy, apparently, was the star of the show, the center of attention, singing verses his pals called for. "This is where men go," Pete told himself; "this is what men do" (1994, p. 17). Billy's friends bought him more drinks and urged him to sing more songs as they slipped young Pete nickels and dimes; eventually his father told him to go home, and he did—with a fortune of coins in his hand. On such occasions, Pete made a visit to Foppiano's candy store to sample the Mary Janes and Sky Bars and purchase Superman, Batman, and Plastic Man comic books. The comics taught him that even an ordinary mortal can imbibe a magic potion and morph into an extraordinary hero. Hamill, the writer, associates this magic potion with alcohol, implying that his father's personality came alive under the influence, but, unlike what happens in the comics, the ultimate price real-life man and boy pay for this gift is impoverishing.

One day while playing with several of his friends, Pete looked up to see his father stumbling toward him, at the arm of another man. Everything about his gait and the expression in his eyes told the boy his dad was seriously inebriated. "He looked at me as if I were a stranger." The other man informed him that his father was all right, "Just drunk as a skunk." The son of the candy store owner began taunting him. "Your old man's an Irish drunk!" which caused Hamill to attack the boy and receive punches in the face and a bloody nose. He ran inside, feeling shamed. Behind him, he says, "everyone was laughing" (p. 21).

The neighborhood bars were filled with drinking men. After American military forces dropped atomic bombs on Hiroshima and Nagasaki, the war ended for good, and the neighborhood celebrated with a huge, noisy block party. Saloonkeepers lined the sidewalk with kegs of free beer, and everybody sang and danced. Pete found his father passed out on the stairwell. "And so the pattern had begun." When there was a celebration, you got drunk; when there was a victory, you got drunk. "Part of being a man was to drink" (p. 58). The local bars were "ceaseless rivers" of alcohol (p. 62). One day, intrigued by the ubiquity of drinking and the magical transmogrification it seemed to spawn, Pete took a sip of a beer from a glass that had been sitting on the kitchen table. The taste repulsed him; it was sour, bitter, and the smell was vile. *Is this all there is to drinking beer?* he asked. *What's all the fuss about? Why would anyone do it?* He took another sip, then a third, expecting some remarkable transfiguration. Nothing happened. Sour taste or sweet, he tells us, "I had taken my first drink of beer" (1994, p. 74).

As a thirteen-year-old, Pete learned to be a tough guy, he learned to "curse, to tell jokes, to play ball." He wanted to be "a man in the world, but a man cleansed of all stupidities. I didn't want to be like my father. I didn't want to be a drunk. And yet drinking started to seem as natural to real life as breathing" (p. 107). Drinking with his pals became commonplace; eventually he learned to like the taste of beer. He consoled himself that he never got drunk, never staggered or passed out. But he knew that he was being changed (p. 114). He talked more, swaggered, admired the local gang members, and yearned for a girlfriend. He developed a hobby—cartooning. Milton Caniff, who created *Steve Canyon* and *Terry and the Pirates,* became his hero.

One evening after dinner, while he was sitting at the kitchen table attempting to draw a cartoon, his drunken father lurched through the room, causing Pete to ruin a line. In a rage, he tore up the drawing, threw the ink bottle against the sink, and stalked out. He blamed his father for his mistake. Among his pals, he began drinking "to get rid of something." That gave him a delicious sense of joy. "I could drink until I got drunk because it was somebody else's fault. If I downed too many beers, it was my father's fault; if I staggered, it was his fault; if I fell down in the grass in the park: it was his fault." He pictured himself as Bogart in *Casablanca,* "in a pool of bitterness, drinking his whiskey. I would be like that. I would just drink, quietly and angrily, and say nothing. . . . In the year that followed, I did a lot of that" (1994, pp. 114–115).

The winter of 1950–1951 found Hamill in the company of Jenny, with whom he had begun having intercourse; drinking, he learned, was an essential part of the sex. He drank three or four beers "to feel confident," and Jenny drank three or four "to have an excuse for letting me do it once again. It was as much a ritual as the Mass." Sometimes he bought condoms, sometimes he bought a quart of Ballantine's. He contemplated his future. "Do what everybody else does," he told himself, "drop out of high school, go to work, join the army or navy, get married, settle down, have children. Don't make waves, don't rock the boat." That was how every neighborhood story ended: "Come on: let's have a fucking drink" (p. 146).

He did not know it at the time, he tells us, but drinking, he came to realize, was part of being a man; an essential ingredient of sex; the glue of friendship, conviviality, and sociability; the motivator and reward for hard work; the spark and source of celebration; and solace for death and defeat. "Drinking gave me strength, confidence, ease, laughter; it made me believe that dreams really could come true" (pp. 146–147). Hamill dropped out of high school, got a job at the Brooklyn Navy Yard, did a man's day's work, and got his own room, lived his own life (p. 149). He was sixteen, but he could lay his money down at the bar with grown men without being asked for a draft card.

Before long, he found his own bar, his special place to drink, a club where he hung out. "I wanted to be part of the widening fraternity of drinkers." On Saturday night, "with the jukebox blasting and the beer flowing, we'd all get roaring drunk." The drinking, he says, left "permanent holes" in his memory. He remembers lurching home, the streets undulating, the lampposts swaying; he remembers that the ceiling rose and fell as if he were in the middle of the ocean. Most of all, he says, he remembers the "heady" feeling at the bar, when he pushed quarters across the wet surface, the feeling when the bartender "bought me a free round." Best of all, he says, was that he could get drunk for a dollar and a half (1994, pp. 166–167).

After a stint in the navy, a stretch working in graphic design, and most of two semesters at Mexico City College on the GI Bill and an arrest for an episode that was more than a misunderstanding and less than a felony, Hamill fled Mexico, returned to the neighborhood, to his usual drinking routine, and agonized over the dilemma between commerce, mainly in the form of graphic design, and art. "I drank a lot. I got laid a lot. . . . I never thought of myself as a drunk; I was, I thought, like many others—a *drinker.* I certainly didn't think I was an alcoholic" (p. 212). He got a freelance layout job putting together a magazine, for which he wrote his first full-length article, on José Torres, an intelligent, articulate, personable middleweight. "That was it. I was a professional writer" (p. 214). He sent a letter to Jimmy Wechsler, the editor of *The New York Post* in response to his reading of Wechsler's recently published book, *Reflections of an Angry Middle-Aged Editor.* After writing a tryout article for Paul Sann, manager of *The Post*'s city desk, who read and commented on his piece, he was hired.

"Naturally, I got drunk in celebration" (p. 224). But there were limits on the stereotype of the hard-drinking reporter. One Saturday night, Hamill's cronies at *The Post* threw a big party at a local hangout. Revelry prevailed, and the party lasted until dawn. On Sunday, Hamill continued drinking and reported to work, half-drunk, at one in the morning on Monday. He stumbled into a trash barrel, attracting some attention. With Al Davis, an editor, standing over his shoulder, he began typing, hitting his fingers between several keys. "*I think you better go home,*" Davis said. "*Don't you ever do this again,*" he whispered. "And I didn't" (1994, p. 227). But this did not stop Hamill from drinking. He simply timed his drinking so that his inebriation did not fall under the shadow of his on-the-job performance.

Hamill got married, had children, free-lanced across the globe, returned to *The Post,* wrote a column, covered the war in Vietnam, and alienated his wife with his "combination of drinking, machismo, intellectual bullshitting, and flattery" (p. 247). She asked for a divorce; he hung out at the Lion's Head, a West Village bar, and continued the drinking and bullshitting. Hamill got his own apartment and began dating. He began noticing "odd little signs of deterioration" in his physical coordination and condition—spelling mistakes, a hand tremor, muscular twitches, lack of feeling in his legs. He could feel his body sending him a message. "I just wasn't ready to hear it" (pp. 254–255).

One New Year's Eve, at a party at a bar named Jimmy's, Hamill was seized by a detached feeling, as if he was performing his life rather than living it (p. 256). His hand trembled so much that he feared that the camera would record it. Several gangsters came in, smoking cigars, their molls snapping chewing gum. "I stared into my glass, at the melting ice and vodka-logged lime. And I said to myself, *I'm never going to do this again.* I finished my drink. It was the last one I ever had" (p. 257). He had to survive numerous tests of will (p. 262). At his father's seventieth birthday celebration, whiskey was passed around, and as usual, his dad sang a song. "I was forever Billy Hamill's son, but I did not want to be the next Billy Hamill. He had his life and I had mine" (p. 263). As the months wore by, he realized that he had successfully stopped drinking. He had "replaced the habit of drinking with the habit of nondrinking" (1994, p. 264).

On a snowy January afternoon, five years into his sobriety, he wandered into a nearby Brooklyn park. He stood under a pine tree, imagined people in his past, all having a whooping good time, and he heard his father singing. "I loved my life, with all its hurts and injuries and failures. . . . I was home. I was free" (p. 265). *A Drinking Life* is a perfect triumphalist narrative. It makes his hard drinking understandable, weaving it into the author's upbringing, his cultural background, and his young and not-so-young manhood. It highlights the personal and collective appeals of alcohol, empathetically ushering us into Hamill's emotional and cognitive space. We cheer when he gives up drinking, knowing full well what he missed out on, yet we never condemn him for his earlier transgressions and excesses. While Hamill offers himself up to a warts-and-all portrait—early on, he was, by his own admission, a staggering drunk—his grace, dignity, self-respect, and accomplishments ensure that his readers never regard him as a deviant.

Susan Cheever, "Drinking Was Part of Our Heritage"

Susan Cheever is the daughter of John Cheever, a successful and critically acclaimed short story writer and novelist, and herself an accomplished and well-known author. John was an alcoholic, and when Susan was six, her grandmother taught her how to make the perfect dry martini. She grew up in an upper-middle-class suburban household marked by a shabby, WASPy gentility. "Every evening at six o'clock," she explains, "the grown-ups in the suburbs would prepare for what they called their preprandial libation" (1999, p. 17). She became "well acquainted with the miraculous medicinal powers of alcohol" (p. 17). Her ancestors came to America on the *Arbella* in 1630, setting sail with three times as much beer as water, along with ten thousand gallons of wine. "Drinking was part of our heritage," she explains (p. 17).

During a period of several years, her father "was drinking all the time" (p. 50). "No one imagined that he was an alcoholic," she tells us; during that stretch, he had written one of his most successful short stories, "The Swimmer," later to be turned into a film (1968). One day, John picked up his children at the airport in a car he had bought with the money he was paid for the screen rights to one of his novels. "My father's driving was erratic, and suffered when he frequently turned around to make a point. He smelled of gin, and in the confined space of the overheated car the smell was so thick it was almost tactile" (p. 51).

When she was thirteen, Susan drank her first alcoholic beverage, grappa from a thick green goblet. Her father had just completed "The Sorrows of Gin," a short story about drinking. She found that gin relaxed her bronchial spasms brought on by an attack of asthma. Growing up, she tells us, "drinking seemed as much a part of life, as ordinary a part of life, as eating or even breathing" (p. 32). Her father drank; her mother cooked. And at home, "we laughed while alcohol twined itself around us like a choking, deadly, invisible vine" (p. 33). There were, she explains, "plenty of early signs." People falling down stairs. Scuff marks on the walls from flying feet. Guests who came for lunch and had to be put to bed. Terrible fights, disagreements that morphed into "an apocalyptic rage" (p. 33). And when others around her drank, Susan drank as well. It never occurred to her "that there was any connection, any connection at all, between the problems I had—at school, with men—and the way I drank" (1999, p. 33).

Susan pin-points the exact moment when she discovered what all the fuss about drinking was about. She and her First Love were apart, and she sat in her parents' dining room feeling "skinned and lonely." She realized that her boyfriend did not love her. "I felt a tearing sensation, a yearning that was almost physical. Then my father walked toward me with a gin and tonic. It was a hot, hot afternoon. I took a sip. The drink was fizzy and tasted of sugar and quinine and then, almost as an aftertaste, the steely gin. I took a swallow, gulping down the sweetness to savor the metallic taste of the gin. I began to feel better. The yearning lessened. . . . I could feel myself relaxing. . . . There would be many men in my life, I knew. I was young, beautiful, smart. . . . My father turned on the record player, and the buoyant strains of Handel filled the room. . . . I was swept away in the feelings of the music and the heat and the cool glass under my fingers and the taste of gin. I was swept away from my pain, from those sharp, terrible feelings; I was swept away for many years" (1999, pp. 33–34).

When Susan was in her twenties, she accompanied her dad to an Alcoholics Anonymous (AA) meeting. "I loved the stories I heard about hiding bottles, and about the ways people disguised their drinking while leading apparently normal lives as bankers or teachers or housewives. . . . Sometimes the stories sounded like my story, but there was always some detail that was too bizarre to fit into my life. There was always something in every story that allowed me to keep my distance from the idea that I might be an alcoholic. I thought that to be an alcoholic, a person had to be in terrible trouble. . . . No one had ever said much about my drinking" (p. 123). But the drinking continued. There was no drama in her drinking, she said, just a slow deterioration of her sanity and good judgment. At the age of thirty-nine, after the birth of her daughter Sarah, her daughter's pediatrician suggested that she stop drinking. She says that she was not even aware that she *was* drinking. Yes, knew that she had problems with men—there were, she explains, months when she "sometimes" slept with three men in the same day (1999, p. 159)—though at the time, she connected the fact of her promiscuity with the condition of clinical depression. But she had another child, began drinking again, and once again denied that she was an alcoholic, blaming her problems on the men in her life. Alcohol, she finally realized, had control of her life, and at some point she put her faith in God—and stopped drinking. Susan Cheever's is the classic redemption story, perhaps a little too pat to work as drama, but tidy enough to serve as the classic AA tale. And the compulsion—as well as the redemption—serve handily as exculpation for her sin. As she told herself, she was not evil or immoral—just sick. *Note Found in a Bottle* offers a cautionary tale—Susan offers us a lesson she learned first-hand—and it took courage to write it and the volume on her other addiction, sexual promiscuity. We put the book down gripped by the feeling that Susan Cheever deserves our respect.

Steve Geng, "I Was Romanticizing Lives of Crime"

How does the author of a drug abuse memoir establish his bona fides as an authentic survivor of addiction, yet ingratiate himself with his readers as a sympathetic character? James Frey tripped over this dilemma in his hyperbolic *A Million Little Pieces*—he was not as much of an abuser as he claimed, and his tough-guy swagger was more Hollywood and Madison Avenue than James Frey. The reverse is true of Steve Geng, who comes off as the genuine article and, while his heroes seem to come out of a Damon Runyon story, his characters actually populate our gritty real-world streets rather than the lyrics of *Guys and Dolls.* For decades a compulsive on-and-off again heroin abuser, a thief, and a revolving-door resident of the state's correctional institutions, Geng is just about the last writer in the world we would expect to employ deviance neutralization. He survived getting sucker-punched by his father; being set on fire by an angry girlfriend; and receiving a hammer in his skull, put there by the brother of another angry girlfriend, along with assorted beatings and other rough handling by representatives of both sides of the law (2007, pp. 139, 171–172), not to mention being infected with the AIDS virus. Why should he make an effort to win us over? Why should he care?

Scott and Lyman (1968) divide their domain of accounts into only two categories—*excuses* and *justifications,* excuses being admissions by the actor that the behavior in question is blameworthy, but offering extenuating circumstances for their enactment, while justifications are those that the actor denies are wrong, not falling within the orbit of deviance at all, while offering a satisfying reason for their enactment. An excuse would be an office worker admitting that she had done a bad job that day but claiming that she had the flu; a justification would be exemplified by a Mafia soldier or a Wild West gunslinger who answers an objection to his murders by arguing, "I have never killed a man who didn't deserve to die" (Joey, 1973, pp. 23, 73; Hardin, 1961). For my money, Scott and Lyman's bifurcation offers a scheme that is a bit too neat, too tidy by far, inasmuch as the constructors of real-world accounts advance a vastly richer and more varied array of verbalizations than the authors lay out in the simple formula explicated in "Accounts." Along these lines, then, I would like to present the drug addiction narrative spun out in Steve Geng's *Thick as Thieves* as exhibit A. It is neither an excuse nor a justification but represents the author's attempt to enable the reader to understand what impelled him into heroin's voluptuous embrace.

When William Burroughs was thirteen, he read *You Can't Win,* a pseudonymously written memoir by one Jack Black, burglar, thief, and drug addict. Inspired, Billy began writing stories about pirates, murderers, gunslingers, gentleman explorers—and a young man who fell into the hands "of a sinister hypnotist who plied him with marijuana injections" (Morgan, 1988, p. 202). Thereafter fascinated by lowlifes, renegades, hustlers, delinquents, and criminals, Billy entertained the notion of becoming a writer. The characters he met, the places he lived, the events he observed, the drugs he consumed—all seem to be experiments in living, designed to provide the writer with engaging literary material.

Geng seemed to have followed the same path, except that the books he read were the plays of Jean Genet, Ayn Rand's *The Fountainhead*—which justifies extreme behavior in response to limitations on one's freedom—and William Burroughs's *Junkie*; the music he rapturously listened to was jazz played by Chet Baker, Gerry Mulligan, Miles Davis, and John Coltrane—substance abusers all; and the movies that captivated him included *Rebel without a Cause, Breathless,* and *Psycho.*

As a teenager, he lived in Germany and France—his father was a serviceman stationed in Europe—hung out with scampish GI buddies, zoomed around in his Citroën, bought hashish from Africans, and engaged in numerous sexual encounters with prostitutes. "I figured I might as well pursue what I knew best—a life of crime and self-indulgence. The hipster, the hophead, and the hustler were fast becoming my role models" (2007, p. 66). Back in the United States, he fell in with delinquents and druggies and found himself using Methedrine and boosting cars, and in San Francisco, the inevitable happened—he and a pal were arrested. He catches sight of an older inmate, whose face he studied. The "creases and scars on his ravaged face, a tragic story detailed like a map in the harsh glow of prison lighting," impress him: It was as though "I was seeing a potential version of myself in thirty years" (p. 76). Assessing his experience in the jail, Geng muses that aside from the pathetic old dude, "it was not a bad time. It was the first of many incarcerations, and I relished my ability to find a kind of beauty in such things" (p. 77). Whenever he sees something positive in his misfortunes, Geng always uses the active voice, but he often describes the negative side almost as a passive observer. "Something clingy and dark had followed me from that county jail and I sensed its proximity, pursuing me" (pp. 77–78). Once, after a man has picked him up and taken him home, he spends the night, and in the morning, when the man leaves for work, Geng raids his refrigerator and medicine cabinet and swipes his Rolex. "Why the hell anybody would want to go to work was simply beyond me," he declares (2007, p. 81).

Here is what Geng said to me in a face-to-face interview in New York City in October 2008 about his fascination and identification with transgressive characters and deviant behavior:

> I had this romantic illusion about these underworld characters. And so my romantic imagination was just flying open, my antenna running around a hundred miles an hour, running around the streets in Pigalle [in Paris]. I was impressionable, and so this stuff was imprinted on my memory. Like the *clothes* people wore were, like, *dazzling* to me. . . . So I was really *riveted* on the details. I thought, "Whoa! Look at that guy's *shoes*." And the stuff was really impressive to me. And another thing was dialogue, how I remember little details of what people said. . . . I can remember little jazz riffs on the saxophone and the way people spoke. . . . I could mimic this other world of, like, *sounds*. And the detail of people's shoes on a rainy night in Paris. And all those sleazy underworld characters. Wow! It was always like I was thinking, somewhere in the back of my head, "I've got to remember this for the story I'm going to write." But that was really just a justification for wasting a lot of time [*laughs*] in all those places. . . . I had a life that was pretty interesting. It was all over the map. I led a life that kids who grew up in the '60s wish they could have had. . . . Lived like an outlaw. . . . I mean, everything about life that was going on in the '60s was empowering and riveting. We loved drug experimentation, protests against imperialism [*laughs*], you know. And the war in Vietnam and so on and so forth. It was about striking out at the establishment and creating a new freedom. And so being an outlaw was highly valued in those days, in that generation particularly. So I just *went off* in that way. For no particular reasons, I was going to become an outlaw. I did it because it looked like fun. I became a shoplifter 'cuz I was *good* at it and it was *easy*. A lot of my decisions were made because it seemed, like, daring. But underneath, it was also because it was easy to avoid responsibility by being a thief. You get arrested; the state takes care of you. They lock you up; they give you three hots and a cot, you know [*laughs*]. You sit around with the wise guys and trade war stories. It was all romance to me; I didn't do it to make a political statement. I mean, I was drawn to the dark side, the seamy side of life. And so I had this roller-coaster life that was full of adventure and

> near-death experiences. And [it was] the life that [other] kids wish they could have had. And I did it, and I was good at it. So I didn't have to make anything up. . . . I mean, [I] *really* had a wild life. I was locked up in jails that were *underneath* jails, you know [*laughs*]. Bizarre places where they stripped you of your clothes and threw you to exist on a little, cold, metal *slab.* It was pretty horrible. So [*laughs*] there's a kind of outlook that you get from having endured in spite of the fact that most of my misery was of my own causing. I don't know if James Frey's book [*A Million Little Pieces*] would have sold as well if it had been a novel. . . . Because I had read these guys like Jean Genet and William Burroughs and [Jack] Kerouac, guys that had gone out there at the edge of human experience and then written very compellingly about it, very poetically. And so I thought of doing the same. . . . [There's] a saying: You become what you behold. And after I had surrounded myself with enough criminals over the years, I actually became one and started to believe that I really was incapable of having a legitimate life. And so I had to shield myself from the remorse and a kind of responsibility for what I had done to myself. . . . And, you know, you think back on times of hardship when the cops were beating me up in a tenement hallway, and you sneer and go, "I toughed it out. I'm a standup guy." This was, like, a merit badge, you know. What is it? *The Red Badge of Courage.* This was like some false courage, bravado that criminals have about the hardships they endure at the hands of the police. And I fell right into that.

Greek drama rendered tragedy inevitable; Oedipus, Antigone, and Medea were predestined to play out a certain fate, having inescapably chosen the wrong path at a critical juncture. Likewise, Geng's narrative makes him seem foreordained to fall under the rapture of heroin. "If God made anything better than this," said a companion of his about the drug's intoxication, "He kept it to himself." Says Geng, "I felt like I finally found what I was looking for. . . . Hell, this was better than sex" (p. 84). And the high he got from injecting perfectly dovetails with the requisite accompanying lifestyle of the thief, the outlaw, the renegade. "I thought it was all a fascinating adventure," and "the characters were deadbeat and Runyonesque. . . . I was thrilled with the lifestyle, proud as punch of my shoplifting prowess, and my ability to score junk all over town. . . . Life couldn't have been sweeter" (2007, pp. 86, 89, 91–92).

Geng's narrative takes on a more bittersweet urgency, given that its spine is wrapped around the story of his relationship with Veronica, his sister, a brilliant and talented writer who died at the height of her powers of a brain tumor in 1997. It was her success that planted the seed in Steve's mind that he too could write and that made it possible for him to place his manuscript into the hands of an editor with enough influence to get it published. It is significant that, during the last year or so of her life, she turned her back on her brother and refused to have anything to do with him; his voice-mail messages went unanswered. It is possible that her deteriorating medical condition played as much a role in her iciness toward him as Steve's illegal behavior and tattered lifestyle, but he did not clean up until after well her death. In the months after Veronica's funeral, he says, he indulged in his sorrows by staying stoned. "She was my closest friend, my jazz buddy, movie goombah, writing mentor, confessor, and my female ideal" (p. 277). Ultimately, in the months after she died, he realizes that her shunning of him was "her parting gift, an unresolved longing that could not be mended, except perhaps through the labor and love of writing" (p. 290). He recalls having watched a movie about Thelonious Monk with Veronica, who referred to Monk's playing, "That's what I want to do with writing, Steve. . . . I try to, but I'm not quite that good" (2007, p. 292). The narration of his loving, admiring relations with his sister draw us empathetically into his story, enabling us to feel that he is a sympathetic character. In effect, Veronica becomes a beacon, a lodestar, and hence, a means of neutralization that considerably softens our feelings toward Geng, his heroin addiction, and his thievery. In the end, what counts is this: It works. We feel satisfied in the reading and confident about the author's redemption.

William Cope Moyers, "I Was Doomed to Fail No Matter How Hard I Tried"

William Cope Moyers, a former journalist, is a spokesperson for Hazelden, the drug addiction foundation; the author of *Broken,* a memoir about his own "addiction and redemption"; and the son of Bill Moyers, former White House press secretary for President Lyndon Baines Johnson, noted television news commentator, author of a dozen books, and currently president of the Center for Media and Democracy. Cope gives many dozens of speeches a year about his addiction to crack cocaine (and alcoholism) and his recovery. The speech in which he first revealed his addiction was to the local Rotary Club, which prompted an editor at *The St. Paul Pioneer Press* to invite him to write an op-ed for the newspaper; the piece took the AA position that drug addiction is a disease, not a freely chosen moral behavior. One of the letters Moyers received in response to his op-ed accused him of shirking his moral responsibility by "foisting the blame" for his use of psychoactive drugs off onto his disease—the well-known "my illness made me do it" excuse (2006, p. 326).

Both throughout this book and in the sections on alcoholism and drug abuse, I insist that I most emphatically do *not* engage in putting the blame "back where it belongs," on the immorality of the drug abuser and addict. I have no idea whether or not the disease metaphor is valid. Our focus here is looking at the ways in which stigma neutralizations are constructed, how they are used, and how they function. *Whether it is valid or not,* the disease metaphor *functions* as a means of deviance neutralization. It enables the addict and former addict to say, "I am not an immoral person; I have (or had) a disease in the same way that a cancer patient has a disease," which tends to result in most audiences expressing and feeling more positive sentiments toward the speaker or writer than when no explanation is offered. Moyers himself is cognizant of the overlap between the two conditions and their radically different public images when he points out the differences in public reactions to cancer victims versus addicts and former addicts (pp. 331–348). And this may or may not be why such neutralizations are used—but *it is the way they work.* The disease metaphor explains but does not justify; hence, it is a *specific* technique of deviance neutralization—but it is neutralization nonetheless.

Most of us harbor a system that holds that, unless accounted for, all transgressive or untoward behavior is elective, freely chosen, an outcome of a moral choice: Do I want to engage in "bad" behavior or not? Moyers recalls the harangue from a physician and family friend that he experienced at one of the facilities where he was treated: "*What was wrong with you?* she was really saying, and her sentiment was secretly shared by everyone, including me. What was wrong with me that I would willingly choose to use drugs and destroy my marriage and my life? How could I be so weak, so thoughtless, so self-centered? Why couldn't I just exert some willpower and strength of character and stop this self-destructive behavior?" (2006, pp. 339–340). As Moyers says, the addict and ex-addict face stigma, and this is a determinant of much of what many people do in relation to them. "I never felt ashamed of having cancer," he explains, but "with addiction, shame filled me up and emptied me out over and over again" (p. 342). He invites his readers to join in on breaking down the "wall of shame, stigma, and discrimination" that prevent addicts and alcoholics from "finding their paths to recovery" (p. 365). *Broken* is as much tract as memoir—addiction treatment is hugely underfunded compared with treatment for medical conditions such as cancer, and stigma, which is, Moyers feels, part of the reason for this—the author issues a call to action to help cure and treat substance abuse by funding treatment facilities in every town in America.

Why did Moyers use and become addicted to crack cocaine? Why did he succumb and not other member of his immediate family? Likewise, all of his college friends drank and used illicit drugs, as did many of his coworkers on the papers that employed him to write news stories. None of them developed habits; he did. "Why couldn't I stop? What was wrong with me?" (p. 296).

Lots of addicts he was in treatment programs with responded positively to their programs and became abstinent after discharge. He plagued himself with these "Why?" questions year after year but finally gave up the effort. "There were no answers to these questions. That was the answer. There are no answers" (p. 297). Saying that he did it because he had an illness covers a great swath of territory.

The disease concept has many critics. Conrad and Schneider (1992, p. 273) argue that referring to and treating deviant behavior, including alcoholism and other forms of substance abuse, as a medical condition is a political and ideological rather than a scientific matter. Shaler (2000) writes that "addiction is a choice"; Davies (1997) argues that addiction as a disease is a "myth"; and for Peele (1998), the "meaning" of addiction is that it encompasses a cluster of negative behaviors that have been reinforced over the years—hence, Moyers's raging torrent of desire experience—that can be overcome by reinforcing different patterns of behavior. Just as using and becoming dependent on psychoactive substances are decisions, abstaining from them is a choice as well. And one of the functions that *calling* addiction a disease serves is to deflect responsibility from the abuser to the illness and hence remove not only free will but also the stigma for the abuser. But it may *also* be true that destigmatizing dependence serves a positive role in facilitating treatment—a therapeutic strategy that fosters a kind of "noble lie" to sustain the treatment industry and ease the addict's transition to abstention. Who could have imagined that an exploration of stigma neutralization and vocabularies of motive would have such consequential implications? Moyers turned his painful, horrendous experience into the impulse to help others who suffer as he did, and for that, he merits our admiration.

William Cope Moyers says he was an addict: *is* an addict, will always *be* an addict. This might seem like a self-serving redundancy. He is an addict because he is an addict. He is an addict because he uses, and he uses because he is an addict. Now that he does not use, he's *still* an addict because he can't use without becoming addicted. To him, this is no redundancy: Being "an addict" means that he suffers from an illness. "Addiction is at the core of my being, and I cannot escape its terrible truth. . . . I can no more leave it behind than I could remove my lungs and still breathe or cut my vocal cords and continue to talk. My disease is less about the drugs I took than the reason I took them—to blot out pain, to alter reality, to change perception, to numb my fear" (2007, p. 208). Moyers's disease stuck to him "like a blood-sucking leech" (p. 212). Like the eruption of a volcano, the disease touched off a "desperate hunger," a "consuming thirst," an "unbearable craving," a "furious yearning," an "excruciating need that grabs you and shakes you and won't let go." It is a "howling internal torment that overrides the need for food, for water, for sleep, for love" (p. 278). "Good people can have a bad illness" is the slogan that the treatment community frequently uses to explain the phenomenon of addiction, a saying that is both self-evidently self-serving and almost certainly true. The "it's not me, it's my disease" justification is self-serving in that it is a form of deviance neutralization—but that does not mean that it is false. Even in abstinence, his condition "sticks to him like a leech" because if he so much as samples a taste, he will be hurled, willy-nilly, back into the maw of catastrophic abuse.

In 2000, Moyers developed a skin melanoma, which forced him to face the possibility that he might have a fatal disease. After a relatively simple operation, he was diagnosed as entirely cancer-free, but the experience gave him an occasion to compare cancer with drug addiction in a number of crucial respects. Both are life-threatening diseases, but, as he insists, they are "as different as night and day" with respect to public attitudes toward their "victims" (p. 337). Nobody admonished or blamed him for the cancer; nobody said it was his fault. He received countless offers of sympathy and support from friends, family, and strangers alike—they called him "courageous"—and cancer never eroded his self-respect or undermined his sense of morality. "I felt more loved and accepted during that difficult period than I have ever felt in my life" (p. 338).

"It was a completely different story with my addiction," he tells us. Accused by others of self-indulgence and a failure of character, he felt shame and guilt, stigma and humiliation and began to feel that he was responsible for causing his addiction. He became convinced that it was the disease that forced him to use drugs and become addicted, and that he was not responsible for it, nor should he be blamed for it. This realization took the burden off his shoulders and enabled him to become abstinent, then, now, and in all likelihood, for the remainder of his life. It is a redemptionist, triumphalist, "feel good" story that has a dramatic, coherent arc—from innocence to temptation, surrender, suffering, redemption, and relapse—several times, and, ultimately, triumph. This story is made all the more poignant when the reader learns of Henry, a son born with a birth defect, saved by surgical intervention, and his wife's clinical depression, cured by a five-month program of treatment while separated from the family. Nothing I say here detracts from the agony that Moyers suffered during addiction and the respect we owe him for his victory over painful, debilitating circumstances. But at the same time, his invocation of the addiction rhetoric serves to vindicate him in the eyes of the therapeutic subculture and makes him an effective spokesperson for the cause of abstinence.

Accounting for Substance Abuse

Jack London became a drunk because, he says, it was the manly thing to do. Companionship, with "drink in hand"! DeQuincey became an opium addict in the effort to cure an illness. Like London, Hamill engaged in an act of masculinity—to be in the company of other men. Cheever did it because her family did it—every night; it was a family tradition. Geng says he did it, like William Burroughs, to be cool—*literarily* cool, to follow in the footsteps of his favorite writers and jazz musicians. Moyers did it because he was in the grip of an illness; he could not help himself.

Do these explanations "sell"? Are they convincing? Do their audiences honor them? The authors would say they worked for them and they should work for their audiences, including those who are substance abusers. Still, saying that some *chose* to consume an addicting substance invokes free will, yet in the end, they became addicts and abusers, which is the opposite of free will, seems a contradiction. Seymour Fiddle, a drug therapist, wrote of *existential* drugs (1967) in precisely this vein. These are drugs that some among us use to test themselves. They go out onto the edge and find out what they are made of. They challenge their strength of will, moral fiber, the laws of nature—toy with to the point of no return. They test their friends to find out if they will pull them back if they are challenged. Yet, ironically, in pursuing the limits of their freedom, they end up finding themselves distinctly unfree. They become addicted, dependent, both abusers and abused. Some feel their justifications absolve them from condemnation. But among the memoirs we are likely to encounter along these lines is that their neutralizations have in common a *redemptionist* vocabulary. Memoirs about substance abuse draw out of the writer the vocabulary of transformation. They are saved, they are cured, they are now straight, they are not under the oppressive yoke of addiction. (DeQuincey was wrong about his condition, but addiction was poorly understood in the nineteenth century.) None attempts to normalize addiction; none feels it is a good idea for others or for society as a whole. None is a proselytizer. Some apologize; some do not. Some make excuses; others do not. And some do miss getting high. But all of them say that they face the reader now no longer under the influence of addicting, mood-altering substances, and all say they are better persons for it.

6
Sexual Transgressions

SEXUAL ACTIVITIES provide a rich, fertile greenhouse of specimens of transgressive behavior; in few areas of social life can a member of virtually any society engage in so many varieties of normative infringements. Though some critics, most notably Alexander Liazos (1972), have complained that sociologists of deviance devote too much attention to sexual violations, the fact is, all of us are subject to a great many sexual norms, and erotic unconventionality is likely to get us in trouble. Most of us love a good sex scandal, and many of us consider past or current sexual violations as a disqualification for a wide range of conventional roles, especially those that entail dealing with children and those that demand adherence to certain "ethical" standards. Most societies set and enforce a substantial array of sexual dos and don'ts, and the range of completely acceptable sexual acts is fairly narrow. Over time, of course, the sexual rules are loosening up—normative constraints are not nearly so narrow now as they were, say, in the 1950s: Sex before marriage tends to be the norm and is pretty much taken for granted; a variety of sexual positions is considered normal, even desirable; in most school districts, a known homosexual can hold a job as a teacher; and most faiths accept known gays as clergy. Still, sexual transgressions cause more uproar here than in, let's say, France. It is clear that violations of the sexual code constitute a *major* form of deviance.

Consider the Bible's sexual prohibitions. True, for most of us, The Holy Bible is not our primary source of sexual norms; in fact, many people consider most of the injunctions in the Bible as more or less irrelevant for their lives. Still, if we want to understand how sexual norms work—especially where they came from—the Old and New Testaments are not bad places to start; they give us a clue to what is considered wrong. The Bible contains sixty-nine passages that refer to adultery, adulteries, adulterer, adulterers, adulteress, adulteresses, and adulterous, and we can find forty-four that refer to fornication, fornications, fornicator, and fornicators; in addition, the Holy Book explicitly prohibits sex with one's father's wife, daughter-in-law, mother-in-law, sister, father's daughter, uncle's wife, and brother's wife—not to mention animals, another man, and one's own wife during menstruation. It is interesting that these prohibitions are spelled out almost entirely for men, far less for women. In ancient Israel, women were expected to adhere to religious law—though they were are regarded as truly evil when they did not—whereas men frequently strayed and needed to have the rules spelled out for them. Several of these injunctions carried a penalty of death, in some cases, by stoning. Clearly, the control of sexuality and the punishment of deviant sexuality were major tasks of the prophets. And the fact is, the importance of certain sexual taboos remains in place today.

To repeat what I said in the Preface, sociologically, the term "deviant" describes *what, or who, is likely to be condemned within a given context, by a given audience.* In the United States, in many contexts, homosexuality and homosexuals are still likely to be condemned. Most fundamentalist and evangelical Christians, rural dwellers, Orthodox Jews, devout Muslims, and conservatives consider homosexuality a sin, an abomination, a perversion. True, a (bare) majority of Americans do not condemn homosexuality, considering it an alternative practice, but this tendency veers off in a negative direction fairly quickly if one strays too far from mainstream opinion. Hence, the title of Minton's book, *Departing from Deviance* (2002), is appropriate here: Dominant public attitudes toward homosexuality are changing, but they have not reached the level of full acceptance. Is "gay the new normal" (Rauch, 2011)? Not quite, but it is getting there.

Consider adultery, condemned not only in the Bible but also informally virtually everywhere in the Western world and in most other places. In a review of Ernest Hemingway's *A Moveable Feast* (1964/2003), Alfred Kazin, a literary critic, expresses his suspicions about autobiography as a form of literature. Great works of art tell the truth, he argued; autobiography cannot serve the same mission because the writer, especially one as great as Hemingway, can hide and shade and edit and condense and omit the crucial details of his life to his own advantage. "The defect of autobiography, as compared with formal fiction," says Kazin, "is that it must always justify the narrator—probably that is why it gets written" (1964, p. 57). But the astute reader can peer between the lines and find the seams, the places where the autobiographer jiggles and juggles a rationale for his untoward behavior. This is where the sociologist of deviance steps into the picture.

In 1921, Ernest Hemingway married Hadley Richardson; in 1925, when the couple lived in Paris, he began having an affair with Pauline Pfeiffer. He blames his adulterous behavior on an unfortunate conjunction of his own innocence and the devious seduction of "the rich." He constructs the foundation for his dishonest and artful dodge by describing the intoxicating beauty and danger that lay on the Austrian mountainside. Skiing, he says, "was better than any flying or anything else, and we built the ability to do it" (1964/2003, p. 207). He makes the experience sound and *feel* wondrous and exhilarating.

But abruptly his description takes on an insidious cast: "New people came deep into our lives and nothing was ever the same again" (p. 207). "Under the charm" of the rich, he explains, "I was as trusting and as stupid as a bird dog who wants to go out with any man with a gun, or a trained pig in a circus who has finally found someone who loves and appreciates him for himself alone." The rich use a trick to deceive a man such as him: "An unmarried young woman becomes the temporary best friend of another young woman who is married, goes to live with the husband and wife and then unknowingly, innocently and unrelentingly sets out to marry the husband. When the husband is a writer and doing difficult work so that he is occupied much of the time and is not a good companion or partner to his wife for a big part of the day, the arrangement has advantages until you know how it works out. The husband has two attractive girls around when he has finished work. One is new and strange and if he has bad luck he gets to love them both" (pp. 209–210).

Kazin is right: This is dishonest, self-serving writing, and it fails as literature. Hemingway describes himself as a young writer, "perfectly innocent," a devoted husband with a wife and small child named Bumby. When he published his first novel, "the rich"—and the woman who was to become his second wife—moved in on him like sharks, devouring him and his marriage with Hadley. He lays the blame on others, not himself, and the reader remains unconvinced. Pauline was single when she met Hemingway, she was already in Paris on a reportorial job for *Vogue,* and she was a practicing Catholic for whom adultery was a mortal sin (p. 177). Hemingway was sexually aroused by her (p. 173), and he convinced her to go on long walks around Paris. The litany of Hemingway's dishonesties is long and self-evidently discrediting.

But as Kazin says, Hemingway is an extremely artful writer, and his justification is devious, subtle, and cunning. He has to go to New York to "rearrange" publishers. Returning to Europe, he stops off in Paris because the woman he was in love with is in Paris and, he says, "I did not take the first train [to Austria, where Hadley was], or the second or the third" (Hemingway, 1964/2003, p. 210). The reader is temporarily taken aback. Why *didn't*

Hemingway take that train? Was he, a grown man, not capable of stepping up off the platform and onto that train? Or was he mesmerized, hypnotized, acting as if in a trance? Hemingway muscles away such questions with a romantic description of his wife. When he saw his wife again standing by the tracks as the train arrives, he tells us, "I wished I had died before I loved anyone but her. She was smiling, the sun on her lovely face tanned by the snow and sun, beautifully built, her hair red gold in the sun, grown out all winter awkwardly and beautifully" (p. 210). After Hadley declares her love for him, he says, "I loved her and I loved no one else and we had a lovely magic time while we were alone . . . , and it wasn't until we were out of the mountains in late spring, and back in Paris that the other thing started again" (pp. 210–211). The "other thing started"? Note the passive voice here, the absence of agency in this statement. Why isn't Hemingway saying that he, Hemingway, actively "started up" with Pauline? He concludes *A Moveable Feast* with the following words: "Paris was always worth it and you received return for whatever you brought to it. But this is how Paris was in the early days when we were very poor and very happy" (p. 211). This is how Paris "was," indeed. We know Hemingway to have been an active, forceful, and importunate man, and the implication that he played a passive, secondary role in this marriage-destroying romance rings as false as a brass coin fobbed off as gold. Although some observers might question the motives of the editors and publisher in putting out this posthumous volume, it almost certainly reflects the author's on-the-page attempt to justify behavior he considered discreditable, as did relevant and potentially critical audiences.

In these passages, Hemingway uses blatant devices of deflecting blame. The nameless and faceless rich are guided to the writer by charming but empty "pilot fish" (1964/2003, pp. 207–209). Like a virtuous, naïve, and hapless army, Hem and his wife had already been "infiltrated" and passively disarmed by the enemy by means of a "trick," "the oldest trick there is," and, hence, they were helplessly conquered, willy-nilly. Hemingway is "trusting," "stupid," and, taking him at his word, innocent. All his flaws are manly flaws: bravery, honesty, impulsiveness, naïveté, misplaced trust, and blundering insensitivity. The flaws of the "pilot fish"—and his second wife—it seems are, to Hemingway, the flaws of women: guile, intrigue, dishonesty, cunning. But a close reading of his passages forces us to realize that it is Hemingway who is cunning, not Pauline, not the "pilot fish," and not the rich, and it is he who feels called upon to weave a web of justification more telling than his sins. I would put the matter in a slightly different way: To the extent that memoir fails as art because it is self-serving, the interests of the sociologist, literary critic, or kindred observer interested in how writers justify their own wrongdoing are served, because self-justifications are *data* about the use of recitations of deviance neutralization. To the extent that the autonarrator employs contrivances that exculpate perceived wrongdoing, this not only demonstrates that such ploys are common but also helps us assemble a richer picture of how and under what circumstances they work, among artful writers as well as the artless, since the more of them we look at, the better we understand them in their infinite variety. Clever deviance neutralizations may activate the critic in the literati, but it brings out the sleuth in the sociologist.

Prostitution is, of course, a major form of sexual deviance; the bookshelves virtually groan with the memoirs of former whores. Perhaps the "mother" of this genre is *The Happy Hooker* by the former call girl and madam Xaviera Hollander (1972/2002). She pioneered the positive presentation of sex for pay, earning enmity from moralists and feminists the world over. But as open and candid as Hollander's life story is, she does employ neutralization devices throughout her narrative, which stretches from innocence to retirement and beyond. Xaviera was engaged for several years to a wealthy financier who, it turns out, was engaged to another woman; it became clear to her that her lover had no intention of marrying her. Treated contemptuously by her supposed future mother-in-law, treated abusively by her fiancé, she broke off the sham engagement and took solace with other men, often while her paramour was away on business. At some point, some of her sex partners offered her gifts, including money. She spent a weekend with "an expensively dressed, distinguished-looking Englishman" named Evelyn St. John (p. 75). When he handed her a hundred dollar bill, she was shocked. The next day, he bought her eight hundred dollars' worth of clothes, and, making the connection between sex and money, she soon sought employment with a whorehouse madam—and the rest, as the saying goes, is history. While Hollander does not apologize for having been a whore, she does explain the contingencies that influenced her career choices.

Jenna Jameson, a former stripper and porn actress, uses much the same device of stressing the role of contingencies in narrating her career path (2004). She "chose the darkness" in the form of a boyfriend, a tattoo artist, whose life—radically different from her pampered, safe, suburban existence—was "so dangerous, so free, and so sad" (p. 12); it was he who led her into a life of evil-doing. The book narrates a sad and squalid tale of maternal death; paternal alcoholism; the suicide (or possible murder) of a friend; a gang-rape and rock-throwing assault at sixteen by members of her high school football team; another rape, the same year, by her boyfriend's biker uncle; her own crack addiction and alcohol abuse; and many emotionally shallow relationships. For a time, Jenna worked as a showgirl, her mother's profession (her mom died of cancer when she was four), but her boyfriend persuaded her to become a stripper, and she quickly learned how to hustle customers. "It was a high to get the upper hand over a customer. They were dumb, they were drunk, and they deserved it. . . . If those guys are going to victimize us, we're going to totally victimize them" (p. 48). Stripping turned out to be an ego-boosting experience; after remaining passive, being manipulated and taken advantage of, she learned how to "take control" of other people and her life. And then there was the money; she earned thousands a night, while her lazy, unmotivated colleagues earned only hundreds. She was dedicated, hardworking, and extremely successful, she says—thereby turning a vice (getting naked in front of ogling, drunken middle-aged men) into a virtue (earning a lot of money). The step from stripping to making pornography seemed natural.

One of the most successful porn businesswomen of all times, Jenna Jameson regards herself as no different from any other venture capitalist around the globe: She is in it the for money. Upon its publication, *Publisher's Weekly* predicted that *How to Make Love like a Porn Star* would become a "low-brow classic"—and it has. Jameson, who is a genuine porn star, suffered to achieve riches and fame. Her book was on *The New York Times* Best Sellers List for six weeks; a million websites are devoted to the author; and she is a multimillionaire. However, before cracking open the volume, it is best to keep in mind its subtitle: *A Cautionary Tale. How to Make Love like a Porn Star* is neither an instructional manual nor a feel-good romp through a voluptuous Garden of Eden. At the age of seventeen, she followed in her mother's career as a showgirl and dancer, which soon spread into nude modeling, stripping, and acting in pornographic films; she retired from pornographic performances in 2007 but still produces and distributes Internet and multimedia porn. In spite of its subtitle, read carefully, hers is a tale of triumph and redemption. The "dark side" morphs into a good side, and the bad girl redeems herself.

Roman Polanski, "*Everyone* Wants to Fuck Young Girls"

Roman Polanski exemplifies the talented "bad boy" who has done things that have attracted widespread notoriety, public and media attention, and criticism, even denunciation, for his actions and a cavalier attitude toward his sins. Outside of his films (and in addition to being the husband of Sharon Tate, murdered in 1969 by a band of deranged would-be hippies), he is most famous for having been convicted of committing the crime of "unlawful sex with a minor," a thirteen-year-old, then becoming a fugitive from justice by fleeing to Europe. Polanski wrote a quasi-memoir, quasi-autobiography, *Roman by Polanski* (1985), in which, in three chapters, he offers an account of this incident, not a "mea culpa" in the strict sense of the term, but an attempt to set the record straight, to present his point of view, and to establish counter-arguments to the many critics who have savaged him for his supposed malfeasances. Polanski's rendition of the event strikes the reader acquainted with autonarration as far more candid and forthcoming than most of its cognate representatives. It is also an outstanding specimen of deviance disavowal. And the sphere in which he most strikingly employs this form of reasoning is his sex life. A Lothario as prodigious as Polanski, whose sexual targets have been as unconventional as his were, is almost predestined to engage in behavior the public interpretation of which clashes with his self-image as a charming, magic seducer. This is precisely what happened following the events of March 10, 1977. It *almost* goes without saying that the criminal charges against Polanski entailed sex with a minor, commonly referred to as statutory rape, a crime of violence—and moreover, her testimony indicates forcible rape as well—but in his mind, he was arrested and charged for "making love," that is, having sex.

The observer has access to two first-hand versions of the pivotal events in question—Polanski's, as narrated in *Roman by Polanski,* and that of the thirteen-year-old girl, Samantha Gailey, presented as testimony in the case's court hearings, of which portions appear in Toobin (2010) and Sanford (2007, pp. 218 et seq.).[1] The broadest outline of the story is uncontested: A man in his forties gives alcohol to a thirteen-year-old girl and has sexual intercourse with her. Simply on the basis of these admitted acts alone, Polanski committed several crimes: statutory rape, furnishing alcohol to a minor, and having sexual intercourse with said intoxicated minor. In his memoir, Polanski freely admits to these crimes, although he does not consider them criminal. And he lays out a narrative that clearly states that Samantha was entirely willing to engage in sex with him, indeed, even acted seductively. Although Stanford (2007, p. 217), one of Polanski's biographers, mentions some aspects of the director's narration as "self-fabulism" (p. 217), he does argue that "there are so many discrepancies, distortions and outright falsehoods in the various accounts of the case that the whole thing has come to resemble one of those morally ambiguous tales like *Rashomon*"—a 1950s Japanese movie about a trial that portrays various versions of a rape (p. 217). To most observers, the details of Samantha's testimony to the grand jury, combined with Polanski's glaring omissions, make her account credible and Polanski's suspect. Still, all we need to know is that a man in his forties supplied alcohol to a thirteen-year-old

[1] Grand Jury of the County of Los Angeles, State of California, *The People of the State of California v. Roman Raymond Polanski,* "Reporter's Transcript of Grand Jury Proceedings," Thursday, March 24, 1977. The transcript is available online; it contains testimony from eight witnesses aside from Samantha: Kim, Samantha's sister; Susan, their mother; two police officers who arrived at the scene and investigated the case; a forensic chemist; a forensic criminalist; a police photographer; and an emergency physician, who examined Samantha after the assault.

girl and had sexual intercourse with her. How old she looked, whether she was completely willing or only reluctant, and what her mother did are not irrelevant—but they never *exonerate* Polanski, they never *justify* his act, and they never take him off the hook with regard to his criminal culpability. We can, however, fathom how he presents the case in his memoir *in the light* of these basic and irreducible facts.

The Polanski–Gailey narratives begin with the publication of the 1976 Christmas issue of *Vogue,* which featured the oeuvre and personality of one Roman Polanski. The issue proved such a talked-about and commercial success that Gerald Azaria, editor of *Vogue Hommes,* another Condé Nast publication, asked Polanski to contribute an article or a layout to its pages. At the time, the work of David Hamilton, an English photographer who snapped gauzy, romantic nudes of tall, thin, coltish, faunlike adolescent and barely pubescent girls—several of which had appeared in a recent issue of *Vogue Hommes*—was popular and chic, albeit borderline pornographic. Polanski suggested to Azaria that he do a more realistic shoot of adolescent girls, showing them "as they really were these days—sexy, pert, and thoroughly human" (Polanski, 1985, p. 358).

Azaria loved Polanski's suggestion and several times during the next few weeks, the two discussed the details of the assignment. In Los Angeles, Henri Sera, a photographer, director, and friend, dropped by to visit Polanski and offer congratulations for the *Vogue* Christmas issue. Polanski told Sera about the *Vogue Hommes* job; in response, Sera suggested a possible model—Samantha Gailey, whose older sister, Kim, he had been dating. Samantha, Sera claimed, was a "fabulous-looking" teenager who aspired to be a model and had already appeared in a TV commercial (p. 359). Sera gave Polanski the Gaileys' phone number. Several days later, Polanski called Susan, Samantha's mother, a former and would-be actress, who invited the director to visit her house the following day. (In his memoir, *Roman by Polanski,* the author refers to Samantha as "Sandra" and Susan as "Jane.") In his account of their meeting, Polanski says he was somewhat disappointed by Samantha—"a good-looking girl, but nothing sensational" (p. 360). He showed Susan the *Vogue* issue and explained the ideas that he had for the forthcoming shoot. They agreed that Polanski would call in a few days and arrange a date.

Polanski arrived at the Gailey household lugging several cameras. Susan had set up a clothes rack in the hallway laden with garments with which to outfit Samantha for the shoot, which establishes the mother's active acquiescence in the events that followed, since she had heard Polanski's ideas about the feature's theme. Roman tossed the gear and clothes into his car and, with his subject, drove off to the hills directly above the Gaileys' house. On the way, Polanski noticed a bruise ("or rather a love bite") on Samantha's neck. He asked if it was the result of her "taking karate lessons" from her boyfriend, "Chuck." Samantha laughed. "It was Chuck all right," she said, "but it wasn't karate lessons" (1985, p. 362). Here, clearly, Polanski is hinting at Samantha's sexual sophistication and experience. In the next paragraph, again, the director notices that, as she changes her blouses for the shoot, Samantha is not wearing a bra "but seemed entirely at ease—not in the least embarrassed" (p. 362). Likewise, in the next paragraph, Polanski describes several boys on motorcycles twenty or thirty yards away "gawking" at Samantha posing topless. He mentions that she ought to put her blouse on. "They don't bother me," she replied. He insisted, feeling that her nonchalance was an attempt to appear "worldly and sophisticated beyond her years" (p. 362). In Polanski's narration, it is he who is the prim and proper one and Samantha who is wild and reckless, teetering toward an experience that perhaps she could not handle. Her provocative poses and glazed stare, too, were designed to enhance her sex appeal (p. 363). Again, Polanski is attempting to cover his flank with respect to his instrumentality in an accusation of rape: *She's responsible for what happened; I'm not.* The fact is, at several points in Samantha's grand jury testimony, she insists that she took off her clothes at Polanski's often gruff insistence; his account has her casually initiating her acts of nudity—changing in front of him, going braless, unceremoniously removing her blouse.

Ten days later, Roman called the Gailey household to arrange a second session. Polanski showed up on the appointed day, at four in the afternoon, quite late for natural-light shooting. In the car, he broke out a slide viewer so that Samantha could inspect the previous session's pictures but insisted that she wear a seat belt—an interesting detail again attempting to establish the girl's character as reckless and risk-taking and his as responsible and careful. Samantha then described the "bad" or "fun" crowd she hung out with—the pill-poppers, drinkers, boys and girls who defied adult authority. As for her, she said, she liked champagne, had tried Quaaludes—even stealing some from her older sister, Kim, who had been "institutionalized" for taking so many (1985, p. 365)—and had had sexual experience with her boyfriend, Chuck. "We went to bed right away," she explained. According to Polanski, Samantha stated that she first had sex at the age of eight, with "a kid down the street" (p. 366). Polanski tells his readers that these revelations "shook" him—once again, attempting to establish that he is the traditional party here, while the young teen was ostentatiously displaying her precocity, maturity, experience, and sophistication. I *committed rape? With* this *young woman?* Polanski seems to be asking the reader. *Not on your life,* he answers.

Realizing that the sun had dipped too low behind the trees above the canyon, he called Jack Nicholson, who owned a house on the other side of Mulholland Drive, which had better light. The call was routed to a neighbor, and

Polanski explained his request, which she complied with, admitting Polanski and Samantha to Nicholson's house. Samantha said she wanted something to drink, so Polanski found some champagne in the refrigerator, asked the neighbor if he could open it, and poured himself, the neighbor, and Samantha a drink. The teenager noticed a Jacuzzi behind the house, next to the swimming pool, which she thought was "real neat." Polanski replied, "Later. . . . Let's get on with the pictures," at which point the director began taking some topless indoor shots. When Samantha took off her jeans to change into a dress, Polanski said he "could sense a certain erotic tension between us" (p. 368). Repeating the central theme to establish his decency, caution, and consideration, before shooting Samantha in the Jacuzzi, Polanski says, he called Susan to explain that the shoot was running longer than expected; if she wanted Samantha back, he would drive her home. Samantha spoke with Susan, sounding, according to Polanski, "quite relaxed." Then Samantha undressed and climbed into the Jacuzzi, exclaimed how hot it was, and began posing; Polanski took a few shots, but the light had grown so dim that the meter read zero exposure, so he stopped shooting. Polanski says he then "stripped and plunged into the pool," swam a few lengths, then stopped at the Jacuzzi end, where Samantha remained. She "was looking at me oddly" and told him that she "didn't feel good," explaining that her asthma was acting up and she had left her medication at home (p. 369). Polanski warned her not to spend so much time "in all that steam" and told her to get out of the Jacuzzi and into the pool, which she found too cold. Wheezing, she walked to a dark guestroom to dry off; Polanski followed her, and she told him that she was feeling better. In her disposition, Samantha tells the judge and the grand jurors that she never had asthma, that she had faked its symptoms, and that she told the director that she wanted to go home to take her medication—clearly a ruse to get out of Polanski's importunate clutches. In addition, she said, she kept her distance from him, even in the Jacuzzi.

According to Polanski's account, Samantha grabbed a towel and walked into the guesthouse and he followed her, and then "very gently, I began to kiss and caress her. After this had gone on for some time, I led her over to the couch. There was no doubt about [Samantha's] experience and lack of inhibition. She spread herself and I entered her. She wasn't unresponsive" (p. 369). When he asked her if she "was liking it," Polanski says that she replied, "It's all right." Soon after, they heard a noise in the driveway; they froze, listened, then resumed, and at some point "it was all over" (p. 369). Samantha Gailey's account, given to the grand jury in 1977, was very different. She says Polanski told her to go to the guest room, which she did; when he came in, she asked to be taken home, and he responded that he would take her home "later." He reached out for her and began kissing her and then yanked off her panties and performed oral sex on her; she told him several times, "Keep away," begging him to "stop it." Polanski began having intercourse with her, during which he asked if she was on the pill. When she said no, he said he would not come inside of her; instead, he "went in through" her anus ("He put his penis in my butt"), in spite of the fact that she again told him not to. She did not fight him physically, she says, because she was "afraid of him" (Toobin, 2010, p. 150). Polanski's account does not mention the methaqualone he gave Samantha, the oral sex he performed on her, her "begging" him to stop, the anal sex, and generally, her reluctance and unwillingness to go through with the act. It is her account, not Polanski's, that strikes the reader as the more valid. And yet, *Roman by Polanski* strikes the reader as containing lies not so much of commission but of omission and shading.

Anjelica Huston, who had previously been dating Jack Nicholson, had entered the house and was in the living room; embarrassed by her presence, Samantha rushed through the house and got into the car. When Polanski came out to take her home, she says, she was crying. On the drive back, Polanski claims, she chatted about her drama teacher, a Shakespeare play she was studying at school, and her guitar lessons—all of which establish that what happened at the pool was "no big deal." She and Polanski made vague plans to see one another again. Before reaching the house, Gailey told the grand jury, Polanski said to her, "Don't tell your mother about this, and don't tell your boyfriend either. . . . This is our secret" (Toobin, 2010, p. 150). Back at the house, he showed Susan and her boyfriend slides of the first shooting session. Polanski tells us that he could sense a change in their attitude toward him (1985, p. 370). They seemed to like the pictures, so it must have been something else, he reasoned. But when he got back to the hotel, he received a "rather puzzling" phone call from Henri Sera, the original contact with the Gaileys, who told him that Susan thought the photographs were "horrible"; she was especially appalled by the topless shots. Polanski asked Sera to come and view the pictures himself, which he did, declaring them beautiful.

The next evening, March 11, after Polanski met some friends in the hotel lobby for a theater date, one asked him for a Quaalude, so he went up to his room and fetched one. Just before leaving, "a man in a bowling shirt" (a social class signifier) approached Polanski and flashed a badge. He was from the Los Angeles Police Department. "Can I talk to you?" he asked. "I have a warrant for your arrest" (p. 371). Polanski handed his companions the theater tickets and asked the officer what he was being charged with. All he heard in the reply was the word "rape." Shocked and bewildered, he repeated the word. The detectives asked to search his room; while walking to the elevator, Polanski tried to ditch the Quaalude he had retrieved for his friend, but one of the officers saw him and demanded that he drop the pill into his hand. The police searched his room and set the cameras, slides, undeveloped film, and Quaaludes aside. They asked Polanski if he knew why the complaint had been lodged, and he said no. "I was incredulous; I couldn't equate what had happened the day before with rape in any form" (p. 373). Unaware of the gravity of his situation, he felt that "a thorough airing of the circumstances" would exonerate him. The detectives asked if Polanski would accompany them to the scene of the alleged crime, Nicholson's guest room, and he complied. Going over his case with two lawyers, Polanski reflected on his experience: "Nothing in my life had prepared me for the idea that I might be a criminal" (p. 375).

In a grand jury hearing, Samantha testified that Polanski had given her "part" of a Quaalude before having sex with her. She admitted to having "sampled" a Quaalude once before and having had sex twice during the previous year. The methaqualone had made her dizzy, so she simulated an asthma attack in a failed attempt to induce Polanski to take her home. Polanski was charged with six counts: furnishing a controlled substance to a minor, committing a "lewd and lascivious act" on a minor, unlawful sexual intercourse, "rape by drugs," "perversion," and sodomy (Leaming, 1981, p. 173). To the defendant, each charge sounded worse than the last. "If the tinted plate glass windows of his thirty-third floor office hadn't been sealed, I might have jumped there and then" (Polanski, 1985, p. 377). How had the incident come to the attention of the police? Samantha told her boyfriend that she had had sex with Polanski; her sister, Kim, overheard the conversation and told Susan, and Susan called her accountant, who recommended a lawyer, who advised her to tell the police. Polanski insisted that he had not gotten Samantha drunk; she drank only a little champagne, and the bottle was still half-full when they left. Her prior sexual experience, he says, presuming the account she narrated to him was accurate, was "very different" from the mere two episodes she reported to the grand jury (pp. 377–378). Overnight, Polanski tells us, he had become "the notorious Hollywood rapist," he had "crossed the fine line between decent folks and scum." He was unjustly accused and mistreated by the press and the criminal justice system.

At his initial appearance before Judge Laurence Rittenband, outside the courtroom, he had to "run the gauntlet of a big posse of TV cameramen, photographers, and reporters, who charged at me like wild beasts" (p. 379). And later, in Los Angeles, as Polanski placed flowers on the grave of Sharon Tate, his murdered wife, a man with a German accent "jumped out from behind some bushes and started snapping pictures." The click of his shutter "sounded like machine-gun fire." Yanking the film from the camera and parodying a defense used after World War II by former Nazi concentration camp functionaries, he said to the photographer, "I know, you were only obeying orders" (pp. 383–384). The author's rhetorical juxtapositions are almost startling: his devotion to his murdered wife, her grave (at Holy Cross Cemetery), and the flowers versus machine gun fire, German accent, following orders, and Nazis. We have to remind ourselves what events these chapters narrate—sex between a grown man and a child and its legal aftermath.

Then Polanski was, he says, betrayed by Gerald Azaria, the editor of *Vogue Hommes,* who had given him a bona fide assignment to do the very layout he had been arrested for: Azaria refused to testify on his behalf, because, his lawyer stated, he and Polanski "had no formal, written agreement." We told Interpol, Azaria said, that we "knew nothing" about the assignment (p. 379). Then Polanski was photographed at a Bavarian beer hall, puffing on a cigar, sitting in a crowd, judging by the photograph, supposedly composed entirely of young women—though, as he points out, the picture was carefully cropped to remove the girls' boyfriends (p. 385). In his account, it is the media who are the villains in this drama: They are guilty of doing terrible things to him, while he was the considerate one. He contemplated the prospect, in the event of a trial, of the prosecution's putting Samantha on the witness stand, which would backfire and exonerate him, since she "was a physically mature girl who could easily pass for eighteen" (p. 381)—she was taller than Polanski and had "clearly identifiable breasts" (Leaming, 1981, p. 177). Roman had "already caused her considerable harm," he admits, he "didn't want her to be exposed to a blaze of publicity that would sear her memory for life" (Polanski, 1985, p. 382). Again, Polanski positions himself as the decent and honorable party here.

Polanski does not deny having sex with a thirteen-year-old girl. (Though in his memoir, as I said, he does not mention his anal penetration of Samantha.) He does not deny giving her champagne before the sex act (though he does not mention the Quaaludes). His reasoning is a form of justification: "I didn't do anything wrong." Well, not anything *terribly* wrong. A moment of "lust," perhaps. But of what crime was he guilty? A technical violation—a legal peccadillo, really—rather than a deadly sin: sex with a minor. So why was he being punished so harshly for it? In the state of Georgia, he points out, "unlawful sexual intercourse" applies to only adults having sex with girls age twelve and younger, which, if such a law were in effect in California, would exonerate him altogether. In Los Angeles County, the court sentenced a quarter of men found guilty of statutory rape to probation to no jail time at all, and among these miscreants, many were teachers and policemen, people who are responsible for the welfare of minors (p. 382). He could not be deported for such a trivial offense, he reasoned. This was vitally important, he tells us, because he had his heart set on living and working in the United States (p. 382). Put-upon but ever the considerate, conciliatory, gallant one, Polanski expresses a willingness to accept a perfunctory rap on the knuckles for bad judgment and a technical violation if he will be allowed to get on with his life. In his moral equation, a deal has been struck, an arrangement agreed upon, a peccadillo acknowledged, atonement conveyed, a transaction concluded. Enough is enough.

Picturing all the terrible things that could happen to him as a result of his trials and tribulations, he says, the thought "had never crossed my mind that I should be sent to prison, my life and career ruined, *for making love*" (p. 379; my emphasis). Notice that he does not say that he could not have imagined that he would be incarcerated for giving alcohol and a Quaalude to a thirteen-year-old, and then, forcefully and against her expressed wishes, having anal sex with her, but that he could not have imagined this for the romantic and entirely positive act of "making love." He admits to having succumbed to a moment of "unthinking lust." Perhaps the most revealing comment Polanski made in his effort to nullify the sin of his act is a statement he blurted out in a 1979 interview with Martin Amis that was published in 1980 in a British magazine called *Tatler* and reprinted in 1993 in a collection of the author's long-forgotten essays and then dredged up in 2009, when federal officials renewed their efforts to get Polanski back to California to face the legal music: "I thought, you know, I was going to wake up from it. I realize, if I had *killed* somebody, it wouldn't have had so much appeal to the press, you see? But . . . fucking, you see, and the young girls. Judges want to fuck young girls. Juries want to fuck young girls—*everyone* wants to fuck young girls!" (quoted in Amis, 1993, p. 246). Polanski's justification is disingenuous to the point of self-delusion, comments Amis: "Not everyone wants to fuck young girls. . . . Most people who do want to fuck young girls, moreover, don't fuck young girls. Not fucking apparently willing young girls is clearly more of a challenge" (p. 247). And almost no one who had done so would use such a defense *to* a writer *in an effort to vindicate himself in a case of statutory rape.* Virtually anyone who peruses both documents—Polanski's memoir and the transcripts of Samantha's grand jury testimony on the case—walks away certain of three fundamental facts: The author of *Roman by Polanski* is satisfied that he committed neither a crime nor a seriously sinful act; the director was genuinely baffled by the uproar the case unleashed; and Samantha Gailey did *not* want to have intercourse with Polanski, and he *forced* her to do so.

Judge Rittenband, deciding that Polanski had worn out his privileges in the free world, ordered him to be sent to Chino State Penitentiary to be psychologically tested, during which he would be confined for a ninety-day stay. The district attorney's office had agreed to allow the defendant to plead to statutory rape; though a felony, it was the least serious charge on the indictment (Toobin, 2010, pp. 153–154). Polanski and his attorney assumed that his sentence would constitute the ninety days of confinement, which would be followed by a fine and probation. The psychiatrists who examined him determined that Polanski was neither a pedophile nor a pathological sex offender. "He was a clinically normal adult male who had made an appalling choice when he should have known better" (Feeney and Duncan, 2006, p. 111). Polanski served forty-two days of the confinement and was released, but soon after his release, Judge Rittenband inexplicably decided that Polanski's sentence had been far too light, that instead he should give the felon an indeterminate sentence. In the men's room of a country club, he remarked to Howard Koch, a screenwriter, that he was inclined to send the director "away forever. I can't imagine anything more terrible, more disgusting, [than] having sex with a 13-year-old girl. I'll see that the man never gets out of jail" (quoted in Sanford, 2007, p. 252). He also offered the director a deal: serve the full ninety days and submit to deportation. "I'd rather do anything than go on living the way I had in the past year," says Polanski. "I'd endured disgrace and press harassment, lost two director's jobs, and done time in prison" (1985, p. 400). What would be the point of remaining in America and facing the prospect of further humiliation and punishment? "Why should I go back to jail until I have to beg to be deported? Why not just leave?" (quoted in Sanford, 2007, p. 253). On the last day of January 1978, Polanski caught a plane from Santa Monica to Los Angeles, from there to London, and finally to Paris, the city of his birth. He has not set foot in the United States since.

In short, Polanski's conventionalizing frame is this: The girl with whom I had sex was willing, even eager; her mother practically threw her into my arms; she may have been thirteen, but she looked eighteen; she was sophisticated, even wild, vastly beyond my conservative middle-aged sensibilities; she had already had sex, drunk champagne, and used Quaaludes; my punishment exceeds that which most comparable offenders receive. I have been abused by the press, the legal system, and the public. The American legal system is flawed, unjust, and self-righteous, and vindictive. I do not deserve this punishment, and I am justified in taking flight. I am the victim here, not Samantha. But Polanski does not spell out general principles for us, such as what would happen to the society if statutory rape laws were wiped off the books, or *at what age* a girl possesses the capacity to make the choice to have sex—and at what age the *male* has to be to have sex with a girl of what age. In short, Roman does not explicate a general *theory* of social control or of its administration. He is too wrapped up in the injustices of his own case to spell out such matters. And, with slight variations, his justifications sound very much like those that *every* man charged with statutory rape would utter; it is in the nature of statutory rape that it *elicits* such deviance neutralization devices. Only the details vary.

Since 1978, Roman Polanski has directed eleven major feature-length films, the most notable of which, *The Pianist* (2002), garnered seven Academy

Award nominations, winning three, including Best Director. Polanski could not, of course, receive his award in person without certain arrest and further incarceration. In January 2009, Samantha Gailey, now Samantha Geimer, in her mid-forties and a married mother of three, filed a legal declaration that the charges against Polanski be dropped. Her 1977 testimony to the grand jury, she said, was valid and true, but to continue to prosecute her rapist would subject her to further unwanted attention and trauma. Nine months later, Swiss authorities arrested Polanski in Zurich at the airport, on his way to a ceremony at a film festival there in his honor. In July of the following year, Swiss authorities released Polanski from custody, declaring him a "free man." A deal struck in 2009 between the Los Angeles district attorney and Polanski's representatives fell through over a disagreement about whether the court proceedings could be filmed. At this writing, he remains a fugitive from justice in the United States.

Kerry Cohen, "My Parade of Boys Continues"

Most erotic memoirs published in earlier centuries were made up of the narratives of sexual adventures of men—conquests, if you will—of which the most famous three are Jacques Casanova, *History of My Life* (1798); Anonymous, *My Secret Life* (1888); and Frank Harris, *My Life and Loves* (1925). Prior to the early twentieth century, many women's sexual "memoirs" were fake—*Fanny Hill: Memoirs of a Woman of Pleasure* (1748) was penned by a man, John Cleland—or were thinly disguised fictionalizations; Georgiana Devonshire's *The Sylph* (1778) falls into the latter category. The parading of masculine heterosexual prowess that prevailed centuries ago currently tends to be more frowned upon than it was in the past, and the inhibitions that enjoined women from expressing their sexuality in narrative form have dissolved; currently, women's erotic memoirs vastly outnumber men's. Consider only the tiniest sampling of a half-dozen of the better-known such works that appeared in the twenty-first century: Lynn Barber, *An Education* (2009); Toni Bentley, *The Surrender* (2004); Rachel Resnick, *Love Junkie: A Memoir* (2008); Sue William Silverman, *Love Sick: One Woman's Journey through Sexual Addiction* (2001); Jane Juska, *A Round-Heeled Woman* (2004); and Catherine Millet, *The Sexual Life of Catherine M.* (2003). The contemporary list of well-known men's sexual memoirs is substantially shorter. (But see Ryan, 1995, and Marin, 2003—and note the negative words in the title and subtitle—"secret," "cad," and "toxic.")

Ironically, even so, today, a majority of the population is likely to regard sexual promiscuity in women as a form of deviance. Female friends counsel one another not to "go too far" into the realm of "sleeping around"; a male companion is likely to condemn his girlfriend, post-hoc, for having sex with "too many guys"; a mother is likely to be made to feel uncomfortable when she learns that her daughter is "the talk of the town" because she is known to have had too many—or any—one-night stands. Being called a *slut* is one of the most hurtful accusations a woman or girl can experience. Leora Tanenbaum entitles her book on stereotyping and the sexual double standard *Slut!* (2000). Stereotyping, true—but a social reality nonetheless.

One of the more common deviance-excusing rationales—relevant to any and all seemingly compulsive behaviors, and perhaps most exquisitely and least convincingly applied to sexual promiscuity—is the invocation of "addiction": *I couldn't help having sex with so many men, because I was driven by an addiction over which I had no control.* "'I didn't know what I was doing,'" writes Susan Cheever in her essay on sexual addiction, "doesn't sound like much of an excuse. But this almost otherworldly suspension of the will is actually a symptom of addiction. An addict is someone who comes to, who regains normal consciousness . . . and asks what happened, not to evade responsibility but because things that happened really seem to have happened to someone else. . . . Normal people find it hard to believe in the addictive trance" (2008, p. 54). Cheever explains that neurochemical changes in the body take place during sex that are remarkably similar to those that fire the engine of drug addiction—pleasure centers in the brain are activated, hunger is generated, satiation and satisfaction is temporary, only to be repeated by hunger again after a few hours. "Adultery," she tells us, "is the drunk driving of sex addiction" (p. 73). Of course, all of us experience these chemical reinforcements, but only a few of us become sexually compulsive with multiple partners, which leaves us with the same puzzlement as before—and feeling very much that Cheever's explanation really is an evasion of responsibility. Would we accept the same justification if Cheever were a man? Probably not. Still, men who claim to be or have been sex "addicts" use the same vocabulary. Michael Ryan, the author of *Secret Life,* the exceptional recent men's sex memoir, claims that a mesmerizing, importunate, "inexorable pull" from an "electronic magnet in [his] solar plexus," "beamed in from Mars," had been "switched on," putting him in "a kind of trance," and commanded him to engage in sexual behavior (1995, p. 3).

"I woke up with a headache, as well as the cotton mouth and disturbed stomach of a bad hangover," Cheever tells her readers, describing the morning after one such "addictive" encounter the night before. "I had forgotten to lower the shades, and morning light streamed mercilessly into the room onto the tangle of sheets . . . and on the man who seemed much older and seedier than he had in the romantic dim light of the night before" (2008, p. 79). The details of this sordid scene are meant to provide the reader with convincing evidence of Cheever's compulsivity, her complete lack of will—her addiction.

But we are all wired up to receive pleasure, and all of us want more after its reinforcement has run out. Why her and not her sisters? Perhaps, for Cheever, the justification offers self-exculpation, but it is unlikely to fly for most of the rest of us. But such is the beauty of deviance disavowal: As undergraduates frequently parrot back to their sociology and anthropology instructors, "Everything's relative."

Loose Girl: A Memoir of Promiscuity (2008), by Kerry Cohen, following the "addiction" justification, offers a stark, almost shocking contrast to that chronicled in its mirror opposite near-twin, Chelsea Handler's *My Horizontal Life* (2005), on the experience of a young woman who has slept with a substantial number of partners. Handler followed up with *Are You There, Vodka? It's Me, Chelsea* (2008), itself loosely dramatized by a television comedy, *Are You There, Chelsea?* (2012), based on the author's comic persona "as a slutty, foul-mouthed lush" (Stanley, 2012, p. C1). Cohen is the superior writer; indeed, she is a professional writer, with an MFA (master's in fine arts) in creative writing and a published novel on her résumé, while Handler dropped out of a community college after one semester and supports herself as a comedian and an actress. Handler unfolds a series of discrete episodes rather than a narrative arc: She remains the same person at the end of the book as at the beginning. And while she fails to make the trivial distinction between "like" and "as," using "nauseous" when she means "nauseated" (Handler, 2005, p. 19), trots out overworked clichés ("swinging from the ceiling fan," p. 47), and flashes cardboard stereotypes, hers is nonetheless the vastly better and more entertaining book. Cohen's explanation for sleeping around strikes the reader as a bit too pat; her tale of "recovery" from promiscuity to monogamous marriage emits an odor of sanctimoniousness, self-righteousness, and piousness. Above all, Cohen's tale is redolent of seriousness; after all, her redemption story entails *saving her life.*

Consider the cover picture intended to depict the theme and content of *Loose Girl* (the hardback version). The highly stylized photograph, in stark, high-contrasty black and white, depicts a slim, petite young woman, from about the sternum up, with long, dark, straight hair and pale, white skin, dressed in a black slip. Her hair half-obscures her face; her eyes, which we cannot see, are downcast; and what we can see of her mouth indicates that she is unsmiling. The background is a harsh, bleached-out white—the total absence of color—and the title of the book, in typescript, appears in black above a horizontal line slightly above the woman's head, the subtitle, in red, below that line. The image is completely contextless, as if a completely singular woman appeared out of nowhere with no social, cultural, or geographical anchoring of any kind. The image conveys a sad, severe, glum girl who is superficially and glossily sexual.

The contrast between the two books' cover photographs is instructive. Given that their subject matter is nearly identical—"promiscuity" appears in Cohen's subtitle, and "one-night stands" in Handler's—the cover of *My Horizontal Life* (the paperback edition) forcefully contrasts with Cohen's. Handler's cover contains twelve photographs arranged in four rows of three per row; in each row we find two pictures in color and one in black and white. All convey the same "bed" theme and include depictions of the following: a rumpled bed and pillows; a note resting on a pillow on which is written a man's name ("John") and his telephone number (indicating that Chelsea woke up after her companion departed and he left her a means of contacting him—perhaps it wasn't a "one-night stand" after all!); Chelsea sitting on the edge of a bed, her feet shod in two different types of high-heeled shoes; and Chelsea's face in various moods and poses. All are, by conventional standards, realistic—that is, they convey the real Chelsea in or on a real bed, with real pillows, in a real room. She is by turns playful, seductive, pensive, and giggly. Clearly, far from being trapped in the coils of an addiction, Chelsea is enjoying herself, and the mood of these pictures is uncompromisingly unserious; they convey the message that everything contained in this book is likewise unserious.

Cohen displays virtually no sense of humor, and her self-deprecation is deadly serious; contrarily, Handler exhibits a refreshingly and wildly self-deprecating sense of humor. Said Chelsea to a *New York Times* reporter, "I wrote a stupid book about one-night stands" (O'Connor, 2005). She devotes a chapter of that book to her discovery of a "skid mark straight down the center" of her panties, which she tries to hide from Gavin, her lover of the previous night. After checking to see that he is still asleep, she lunges for the evidence, throwing the panties out the window into Gavin's backyard, after which she sees a dog, which she names "Cujo," running into the bedroom, his chompers clamped down on her soiled panties. Cujo proceeds to eat the panties, but not before Gavin spies the offensive stain. "Ew!" is all he can muster as she runs out of the room, claiming that the panties are another woman's (Handler, 2005, pp. 56–59). To elicit a laugh, she describes the colors of an outfit she donned (hot pink, citrus, and lavender) as "summer whore" (p. 167). To convey the notion that New Jersey is not a romantic locale in which to attain adolescence, she asks the reader to picture a "starry summer night at the Jersey shore." Then "violins and a harmonica." Finally, "picture the harmonica up my ass" (p. 13). These are not the words of a writer too proud or vain to make fun of herself.

Handler describes going to a costume party dressed as an M&M, after which she takes a cab to a nearby apartment and, still wearing the costume, crashes on a bed, awakens to the sounds of lovemaking, and, disgusted, rolls out of bed; falls on the floor and crawls out the door; runs down a flight of stairs without her contacts, shoes, cell phone, or purse; sprints down the street to a friend's apartment; throws rocks at his window and attracts his attention; gets her friend to take a snapshot of her in the costume; convinces him to accompany her to her own apartment; crawls through the kitchen window, getting stuck in the process; and eventually squirms out of the costume (pp. 187–196). "Don't take all this too seriously!" Chelsea seems to be telling us. In fact, Chelsea is so lighthearted about her sexual adventures it is difficult to categorize what she does as a form of sexual deviance. In effect, she adopts a postmodernist definition of sexual behavior—beyond evaluation or judgment. It is difficult to imagine Cohen engaging in—or at least describing herself engaging in—such humorously self-deprecating, humiliating antics. Cohen's purpose is too serious for that, too dedicated to the depiction of herself as stumbling toward the edge of an abyss and heroically pulling herself back toward sanity and normalcy. Cohen is a traditionalist; she offers a conventional, pathology-oriented, and most decidedly judgmental attitude toward her sleeping around.

Cohen's explanation for her sexual promiscuity? Her "feelings of uncertainty and confusion" that surrounded her sexuality; it was easy to attract a boy's attention. "What's easier for a girl than to get noticed for her body?" A boy told her, "Boys have to put forth real effort to get laid, while all you have to do is to stand braless to the wind." It is true, says Kerry: "Using my sex appeal was default behavior. . . . I was desperate for attention—any attention—and men's interest in my body was the easiest avenue to being noticed." In addition, Cohen adds the "A" word into the equation: "My story is also about addiction. Addiction to power, to the attempt to control others through my body. It is about how desperate I was to feel loved, less alone, and how, misguided by all those cultural mixed messages, I tried to fill my need with male attention and sex. . . . And finally, how I learned to stop" (Cohen, 2008, p. 3). One gets the feeling that Cohen's book was designed as an object lesson warning early teens to avoid making the same mistakes she did.

At some point, she begins a "new life." One spring, after having completed an MFA, taken a kickboxing class, begun a novel she had been "meaning to write," painted her studio, and run through several boys in her "parade," she takes a plane to New Jersey to visit her dad and sits next to, and makes out with, a "handsome, well-groomed" boy who clearly has an erection inside his pants. "I briefly consider jerking him off under the tiny airline blanket, but he doesn't push for it, and I don't offer" (p. 194). At home, she thumbs through her high school yearbook, wondering if she has changed from her profligate past. "But I don't really know if that's the case" (p. 196). Lying in bed, she wishes to have a boyfriend "to lift me up like a dead thing and breathe me into life" (p. 199). She hooks up with a young man, then tells herself she is bored. "Even during the sex." She wonders why she is still doing this, "after so many years." A boy calls, but the phone does not make a connection. "I make a tentative decision. No more boys for a while. Just to see what will happen" (p. 203). She sits for days in her small apartment, loneliness as her unwanted companion, "a pain intense enough that I keep my arms wrapped around my middle" (p. 203). Her joke with her friends is that she's "calling a moratorium" on her vagina (p. 204).

Cohen meets a boy named Michael, works up the gumption to tell him she does not want sex, and then he announces that he loves her. Then she gets married. Not long after the wedding, she goes out with friends to listen to a band, have drinks, and socialize. Across the bar, she catches the eye of a young man. He looks back, she decides to leave, but he catches up with her. "We were watching each other, right?" he asks her. "I'm sorry," she says. "I'm married." After climbing into bed and nuzzling with her husband, she tells herself, "I don't have to be great at this; maybe I just have to be good enough" (p. 210).

Melissa Febos, "I Took Aim and Flicked the Whip toward Him"

Sex work—sex for pay: being employed to engage in erotic activities. Many people treat sex as a commodity—they buy it; they sell it. Customers pay for it; employees supply it. Of all forms of sex work, prostitution is the most well-known; others include working in a massage parlor, working for an escort service, pimping, stripping, lap dancing, and working in the pornography industry. Melissa Febos describes her life as a dominatrix. The dictionary definition (Merriam-Webster) of "dominatrix" is "a woman who plays the dominant role in a sado-masochistic sexual relationship or encounter." Most members of the society are likely to consider working as a dominatrix deviant; we would consider it shameful, disgraceful, discreditable—as did Melissa Febos and as she assumed others would.

For four years, Febos worked for an establishment she refers to as "the dungeon," or the Dungeon of Mistress X. She wore skimpy leather outfits or black lace corsets or bustiers, stilettos, and fishnet stockings, lording it over crouching, cringing men; tying them up with leather straps and chains; hitting them with whips or paddles; playing out stereotyped, stylized dramas; insulting them; forcing them to engage in degrading activities; sometimes urinating or defecating on them as they whined and whimpered and, eventually, for some, masturbated themselves to orgasm. Febos never engaged in sexual intercourse with her clients, she never took off her outfits—occasionally, only her bra, exposing her breasts—and she did not have an orgasm during these sessions. To her, it was a job; to her clients, it was sex. Being a dominatrix is *sex work.* For this activity, Febos was paid seventy-five dollars an hour. How did she justify her participation in such an activity? Her description balances what her readers are likely to consider sordid, and therefore *intriguing* and *provocative,* with what is conventional, and therefore *acceptable.*

In the late 1990s, Febos moved to New York and enrolled in college at The New School. During her first year there, she thrived. One afternoon, coming home from school, she saw Rebecca, her roommate, talking with a woman. After they parted, Rebecca exclaimed, "You'll never guess what she does!" It turns out the woman, a resident of the apartment next to them, was a professional dominatrix. Fascinated, Melissa thumbed through several SM (or BD—bondage and discipline) publications and saw women with "stony eyes and vampish mouths" who glared at the reader while wearing nurse costumes or burlesque outfits, holding riding crops and ropes, their boots planted on other people's bodies. Unlike the usual pornographic magazine like *Playboy* and *Penthouse,* whose models suggested seduction and compliance, these women "advertised entitlement. *You want me,*" they seemed to be sneering—"*ha!*" (2010, p. 12). Later, she spotted her neighbor at a nearby Laundromat; expecting her at the very least to be wearing tall leather boots, she was struck by how ordinary and conventional the woman looked. Melissa admits to having been "enthralled" all her life by the drug culture; deviant sexual practices; stories about juvenile delinquents, criminals, the underworld; anything taboo and extreme—"the romance of misbehavior" fascinated her (p. 13).

But her enchantment with the dominatrix went beyond the simple allure of deviant behavior, she tells us. The woman worked at an *interesting job*—and she herself did not. Melissa was a college student in a liberal arts program who accepted very little money from her parents, yearned for self-sufficiency, had no job prospects and a profound intolerance for work she did not find "compelling." She "couldn't bear office work or ass kissing" and had no confidence that her limited but excellent academic skills would translate into interesting employment. And besides, she tells us, was a regular speedballer—she shot a mixture of heroin and cocaine, an expensive indulgence. Meanwhile, she thought, her neighbor, the dominatrix, lived under trouble-free circumstances, "in air-conditioned, roachless comfort" (p. 14). Her mandate seemed crystal clear: Talk to her neighbor about getting a job at an SM establishment.

In the first fourteen pages of *Whip Smart,* Melissa Febos offers three deviance disavowal strategies. Strategy one is that she needs the money to live on. Strategy two is that she does not like boring jobs. Strategy three is that she longs for independence from her parents. She also indicates that she has a drug habit, an added incentive to earn a reasonably substantial income. Normally, using recreational drugs would add to rather than detract from her identification as a deviant, but she tells us that often the money that she should use to pay the utility bills ends up going to her drug dealer—implying that she has a *compulsion* to use. Febos offers economic need, along with a couple of strong personal inclinations—the need for interesting employment and the need for self-sufficiency—as reasons why we should not condemn her and her choice of a deviant profession. Money represented security, and she needed to earn her own (p. 13).

Melissa knocked on her neighbor's door and chatted with her. The apartment was indeed air-conditioned. "I had expected to find chains hanging from the ceiling," she explains, "and cages lining the walls—some kind of, well, dungeon" (pp. 14–15). Instead, she saw bookshelves "lined with the same titles as mine," a fine art print hanging on the wall, Ikea furniture, and a copy of *The New York Times Week in Review.* And her neighbor was, Melissa found herself surprised to learn, a law school student. "She looked so *normal,*" Febos marveled. After learning a few basics about the job—including the fact that the job is easy to get but difficult to keep—she was handed two volumes on female domination and left the apartment with all she needed "to make fast money without taking off my clothes" (p. 16). She became certain that she would become a dominatrix. Justification number four: People who work in dungeons are normal, in fact, a lot like me. Later, at parties, she reveled in people's reaction when she told them what she did for a living: "I loved their shock at how normal I seemed, how unlike what they would have imagined" (p. 67).

Febos answered an ad in *The Village Voice*: "Attractive young woman wanted for nurse role-play and domination. No experience necessary. Good $$. No sex." The Dungeon of Mistress X was located near Herald Square in midtown Manhattan; a woman named Fiona showed her around. Melissa was "hopelessly impressed" by its lushness, greater than she had "even remotely imagined," its immense size, ornate rugs, glowing sconces on red walls, marbled floors, and mirrors hung in gilt frames. The actual dungeons were located behind doors—the Red Room, the Black Room, and the Blue Room, two of which had their own bathrooms and the last of which alone measured some seven hundred square feet, all with ten-foot-high ceilings. And they accommodated equipment, stored in appropriate places: a coffin, a hanging cage, a Catherine wheel—a type of torture instrument for crushing the victims' hands and feet—thick chains, clamps, candles, hooks, floggers, paddles, blindfolds, rope, a leather riding saddle, a dog dish, a giant wooden cross, a leather swing that hung from the ceiling, a kind of throne, and mirrors on most of the walls. "Reeling, I wondered how I'd ever remember the names of all the equipment, let alone learn how to use it" (p. 19). In addition, there were three medical rooms—Med 1, Med 2, and Med 3—each with its own specialized type of gear: adjustable examination tables and cupboards filled with syringes, stethoscopes, proctoscopes, wheels with spikes, pincers, clamps, thermometers, tongue depressors, and (in one room) anatomical posters of the male and female reproductive system. Down the hall she found a cross-dressing room and two other cross-dressing rooms for employees, as well as a kitchen, an office, and a changing room. Here is Febos's self-exculpation number five: This is a really classy joint, one of the biggest and best equipped of its kind.

Melissa admits to another compulsion over which she said she had little control: the need to effortlessly seduce and conquer, to induce others to hunger for her, to be in control in a relationship. Acting as a dominatrix (or "domme" or "dom") in a dungeon addresses these needs. Was this compulsion an *addiction*? Her descriptions seem to say as much. If so, Febos's invoking it amounts to another justification for choosing a job as a dominatrix—another type of deviance neutralization. Interestingly, she incorporates her heroin habit into the same explanation. Melissa struggled lifelong with interpersonal insecurity. It was precisely because she felt she incapable of dominating and controlling the people in her life, particularly men, that she took the job at the dungeon—and why she used heroin. Heroin created distance from what she was doing and enabled her to act as she would like to act—with mastery. She was attracted to being a dominatrix—and to heroin—specifically because she was *not* dominant in her everyday life. Once, well into her employment, while crouched on a bathroom floor holding a man's head under water, she experienced "a kind of transcendence. It was that utter alienation from self, a loosening of the glue that made my reality whole. It felt both horrific and triumphant" (p. 92). In her confessions, the reader is made to understand the motivation driving both activities and is less repelled by her choice of them.

SM workers divide sessions into three categories: sensual, corporal, and switch. And each specific session may merge into different categories, since clients (whom dommes call "slaves") request slightly different activities. "Sensual" usually includes playing the roles of naughty, flirtatious schoolgirl or secretary or girlfriend or babysitter; light bondage and spanking, tickling, and nipple play; as well as teasing and denial, often involving a hand job, and rubbing the woman's breasts or ass in the client's face (p. 29). "Corporal" includes smothering with masks, pillows, plastic bags, or Saran Wrap and more vigorous whipping and paddling; more severe and painful nipple pinching and even skewering; placement of the client on a rack or wheel; possible bloodletting; penetration with large dildos—anything that causes serious physical pain. And, of course, corporal sessions are more likely to feature urinating and defecating on the client ("golden showers" and "brown showers"). The "switch" session, as it sounds, entails the client and the worker switching roles.

Given the nature of her employment, Melissa was reluctant to tell her parents about her job, delaying it as long as she could. But when she finally told her mother, she used several deviance neutralization strategies to convince her that it was an acceptable way to make a living. "I don't have sex with anyone, and I don't take off my clothes," she told her mom. She insisted that it was safe. And that it was "like a kind of therapy, reenacting childhood traumas." She said the money was good. She insisted that it had been "great" for her. "It's given me so much confidence. I get *worshipped* for a living. . . . I'm in control of everything that happens. It's *empowering*" (p. 96). She told her mother that as a result of her job, she had made a lot of good female friends; that it had improved her body image. Though her mom nodded, "her face never relaxed" and "her eyes stayed worried" (p. 97). Sometimes deviance neutralization does not work. Febos feels she did not do anything terribly wrong, and in the best of all possible worlds, dominatrixes should not be anathemized.

By the end of her third year, she tells us, "I enjoyed it. . . . Even without the drugs, it could induce an altered state. I was good at it, and as in all things I've done well and with practice, there was a rhythm to be captured. A beat emerges. . . . In it, your movements string together with sound and consciousness to form one long, sinewy stroke." In the dark, "everything else could just fall away, and I would be pure motion, pure drive" (p. 153). Perhaps "love" is not quite the right word, she explains, but it was an emotion "just as strong" (p. 153), an emotion that frightened her—but she was not quite sure why.

But at some point, Melissa recognized that the justifications she had constructed to enable her to work in the dungeon rang hollow. After whipping a man, she walked toward him. She could smell rubber on his breath, and saliva dripped from the corners of his agape mouth. "The dungeon suddenly felt filthy, the film of dust and lubricant that covered it becoming a coating of hypocrisy, of lies and rationalization. . . . The place was so soaked in shame that I could hardly breathe" (pp. 150–151). Staring at the man crouched on the floor as he craned his neck to look her in the face, she whispered, "You pathetic fuck" (p. 151).

Melissa began crossing lines, doing what she insisted to herself that she would never do in a session. Brown showers. Topless sessions. More submissive scenes. One client forced her into playing part of a scene outside, in the street, and he exposed his genitals to her. The whole thing felt unnatural, phony, disgusting. Her "whole body burned with humiliation" (p. 206). Later, they checked into a hotel room. The clerk looked at her as if she was a prostitute. She insisted to herself that she was a dominatrix, not a prostitute, but the clerk could not have cared less, and she "waited to stop feeling like a whore," taking a shower to feel clean (p. 207). She began seeing a therapist to whom she admitted, "I torture people for money and I can't stop." She wanted to punish the therapist for her own shame (p. 234). When she began explaining her activities and her job title, her therapist did not even know what a "dominatrix" was. As she explained it, she could hear herself speaking. "It did not sound glamorous. It did not sound tough, or cool, or sexy. It sounded humiliating" (p. 236). Eventually, her sessions with clients began to feel "like surgery without adequate anesthesia" (p. 240). She stopped working at the dungeon and began taking a few private clients, renting a loft from an ex-colleague. She started having dreams of sessions in "soiled basements and condemned motel rooms, my shame translated into literal filth and disintegration" (p. 247). She realized that her participation in SM was a result of a kind of pathology. She enrolled in an MFA program at Sarah Lawrence and now teaches writing and literature at SUNY Purchase. Though she misses certain aspects of her former job, it gradually receded into the past, belonging to a former life. A strange way around, many of us think, but not too bad a place to end up.

Kirk Read, "I Wanted to Be Shirley Temple"

Kirk Read, born in 1973, grew up knowing he was different. In the fourth grade, he saw Jesse, a seventh-grade boy, in a contest dancing to Michael Jackson's "Beat It," which contains the line "They'll kick you, they'll beat you, and they'll tell you it's fair." The audience sat, "slackjawed, beholding the purely alien being before them" (2003, p. 1); someone muttered the word "faggot," and Read was fully alerted to "what a horrible thing" being a "faggot" must be, even though the boy performed brilliantly and won the contest (p. 2). Later, Jesse, accompanied by several of his female friends, walked past a crowd of students, attracting everyone's stares as if he were a species of "leper messiah" (p. 3). This story contains the essence of the message in Read's memoir, *How I Learned to Snap*: This boy was a queer, he was different, he was special, and he was a rebel—and yes, perhaps a deviant—but in the end, he was triumphant. All at once we know that Read will cast himself into that same light. Virtually every story Read tells in *How I Learned to Snap,* most of the chapters in the book, convey the same theme. In short, it is a "feel good," triumphalist narrative. For Jesse and Kirk, "snapping," meant—snap!—"I am not afraid" (p. 57). When Jesse received his high school diploma, Kirk "could hear the angels snapping" (p. 57). *How I Learned to Snap* is very much like a situation comedy version of a young gay person living in difficult circumstances, about to surmount the hostility of the homophobes around him with his wit, charm, and superior intelligence. The author works rhetorically to locate his readers on his side by advocating a progressive, enlightened position and making us feel good—and superior—about having that experience. This is a clever if overly slickly produced life narrative.

But Read has a pesky, flamboyant, unquestionably unconventional facet as well, which redeems the book for the more sophisticated reader—and for the more militant gay who wants to see some spice in all this treacly triumphalism. Gays are not just like straight people except that they attract stigma and hostility. They really *do* do different things from the majority—including engage in homosexual acts. Here is where Read radically departs from the bland, assimilationist sit-com mode. At a certain point, *How I Learned to Snap* begins to unfold some of the "nasty stuff" the author does that mainstream readers who feel enlightened because they accommodate gays into conventional society do not necessarily want to be exposed to. One of Read's mini-chapters chronicles this thirteen-year-old's effort to achieve sexual satisfaction by slipping into the bathroom while an elderly, male, *blind* guest is preparing to take a shower. Read takes a box seat on the hamper by the window and watches the man undress, step into the shower, and soap up. As the man lathers up his hair, Read unzips his fly and begins masturbating, hoping to "burn the image of this naked man" into his brain "for future use" (pp. 39–40). But at some point, guilt overtakes him; he realizes he should not be doing this. "It was pathetic, really," he tells himself. "The only way I could find sex was to steal it from the blind" (p. 40). He tries to exit by faking accidentally entering the room, then apologizes, and slinks out, deeply ashamed. It is true that this chapter, like nearly all of the others, ends on an upbeat note, but the *act* he describes seems sufficiently perverted to be off most readers' moral chart. Another chapter, barely a page long, is off the chart not because it describes a perverted act but because it is graphic in describing an act of anal sex—with a grown man, Rich, who is penetrating Kirk, age fifteen—which describes Rich pushing gently and being surprised "when he slid all the way without me screaming." Said Kirk when it was all over, "Let's do it again" (pp. 78–79). A conventional straight person who accepts the occasional gay neighbor or relative, finding him charming and personable, does *not* want to read this scene.

Kirk Read grew up in conservative communities in Virginia; his dad, a military man, a colonel, graduated from VMI—the Virginia Military Institute. Early on in his memoir, he constructs a picture relative to the traditional, literally militaristic setting in which he spent his youth. Anyone who picks up a book narrating a gay coming-out story is already in his corner, very much in favor of his rebellion against his surroundings, but he uses deviance neutralization to further sweeten the pot. At the same time, readers sense that the author feels no animosity or contempt toward the people in his background. He expresses an emotion bordering almost on nostalgia for them; it is just that he always knew he did not belong with them, and at the moment the curtain closes on his book—high school graduation—we intuit that he will move on to a more progressive setting.

When Kirk was ten years old, his parents, fearing he might be too effeminate, shipped him off to a macho camp to promote his masculine development. He was mercilessly insulted for his effeminacy. He was greeted by a torrent of homophobic slurs and fag-baiting; he was, he tells us, "fair game for fights" (p. 7). "Faggot," "little bitch," and "butt pirate" were one boy's favorite taunts. "Fuckin' queer faggot," he growls (pp. 7–8). Before long, the two boys were flailing at one another with their fists which, surprisingly, Kirk got the better of. "Who's the faggot? Who's the faggot?" he screamed, jumping up and down on the mattress he had dumped on top of his opponent. In spite of his effeminacy, his tough-guy performance earned him some respect with the other boys, and with this boy in particular.

In spite of his dad's extremely straight-laced conservatism, his intolerance for homosexuality, and his dedication to the military—his priorities in life were VMI, the army, God, and family, "in that order" (p. 11)—he turns out, the reader discovers, to have been a remarkably decent and empathetic man. Read grew up with a provisional appointment to VMI on his wall—sort of an a priori diploma—and whenever he got angry with his dad, he hurled the appointment down the stairs, often followed by Norman Vincent Peale's *The Story of Jesus* and a juvenile version of the Bible. For him, it was gratifying to see the Colonel's "sacred totems, manhood and God," bouncing down the steps (p. 11). Yes! On one occasion, while his father was watching, Kirk played Madonna's "Like a Virgin" and descended the staircase, "singing, humping the staircase, and generally making my father apoplectic. Making him squirm was one of my favorite things in the world" (p. 12). As usual, the outcome was positive. "Son," he said, "I don't think VMI's cut out for you. Go wherever you want" (p. 12). Who wouldn't side with the little boy sitting in the barber's chair getting a haircut, with a gruff dad barking orders to a perplexed barber? In Kirk's case, along with the insult of getting the usual "bowl-and-bangs" haircut, he had to listen to "the hunting stories and racist diatribes of other customers" (p. 16). At the age of twelve, Kirk rebelled against his haircut regime by announcing that he no longer wanted the usual haircut. "The whole mannish-boy thing was working my nerves. The spinning blue-and-red stripes of the barber's pole were about to be relegated to memory" (p. 16). Notice the juxtaposition Read presents to the reader: On one side, we see traditionalism—a bowl-and-bangs haircut and hunting and racist stories—and on the other, his effeminacy and budding homosexuality. Which do you choose? Read has chosen his audience very carefully.

"Are you a boy or a girl?" a girl in his school's marching band asked him. Kirk called her a "fucking bitch," and she slapped him, "an anemic half-slap." She immediately apologized. "Did I hurt you?" she asked. "You're gonna have to hit a lot harder if you want to hurt," he responded. Tough guy, we think.

One day, Kirk picked out a bright yellow sweater to wear to school. "I could build around that sweater" (p. 18), he thinks. But the sweater attracted a crowd of boys who taunted him, poked him, and yelled at him, "Yellow sweater faggot" (p. 19). "Young homophobes are so creative," he sarcastically comments about their taunts (p. 19). He walked to the public library with the sweater in his backpack and hid in the basement. When he emerged and wandered through the stacks, two boys followed him and pushed books on top of his head. "Where's your yellow sweater, faggot?" they shouted. As Kirk sat in the back seat of the family car, his father told him that his sweater was "faggy." His mom defended the sweater, insisting that both Kirk and his dad were "autumns" and hence the color was appropriate. The next day, his dad wore yellow pants to his office (p. 20). Again, Kirk's unconventionality triumphs over his repressive environment, and the story becomes another occasion to smile. He may be super-effeminate, feels the reader, but at heart, he is a regular guy—not a deviant at all. Well, almost a regular guy.

Kirk manages to see a positive message even in negative experiences. Like so many other teenage boys, with his friends, he got drunk on the booze from his family's liquor cabinet. A drunken, vomitatious evening is followed by climbing on the roof of his house with a female friend to the sound of The Eagles, imagining that the stars were the butane lighters held by concertgoers. "As far as we were concerned, all those people were there to see us" (p. 72). Pat Robertson, a reactionary preacher and would-be politician and neighbor, was on Kirk's newspaper route. He broke Robertson's window by hurling a paper especially hard. The window cost him his entire two-week's salary, but in hindsight, he says, "it was worth every dime" (p. 38). Kirk has fantasies about joining the football team as a place kicker—he is a member of a soccer team—but holds back partly because he assumes his teammates would be ruthless fag-bashers. "I presumed that none of these boys were safe for me to be alone with in a hallway" (p. 109). It turns out that he is wrong, that some of them have close relatives who are gay, and are surprisingly tolerant on the matter.

"I loved the people I'd grown up with and even when they scared me, I held out hope that they'd come around on gay issues" (p. 111). After all, he says, "they're my people, and I can't give up on them" (p. 112). After a party, a football player hands Kirk a mostly empty pizza box; the two sit on the patio and share a couple of slices, attempting to communicate. That night, he tells us, he cut off the lid of the pizza box and added it to his collage. "I'd received benediction, and there would be mornings when I needed to be reminded of that" (p. 115). He subjects his friends, one by one, to "The Talk"—telling them that he is gay. Girls tended to already know that he was gay. A tough guy he told said to him, "Let me give you a hug" (p. 112). And so the narrative flows forward, chapter by chapter, opening with a problematic situation, his insecurity, the stress he experiences and the possible danger or harm he faces, ending with a more or less positive resolution, an acceptance that parallels—and activates—the reader's own acceptance, making Kirk seem less different, less deviant, less "queer," more mainstream, one of "us." Kirk's view of the matter is simple and straightforward: There is nothing wrong with being gay or with gender-bending; homosexuals should be integrated into conventional society and allowed to be themselves. "Live and let live" is his motto; it works for him, and it should work for the rest of us. Not only is Read normalizing homosexuality and effeminacy; he is calling on the straight community to do the same—and he is saying: *Remember all the hell you put me through? Well, I forgive you; you're still a good person, and I'm still your pal—just drop the gay-bashing, okay?*

Aside from a few specific offbeat or unconventional details, the shadow on his narrative—one feature of his otherwise conventionalizing rhetoric that many readers are likely to find at least somewhat disturbing—is Kirk's chronicle of his affair with a much older man. He does not give an exact age to Rich other than to say that his affair with him entailed "intergenerational sex," which means that when he was a minor, Rich was probably around forty. But he does cast a rhetorically mellow light onto his chronicle, rendering it less "bad" than we would think in the absence of such a justification. Sex with an older man, he tells us, "probably sped up my coming-out process. . . . Had our relationship been discovered, Rich could have done time in jail. During the time we were having sex, it never dawned on me that he was literally risking his freedom over me" (p. 58). He agrees that some younger-older sex partnerships entail abuse, but, he emphasizes, this should be judged on a case-by-case basis. For many teenagers, "sex with an adult can be a beautiful experience. It was for me" (p. 59). They are mentors; they are more likely to practice safe sex; they introduce boys to the gay world, to gay culture; and they can literally keep them from becoming "a suicide statistic" (p. 91). Intergenerational sex "saved my life," he informs his readers. Who among us can argue with that? Well, some would.

"Cultural shifts of the past decade," says Read, "have helped to demystify homosexuality. . . . The boys I passed on my way to the cafeteria don't call me faggot anymore." When he returns to his home town, he and the straight guys he grew up with, the guys who used to taunt and bully him, "buy each other conciliatory pitchers of beer. They shake my hand too hard and ask me to tell exotic stories of life beyond the county line. . . . They ask me what it was like to walk the halls alone, with all those people screaming all those years ago." Instead of insults, he says, now "we call each other by name" (p. 228): *Ain't life grand? And aren't you glad you met me? I'm not so bad, and I'm not really so different from the next guy.* After reading *How I Learned to Snap,* the reader feels like embracing Kirk Read.

Accounting for Sexual Transgressions

What do our sexual memoirs have in common? Where do they diverge? None of our transgressive authors cite victims, deserving or otherwise—Polanski explicitly denies Samantha Gailey's victimhood—and only Kerry Cohen excuses her behavior by invoking forces beyond her control. Hemingway externalizes his behavior ("the other thing started again") and, though he is certainly aware he is hurting his wife, he blames others for his transgressions—specifically, the "pilot fish"; the rich; his wife, Pauline; the beautiful women themselves. As for him, he seems more victim than victimizer. Dishonest writing, almost certainly, but grist for the student of deviance neutralization. Hem's justifications represent an atypical example of excusing that we find in the literature, a true "billiard ball" portrait of this powerful and importunate writer. His only transcending commitments were to his own lust. He does not "normalize" exactly, because he does not want either Hadley or Pauline to do what he did. But he did what he did and portrays himself as much like a loyal bird dog in committing the act. Nobody honors the account, and Alfred Kazin feels that in making this argument, Hemingway's literature suffered.

Hemingway has much in common with Roman Polanski in the self-serving justifications he employs. Roman's arsenal of justifications is myriad but not formidable. Readers have to keep reminding themselves that Polanski is deviance-neutralizing having sex with a *thirteen-year-old.* Everyone wants to do it. She was sexually experienced. She looked eighteen. She posed nude, displaying herself before teenage boys twenty or thirty yards away. She had drunk alcohol, taken Quaaludes. She was willing, her mother practically threw the girl in his company. "What else could I do?" he seems to be saying to us, as does Hemingway. And Polanski's account virtually cries out for deviance neutralization. Indeed, the act and the account dovetail with one another the reader regards them as organically intertwined like the tendrils of a creeping plant. Polanski, like Hemingway, feels he should not be blamed or condemned for the act, yet both felt the overwhelming and urgent passion to do what they did. No apology, really; no excuses, exactly. This is simply what a man does. One might also cite the privilege of celebrity.

What Kirk Read did is *not* what a manly man does, and yet his narrative jibes perfectly with all the accounts in this book. Kirk follows his destiny, not his lust. He knows he is different, yet he strives to find common ground with his reader. Most triumphalist narratives offer a triumphalist dynamic—I overcame a deficiency, a disability, a weakness, a shortcoming, and now I am a much better person for it. Read does not follow this formula: He is the same person in the end as he was in the beginning. But he knows his audience; they are either gay or belong to a liberal, anti-homophobia crowd. They love rebellion against authority, and they love unconventionality in measured doses. Kirk fights, he gets drunk and vomits, he loves rock and roll, and he loves his neighbors. Hardly anybody questions Read's right to pen his memoir and to justify his behavior, which *calls forth* a specific kind of explanation of the author's sexuality. Like Hemingway and Polanski, Read is asking us, "What else could I have done?" but we "buy" or honor Read's vocabulary of motives, but not Hem's and not Roman's. Readers feel privileged to have known Kirk Read and delighted that he shared his life with us.

Reading Kerry Cohen's *Loose Girl* and Chelsea Hander's *Horizontal Life* side by side, we are forcefully reminded that neutralizations come in all colors. Cohen makes us believe that she was in the grip of a compulsion that she overcame; it is a transformative narrative that helps us see the deviance in sexual promiscuity and the apology that some girls advance to reduce it. At the same time, Handler pulls off the opposite device; she does not regard sleeping around as deviant or blameworthy or sordid or in the least bit wrong. In fact, she makes extensive use of humor to portray her promiscuity as something of a lark, an adventure, a romp through beds bristling with erect penises and orgasm-laden experiences. What's wrong with that? Nothing, apparently, as Chelsea Handler sees it, and so too does her reader. There is no transformation here; like Read, she is the same person in the end as at the beginning. And why not? Handler goes a long way in *normalizing* what some of us might regard as one sexual transgression after another. She does not apologize, she does not excuse, but we know she does what is right for her.

Melissa Febos is in Handler's camp: She makes what she does seem virtually normal. *She* seems so normal. What she does does not seem all that bizarre. Different, yes, kinky, maybe, but her clients seem conventional, and *in context*—in the parlors and studios where it takes place—their behavior seems inoffensive. Yes, they did sordid, squalid things, but she seems in control, surfing on the waves of their turmoil as they churn and squirm. Her sexuality seems intact, she got what she wanted out of it, she went on to college, to other occupational horizons, and gathered material for a book, and, somehow, it all ends up in such a natural place—different, unconventional, non-mainstream, certainly, but not *dreadfully* deviant.

7
Political Deviance

ODDS ARE that a randomly chosen infant born into an American family will grow up to hold political views that more or less fit into the ideological mainstream: a not-too-strongly committed Democrat or Republican, a liberal, a middle-of-the-roader, or a conservative—somewhere along that spectrum. But if we turn our attention to the statistical minority, the "tails" that trail off at both ends of that continuum, we will find ideologies that convention regards as unacceptable, wrongheaded, even harmful. When members of the society radically or sharply depart from the hump of the normal curve, the interested observer is likely to ask what *explains* this deviation: How did these people come to adopt such ideologically off-center views? And when they interact with persons outside their ideological circles, they are likely to be called upon to *account* for their unconventional politics. Following the paradigm I have spelled out here, such a question typically prompts these ideological outliers to render accounts of such dissenting views; a few will even write their memoirs, contextualizing, justifying, and exculpating their non-mainstream political philosophies, attempting to render such views more reasonable, more veracious, and more ineluctable than others consider them to be. But as we already know, *difference* is not the only, or even an essential, ingredient in *deviance.*

By "political deviance," let us be clear: I do not refer to corruption or other malfeasances by politicians, and I do not mean that *defining* deviance is a political and ideological issue (Ben-Yehuda, 1990; Hendershott, 2002) or that *the way deviance is defined* has important political implications—all quite clearly and self-evidently true. What I am interested in here is that among members of certain categories, groups, and social circles, specific political and ideological positions and actions are regarded as wrong, fallacious, spurious, specious, unsound—the cause for condemnation and punishment of said believers and actors. People treated as political deviants believe that the ideological cause in which they believe is right and that persons who strongly disagree with them are wrong.

Deviance constitutes, let us recall, anything that relevant audiences are inclined to condemn. Politics are always contentious. By their very nature, advocates of differing sides of an argument consider the other position unsustainable or at least arguable; they regard the opposite posture as wrong, ontologically unacceptable, and possibly deviant. And the more the opposite side departs from one's views, the more unacceptable it seems. But let us be clear on this: Political views and programs are "deviant" to the extent that *they offend specific audiences*—one or more designated social collectivities—not because they are abstractly "bad," wrong in some absolute or factual sense. Hence, one's ideology need not necessarily even veer off the mainstream political charts, though that helps; they need only violate the stance of members of particular social circles—which *themselves* may be seen as deviant by the mainstream. As a consequence, the politics of a mainstream liberal *or* a conservative may be seen as objectionable or unwelcome at a convention of revolutionaries. Of course, holders of mainstream views are not called upon to justify their politics to the extent that ideological outliers are. Let us keep in mind that when we refer to a particular figure as a political deviant, we do not oppose *or* take the side of the person so named—but we do recognize that he or she has attracted condemnation, antagonism, hostility, and denunciation from critics, often the regime in power. This "deviantization" is an established fact, and we are interested in how the person so named addresses or answers the charge of political incorrectness.

Political deviants may be rulers, their opponents, or just ordinary citizens—anyone who thinks about, expresses, or acts on civil or ideological issues. The ruling Athenians considered the views of Socrates (469–399 B.C.E.) so heretical that the judgment forced him to commit suicide. In 44 B.C.E., Julius Caesar's fellow Roman senators assassinated him because they believed he had become tyrannical. The subversive teaching of Jesus (first century), a Jewish teacher and prophet, attracted the condemnation of, and execution by, the ruling Roman authorities. Joseph Stalin (1879–1953), one of the most anathemized figures in human history, was a mastermind of Bolshevism; a patriarch of the Russian Revolution (1917); premier of the Soviet Union (1941–1953); liquidator of the opponents of his programs; and responsible for the starvation, massacre, torture, imprisonment, and exile of tens of millions of kulaks, Poles, intellectuals, counterrevolutionaries, religionists, political dissidents and opponents, and ordinary citizens who inadvertently got caught up in the bureaucracy of tyranny and state terror. Adolf Hitler (1889–1945), deservedly the most reviled man on Earth, led a monstrous regime that murdered millions of innocent victims and launched the most ruinous and destructive war in human history; his high command attempted, but somehow failed, to assassinate him. Jacobo Timerman (1923–1999) was an Argentine journalist who criticized his country's military regime and the "dirty war" it waged against its opponents and citizens and was jailed and tortured for his dissidence. Ayaan Hirsi Ali (b. 1969), by birth a Somali Muslim, fled to the Netherlands to escape a forced marriage, becoming a feminist who rejected and denounced Islam and attracted hostility and death threats from devout Muslims. The list of possible candidates of political and ideological deviants is multitudinous.

Recall that we are looking at behavior and neutralizations that form a conceptually coherent and understandable category and so, for this book, we are limiting our candidates to Americans born during the twentieth century. Hence, some of the interesting cases we might think of, such as the ones I just mentioned, are excluded—some did not write memoirs (or ones that survived), some lived in earlier centuries, and none were Americans. But even many American candidates did not commit their narratives to paper (or, if they did, the document has not survived): Aaron Burr (1756–1836), Thomas Jefferson's vice president, whom both Jefferson and Alexander Hamilton accused of treason but was acquitted of the charge in court and who killed Hamilton in a duel in 1804; John Brown (1800–1859), a revolutionary abolitionist of slavery; Cochise (1815–1874), Geronimo (1829–1909), Sitting Bull (1831–1890), and Crazy Horse (1840–1877), American Indian warriors who fought against European American settlement; John Wilkes Booth (1838–1865), assassin of President Abraham Lincoln; and Iva Toguri D'Aquino (1916–2006), one of several Japanese American women dubbed "Tokyo Rose," who was convicted of treason following World War II and pardoned by President Gerald Ford in 1977. The mind reels and staggers when conjuring up what Aaron Burr, John Brown, Sitting Bull, John Wilkes Booth, or Iva Toguri would have said in their reflections and recollections of their lives and views. If only every interesting personage who ever lived wrote a memoir!

Almost by definition, authors who address political issues in the form of accounts feel that they need to convince the reader that they are responsible for their actions and, if wrong, consider justifications a crucial armament in their ideological arsenal. Excuses are mitigating or extenuating circumstances that led the actor astray. To excuse one's political actions or position would mean that one is something of a dupe, a sucker—that one has been bamboozled and hoodwinked. "I may have made a mistake," the actor tells the reader, "but I'm nobody's fool." An excuse denies responsibility, and it is the task of political actors to convince others that they are, above all, responsible, even if they make mistakes. It is not so much that political deviants do not excuse their mistakes—they do—it is that they rarely if ever *admit* to making excuses; they would say that they were misled by the circumstance of unusual and difficult times. It seemed like a very good idea at the time, say Elia Kazan, Malcolm X, Norman Podhoretz, and Cathy Wilkerson about their earlier ideological incarnations. Things were the way they were, I had my feet on the ground, and we still have to be vigilant, they would say now, or at the end of their lives. Here we examine two memoirs by radical authors whose views in the 1960s truly were off the charts and two by authors whose views grew to be more or less mainstream but *at one time* so offended left-wingers that they were *anathemized* or "deviantized" among them in very specific, concrete, face-to-face ways.

Elia Kazan, "I Was Notorious, an Informant, a Squealer, a Rat"

Elia Kazan (neé Kazanjioglu) was born in Constantinople (later to become Istanbul), in the Ottoman Empire, to Anatolian Greek parents who immigrated to the United States when he was four. Here, his father earned a living as a rug merchant. Young Elia excelled academically, attending Williams College and the Yale Drama School. He began working as an actor but soon found his métier in directing, initially in the theater and later in film. His plays and movies usually center on progressive, liberal themes, taking on major issues such as anti-Semitism, racism, the exploitation of workers, alienation, conformity, revolution, intergenerational conflict, political corruption, and injustice. In 1934, disgusted by the injustices of the society, Kazan joined the Communist Party of America, which he and many other artists and intellectuals in the 1930s believed embodied a progressive political philosophy and agenda. The appeal of the Party was understandable; it offered idealism—the promise of a world cleansed of war, racism, class inequality, exploitation, and oppression. But during the late 1930s, the ugly, brutal reality of Soviet-style communism became increasingly apparent in the West, and so intellectuals, writers, artists, and activists who once found communism appealing came to regret their political naïveté and resigned from the American Communist Party. Unfolding events soured all but the most dogmatic of communist supporters, and Kazan, disillusioned by the Party's rigid, authoritarian program, resigned in 1936. To him and other progressives at the time, communism was "the god that failed" (Crossman, 1952). Still, many former communists retained a sense of loyalty to their friends and to their own idealism.

Elia Kazan (nicknamed "Gadge"—for "Gadget"—for his usefulness to the people around him) was the most successful film director of his generation, and he worked with some of the most renowned actors of all time, including Marlon Brando, James Dean, Rod Steiger, Karl Malden, Richard Widmark, Montgomery Clift, Warren Beatty, and Natalie Wood, directing now classic films, such as *Gentlemen's Agreement* (1949), *A Streetcar Named Desire* (1952), *Viva Zapata!* (1953), *On the Waterfront* (1954), *East of Eden* (1955), *Rebel without a Cause* (1955), and *Splendor in the Grass* (1961), which garnered a total of twenty Academy Awards.

In postwar America, McCarthyism reared its ugly head, and increasingly witch-hunts rooted out communists and ex-communists, eliminating them from jobs and positions of authority. Early one afternoon in 1952, a man came to Kazan's house and took a pink sheet out of an envelope and handed it to him. It was a subpoena; in a lowered voice, the man told him that the session would be secret. "You don't tell anyone, we don't tell anyone. We expect you to be a cooperative witness." Kazan had been called before the House Un-American Activities Committee (HUAC) to appear in chambers in Washington and questioned about his associates in the Communist Party. That night, he said, he was unable to sleep (1997, p. 443).

On the morning of January 14, 1952, Kazan took his seat and awaited the questioning. He planned to tell the committee that he had been a Communist Party member for a year and a half and had quit in disgust, that the Party had tried to take over the Group Theater and failed, and that it was unable to influence the direction and program of the theater company. He knew that the members of HUAC would ask him to name the names of the others who were in his "cell," and he resolved to refuse to answer the question. Before the committee opened its session, Raphael Nixon, the director of research for HUAC, conducted a chatty-seeming conversation with Kazan in his office. Nixon "seemed anxious to have me believe that the committee was not out to destroy individuals." He said that members were "particularly sensitive" to the criticism that they "smeared people and ruined lives" (p. 445). When Nixon began pressing him for specific names, Kazan answered that he was eager to cooperate with the committee in every way about himself, but he would not discuss particulars about anyone else. Nixon asked Kazan to reconsider the matter and handed him a copy of the testimony of several other witnesses who had been cooperative.

After lunch and before the members of the committee—who continued to walk in and out, attending to other matters during the session—Nixon began questioning Kazan in detail. Was the Group Theater a communist front organization? Who had recruited him? Was John Garfield, a well-known stage and film actor of the 1930s and 1940s, a member? How about Clifford Odets, a playwright and 1930s and 1940s radical? At some point, Representative Bernard Kearny of New York "urged me to give the committed the names of other Party members in the Group Theater" (p. 447). Kazan refused, saying that Jack Warner, head of Warner Brothers, had already refused to name names, and Warner would cancel any film Kazan might be preparing for (p. 447). "I concluded that what these fellows were conducting was a degradation ceremony, in which the acts of informing were more important than the information conveyed. I didn't doubt they knew all the names they were asking about" (p. 447). At the end of the session, Kazan realized that he was going to be called back before the committee.

During his next session, Kazan began regarding the members of the committee as vainglorious and sadistic, motivated by political opportunism and the lust to advance their careers rather than seeking the truth. At the same time, he also believed the Communist Party to be a "thoroughly organized, worldwide conspiracy" (p. 449). Kazan was caught in a trap, a painful dilemma: On the one hand, he did not want to cooperate with the committee; on the other, he did not want to support the Party by remaining silent.

It turns out that HUAC had leaked the substance of Kazan's sessions all over Los Angeles; his refusal to cooperate was public knowledge. Darryl Zanuck, a major Hollywood producer, urged him to cooperate. "Name the names, for chrissake. Who the hell are you going to jail for? You will be sitting there and someone else will sure as hell name those people. Who are you saving?" (p. 455). At the same time, Kazan was seething with resentment for the crimes that Party members had gotten away with and resentful of the irony that when crusaders revealed these crimes, it was they, not the perpetrators, who were excoriated; they would be accused of "red-baiting." The Party should be "driven out of its many hiding places and into the light of scrutiny," he believed. Would naming who had been Party members with him not "clear the air" about this whole business? Kazan was suddenly struck by the rationalizations he had lived by since quitting the Party in "going along" with its sins, in remaining silent about its truly evil deeds. The truly horrible thing I did, he tells us, was condone his former comrades for holding the Soviets blameless for their crimes for all those years. "Reader," Kazan says, grabbing us by our lapels, "if you expect an apology now because I would later name names to the House Committee, you've misjudged my character" (1997, p. 460). Still adrift on the matter, he sought out the advice of some of his friends. "I'd hated the Communists for many years and did not feel right about giving up my career to defend them" (p. 460). But Arthur Miller, a respected playwright and a former close friend, snubbed Kazan on the street; an actor, Curt

Conway, whom he was about to greet, "suddenly crossed the street away from" him; a secretary who had worked for him for years quit and began working for another director; at a meeting with Kazan, Lillian Hellman, an important writer at the time, "was silent as a coiled snake" and suddenly walked out on him (p. 461). Later he found out that Hellman's diagnosis of Kazan's revelations was simple: "He sold out! He did it for the money!" (p. 462). He felt his motives, however complex, were to do the right thing. At the same time, he says, he "felt like a pariah" (p. 463); among his peers, Kazan had become *deviantized.*

Kazan told his wife, Molly, that he was going to write out the whole story of his involvement with the Communist Party, and he would name the other eight members of his group. He went to Washington and "turned in" his statement. Now, he says, there came "a storm of anger against" him; his friends expressed "sickhearted disappointment." He was, he says, "being unfairly reviled" (p. 464). He asked Molly to write out a position paper for him, expressing his motivation for why he did what he did. They bought space in *The New York Times* and published Molly's statement. "But it didn't change anyone's view of what I'd done. Instead of understanding, it brought me scorn and hardened the antagonism. I soon became the target of a well-organized campaign branding my act as shameful" (p. 465). To some extent, Kazan says, in some quarters, this feeling persists. Because of his ambivalence, he was consumed by guilt; what he did was "correct," but was it "right"? He was not sure.

Kazan received an avalanche of mail, mostly hostile. One letter said that the majority of the people in the Actor's Studio "were thoroughly sickened and upset by your testimony. . . . You slammed the door on some decent people whose only crime is that they think differently from you" (p. 467). *The Daily Worker,* a mouthpiece of the American Communist Party, said, "It is the lowest moment in Kazan's life, one which will haunt him forever" (p. 469). Marlon Brando asked himself, "What am I going to do when I see the man next? Punch him in the nose" (pp. 470–471). Later, Brando made *On the Waterfront* (1954), apparently without punching Kazan in the nose. Still, Kazan stuck to his guns. He says he did not really understand the "intensity" of his guilt in the eyes of his peers. "I believed then and do now that the Communists should not be in positions of control in communications" (p. 469). Kazan's self-justification is simple: *I'm right and my critics are wrong,* a neutralization technique that carried him through fifty years of denunciation and excoriation. *Informing on my peers is customarily wrong, but it's not wrong in this case, because it serves a greater good. It's not really ratting because the authorities already know the names of persons named as communists.* Hence, it is a case of deviance neutralization by means of *exceptionalization.* It is also an *appeal to higher loyalties*—doing what is right, in Kazan's mind.

At the end of *A Life,* perhaps to offset potential hostile feelings that reading it might foment, Kazan directly addresses the reader. "I imagine that, from time to time, you've thought my book unfair, ugly, and hateful. . . . I'm happy—on the whole . . . [and] while I'm no longer treacherous, life is. . . . And if I were lucky enough to have a visit from the good fairy and she offered me three wishes, I'd . . . say 'I have everything I want now,' refuse the treasures I once craved, and ask for only one thing—more years" (pp. 820, 825). Kazan's defense is straightforward: *I didn't hurt anyone; I'm on the side of truth; the cause I denounced was evil; I'm being unfairly persecuted; and you, my reader, have no right to join this screeching chorus.* As he takes us, his readers, into his intimate embrace, we feel more positive about the principled position he took and less positive about his detractors. *A Life* is likely to be considered successful both as a memoir and, even for leftists, an appropriate apologia for his controversial behavior.

Norman Podhoretz, "The Theory Circulated That I Had Gone Mad"

Like Kazan and Malcolm—and St. Augustine—Podhoretz had a conversion experience, and it was that conversion that made a certain circle consider him deviant. And like Kazan, Malcolm, and Augustine, his task is not simply to defend the position he now holds, but to defend that position while explaining how, in the past, he came to his previous, erroneous one. What was Podhoretz's political sin? What made him infamous—a *deviant,* a persona non grata, rejected, shunned, and beyond the pale—specifically among his crowd, the denizens of New York intellectual circles during the 1960s and '70s? And how does he justify his putatively reprehensible behavior? In a phrase, according to his former friends, his sin was *ideological apostasy,* and the explanations and justifications he offers to account for it, and his consequent break with his once close friends, are instructive. Forty or more years ago, Podhoretz traveled in liberal, even radical ideological crowds. But at some point during this period, his position shifted from left-wing to right-wing or conservative—or "neo-con," as his stance came to be known. In short, Norman Podhoretz became a renegade, a turncoat, a defector—a deserter from all that was regarded, *among* members of the social collectivities in which he formerly navigated, as decent, sane, honorable, and moral. What made it even worse, he tells us, is that his desertion stretched far beyond politics. His circle of intellectual friends constituted a "family," a close-knit social group that would often meet at parties and dinners and passionately discuss political and ideologically tinged personal matters. After the break, some of these friends cut him off—perhaps, he says, it would be more accurate to say they "excommunicated" him—while others he cut off or let drift away (2000, p. 3). The result was the same: Over the years that followed, Norman Podhoretz "managed to lose or throw away" dozens of close friendships with "famous people" whose company he had once valued (p. 2). He attacked them in the pages of *Commentary* and in his memoirs—and they in turn attacked him in their writings. The breach with all of them was final and irreconcilable.

Podhoretz's justification for rejecting the radical ideology of the New York intellectual crowd, thereby causing a sharp break with his radical friends—who would subsequently become his "ex-friends" (2000)—is that their politics were indefensible and unsupportable. Podhoretz's justification is that he was right and they were wrong. "I could do no other," he seems to be saying; "my conscience dictated that I do as I did." He had finally, he explains, come to his senses "after more than a decade of experimenting with radical ideas that were proving dangerous to me and destructive to America, not to mention the threat that they posed to my children, and everyone else's as well." As soon as he realized that he "fully intended to carry on with the war I had started against those ideas," he dropped "the exculpatory explanation" for his apostasy (p. 3). Perhaps the central notion that tied his leftist eventually-to-be ex-friends was their "fierce hatred of America," which Podhoretz felt was a potentially fatal ideological position. And the glue of his memoirs—that is, his justifications, his arguments that he was right and his left-wing former friends were wrong—was *precisely* self-exculpation; it warranted what he did.

Dear reader, Podhoretz seems to be asking us, *how could I have done otherwise? What would* you *have done? Sacrifice your ideology?* he asks us. *At what cost? Consider my roster of irresponsible, wrongheaded ideological nitwits,* he seems to be saying. *Consider their positions, consider the* implications *of what they were saying, consider the fact that they placed the very lives of my* children*—indeed, the lives of every one of us—in their irresponsible hands. What would have happened had their politics held sway over our precious society?*

Consider his breaks with Allen Ginsberg, Lillian Hellman, Hannah Arendt, and Norman Mailer. In an age of AIDS, when most of us are now alert to sexual risk and the need to practice safe sex, we are likely to find Ginsberg's encouragement of oral and anal promiscuity irresponsible, reckless, suicidal, perhaps even homicidal. In the face of the revelations of Soviet mass murder, which she swept under the rug years after the facts were known, today, virtually no one can side with Hellman's endorsement of Stalin's policies and programs. Hannah Arendt, who in face-to-face encounters with Podhoretz seemed respectful, even affectionate, spoke ill of him behind his back. It was Hannah Arendt who argued that, during the Holocaust, Jews went to their deaths like sheep, thereby serving as accomplices to evil. It was

Hannah Arendt who argued that without Jewish cooperation, the Nazis would not have been able to murder six million Jews. Dismayed, Podhoretz annihilated Arendt's argument point by point, and when she asked Norman why he wrote the article refuting hers, he replied that he did it out of a sense of "duty" (p. 170). Her condescending smile said it all, and matters between them "were never the same again" (p. 173). As for Norman Mailer's macho pronouncements, the best that can be said is that, in an era when women are considered the equal of men, such posturing has fallen out of favor. Podhoretz found Mailer's wild promiscuity ("both in and between marriages"), his stabbing of his wife Adele, his "constant proselytizing for marijuana" (p. 195), his defense of hoodlums who had murdered an elderly store clerk—these delinquents, Mailer said, should be admired for "daring the unknown" (p. 187)—*repugnant.*

And so it goes: one writer after another, Podhoretz's annihilation of one intellectual folly after another. My position is reasonable, he tells us; theirs is not—hence, my apostasy. I am being anathemized for doing the right thing. Why should I have to neutralize the putative deviance of my politics? They are in the wrong, not I. Who could argue with that? Podhoretz is right, his readers tell themselves; he *did* do the right thing. His detractors *do* seem self-righteous, sanctimonious, and wrong-headed, and in our eyes, *Ex-Friends* valorizes the author's position. But however righteous we might regard the author's convictions, as I have conceptualized the term, Podhoretz *was* a deviant in the eyes of his radical detractors and former friends, and so he felt called upon to defend his position against their charges in his memoirs by engaging in deviance neutralization—more specifically, *normalization.*

As Sigmund Freud famously said, sometimes a cigar is just a cigar, but politics are rarely "just" politics. In a review of *Ex-Friends,* the writer Nicholas Lemann (1999) insists that more than "intellectuals differing over politics" is woven into the book. According to Lemann, Podhoretz—whom he refers to as "the outcast"—possesses a "quite common" pairing of human qualities that causes someone to attack others: hypercriticality combined with hypersensitivity. "Read carefully in the ex-friendships and you often find that what turned things sour was that the other person criticized Podhoretz in a way that he found mystifyingly unjustified and that deeply, permanently wounded him" (Podhoretz, 2000, p. 38). Lionel Trilling, one of Podhoretz's Columbia professors, and Lionel's wife, Diana, urged him not to publish what became his first book, *Making It!* (1967); Hannah Arendt, a highly respected intellectual, also did not like the book; and Norman Mailer, who told Podhoretz he liked it, turned two-faced and trashed it in a review in *Partisan Review.* Justification enough for friends to fall out with one another? Perhaps, but in order to defend oneself from all of this brittle and prickly verbiage, one needs to neutralize attacks on one's ideology—which was precisely Podhoretz's mission in *Breaking Ranks* (1979) and *Ex-Friends* (2000), and one of the many reasons that makes searching out vocabularies of motive such an illuminating exercise.

Malcolm X, "I Never Have Felt That I Would Live to Become an Old Man"

Ironically, though the positions of Elia Kazan and Malcolm X occupy virtually opposite sides of the ideological spectrum, these figures structure their arguments in a virtually identical fashion. Kazan's early membership in and tolerance of communism was deviant to the society as a whole, but within the context of leftist American intellectuals and artists, it was entirely *conventional* and *conformist.* In a way, Malcolm's two earlier incarnations were much the same. His behavior as a street hustler was in agreement with the mini-society that accepted him as a fellow among the clan of street hustlers—good at what he did, cool, sharp, manly, and centered. *In that context,* he was not deviant, though, as with Kazan, he certainly was to the American society at large. After Malcolm's jailhouse conversion, he found himself in much the same circumstance: *To Black Muslims,* he was a brother, he had found the path of truth, righteousness, and honor—he was a man of dignity who brought other men dignity. Both Kazan and Malcolm would have said that at Time 1 (or, for Malcolm, Times 1 and 2), they were *not* deviant among their peers, but at the time of writing their autobiographies, *they were wrong then.* Both fit into their own environments (and were therefore not deviant), *but in the assessment of their lives,* they had come onto a position they now assessed as invalid. In the here and now of their memoirs, in the light of assessing and looking back on their tumultuous lives, they were able to say that their former peers would have considered them deviant, but they *now* regarded their final political positions as correct. And both offer justifications that invoke righteousness and appeal to a higher, transcending commitments or duty. Before, among my crowd, I was conformist but wrong, and now, *to that same crowd,* I am deviant—but I know I am right.

At first glance, *The Autobiography of Malcolm X* (with Alex Haley, 1965) offers itself up as a narrative fairly bursting with self-exculpation. Malcolm *excuses* and *exceptionalizes* his criminal past as a product of his race and background, *justifies* and *normalizes* his black nationalist phase during his Nation of Islam (NOI) tenure, and, just before his death, leaves the picture open to multiple interpretations. Yet Malcolm X, born Malcolm Little, eventually transmogrifying into El-Hajj Malik El-Shabazz, defies simple characterization. Michael Eric Dyson (1996) compares Malcolm X's *Autobiography* to Augustine's *Confessions* in that both reveal an early life of sinful hedonism, the reevaluation of which led to a spiritual conversion. Actually, Dyson goes on to say, the myth that Malcolm's life most resembles is the tale of Icarus—a man in Greek mythology whose father devised wings made of wax and who flew too close to the sun, causing the wax to melt and him to plummet to earth to his death. (Chapter 15 of Malcolm's autobiography, entitled "Icarus," bespeaks the reminder Malcolm made to himself not to make the same mistake.) *The Autobiography* has achieved something of the same mythical status as the Greek tale, and Malcolm, the man, that of an icon. The force of Malcolm X's vision, filtered through a blend of his own words and those of his amanuensis, Alex Haley, is such that his ideology seems almost preordained, his destiny, so to speak, forced upon him by circumstance—that is, the implacable reality of American racism—rendering deviance neutralization almost superfluous. Although Alex Haley's fashioning of *The Autobiography* attracted criticism, a comparison of its voice and the one that emanates from Malcolm's speeches (Breitman, 1966) indicates that this document is the opposite of the ghost-written memoir—in richness, detail, originality, uniqueness, and individual integrity.

It is well known that Malcolm exaggerated his criminal past to make his conversion to the Nation of Islam seem sufficiently remarkable as to provide an object lesson for criminals and other street people. Moreover, Alex Haley smoothed over the disjunction between Malcolm's separatism and Martin Luther King's integrationism and eliminated the anti-Semitic references in the original manuscript, making the book "palatable for latte-leftist audiences" (Biddle, 2011). *The Autobiography of Malcolm X* may be as much fiction as autobiography, though the man grew into the portrait Alex Haley shaped, both in mythology and reality. Virtually everything about Malcolm X and his autobiography was remarkable.

Malcolm Little was born in 1925 in Omaha, Nebraska; his parents eventually had seven children, and his father already had three by a previous marriage. His father, an outspoken supporter of Marcus Garvey, was an early advocate of black pride and self-reliance. Because of Ku Klux Klan threats, his family relocated to Lansing, Michigan, where, again, the family incurred the wrath of white supremacists. Early in Malcolm's teenage years, his mother experienced a mental breakdown and was institutionalized in a mental hospital; the minor siblings were dispersed among a number of foster homes. An eighth-grade teacher told Malcolm that becoming a lawyer was not a realistic aspiration for a "nigger," and he dropped out of school. "I drew away from white people," he said (1964/1999, p. 38). Several years later, Malcolm lived with his half-sister in Boston; he worked at a variety of short-term jobs, including selling sandwiches on a railroad car, washing dishes, and shining shoes. In 1943, when a local draft board interviewed him, he put on an act of insanity and was ruled unfit for military service. By now, Malcolm was wearing a zoot suit and orange shoes and had begun "conking," or straightening his hair with lye. Commenting in *The Autobiography* on his appearance, Malcolm says, "How ridiculous I was! Stupid enough to stand there simply lost in admiration of my hair now looking 'white.' . . . This was my first really big step toward self-degradation" (1964/1999, p. 56). In his late teens, he got drawn into street crime—selling marijuana cigarettes and stolen goods; steering men to prostitutes; committing burglary, and, eventually, armed robbery. Along with his friend Shorty and their two female accomplices, Malcolm was apprehended for a burglary and received a ten-year sentence—the judge, it seemed, was more outraged at the two black men consorting with white women than at their crime of burglary—of which he served seven years.

In prison, his brother Reginald encouraged Malcolm to adopt the teachings of the NOI, which he did, after writing to Elijah Muhammad; in 1950, he adopted the name Malcolm X. In 1952, upon his release from prison, he visited Muhammad in Chicago and was appointed assistant minister of Temple Number One in Detroit. Malcolm X expanded or established more than a half-dozen temples and quickly rose in the NOI's hierarchy, attracting considerable attention and media publicity, not to mention hostility from the mainstream press and much of the public. In December 1963, Malcolm X was asked about the assassination of President John F. Kennedy, which had occurred several days before; he said it was a case of "chickens coming home to roost," which generated considerable uproar among whites as well as among the leadership of the NOI, which had already sent the Kennedy family condolences. Malcolm X was banned from public speaking for three months. His shock at Muhammad's extramarital sexual relations with his secretaries had already alienated him from the NOI's leadership; in turn, Elijah Muhammad had become increasingly jealous of the attention Malcolm received at his expense. Three months later, Malcolm X announced that he was stepping down from his position at the NOI and establishing his own black nationalist organization in order to work for civil rights. Malcolm converted to orthodox Sunni Islam, and in April he made a pilgrimage (or "hajj") to Mecca, where he realized for the first time that Muslims came in all colors and races.

His itinerary throughout 1964 was crowded with speaking engagements all over the world, and during that year evidence emerged of assassination plots by the NOI against Malcolm, and members released statements through its newspaper *Muhammad Speaks* that "hypocrites like Malcolm should have their heads cut off" (Louis X, later Louis Farrakhan), that "anyone who opposes the Honorable Elijah Mohammad puts his life in jeopardy" (John Ali), and that "such a man as Malcolm is worthy of death" (Louis X). In June

1964, the NOI sued Malcolm X to reclaim his residence; the lawsuit was successful, and on February 14, 1965, the house was burned to the ground. On February 21, as Malcolm stood on the stage of the Audubon Ballroom getting ready to speak before the Organization of Afro-American Unity, a scuffle in the audience broke out. At that moment, a man rushed onto the stage and shot Malcolm in the chest with a sawed-off shotgun; then two men shot him sixteen times with handguns. All three assailants were convicted of the murder.

Who was Malcolm X's audience? To whom was *The Autobiography*'s message addressed? During the late 1960s, several students complained to me that several instructors, including myself, had assigned some or all of *The Autobiography* in their courses. Could Malcolm have foreseen that more than half of his readership would be white? *And* that his ideology would be more or less comfortably incorporated into theirs? Probably not, but Alex Haley, his scribe and editor, almost certainly had. He predicted to his editor that the book would "sweep the market like wildfire," that it was "pregnant" with "millions or more [in] sales potential" (Marable, 2011, pp. 331–332). Both Malcolm and Haley recognized the same dilemma—the same balancing act—that all unconventional authors face: The shock, the sting, the surprise of a heretical message should be just so great as to thrill, intrigue, and titillate—but not so overpowering that it offends, outrages, and alienates. And both surely knew that Malcolm's radical message would, statistically speaking, go down more easily with African Americans than with whites; though Malcolm could not have predicted the stupendous size of his white readership, Haley tailored the book as much for liberal and left-wing whites as for blacks. But many of the rhetorical justifications that *The Autobiography* harbors find a common racial ground between the two, such that both audiences see the moral of the tales the author told and recognize the author as more of a prophet than a hate-monger.

It is almost beside the point that many of the particulars laid down in Malcolm X's *Autobiography* were at variance with the literal facts of Malcolm X's life (Marable, 2011), not to mention that in crucial ways, Alex Haley transformed Malcolm's manuscript into a document less threatening than it originally was—as I said, Haley removed almost all the anti-Semitic statements he came across (still, throughout, Malcolm identifies specific Jewish persons as "the Jew" or "this Jew")—but in a very real sense, these transformations seem minor matters. Malcolm X's explanations for his multiple conversions transcend the routine boundaries of ordinary personal justification. He was on his way to a position he had not yet grown into. Given the transformations he had accomplished and his still evolving persona, Malcolm X was a protean character—he not only morphed into different personages; he meant all things to all people. Hence the inevitable question arises: *Which Malcolm X is the* Autobiography *justifying?*

The answer to this question is not straightforward; the best answer is that the man's life and identities are not disjunctive but flow from one to another in a continuous stream, with society changing as Malcolm changed. He uses observations he made during one stage to bolster insights he had in a later one. Consider the fact that his face adorns a thirty-three-cent U.S. Postal Service stamp—in the words of Ruby Dee, a friend and neighbor of Malcolm's, it is a case of "the radical gone respectable" (Shabazz, 1999, p. xii). Or consider the fact that *Time* magazine chose *The Autobiography* as one of the ten most important non-fiction books of the twentieth century. Consider the almost saintly, though conflicted and tortured, character of Malcolm that Spike Lee presented in his 1992 film *Malcolm X.* Not only was the Malcolm X who existed in what I simplistically refer to as "real life" very different from the Malcolm X who was born in the pages of his *Autobiography*; the man we see in the pages of his *Autobiography* is a very different man from the legend that Malcolm X has become. Still, *The Autobiography* is a document that yet lives, that people still read, talk about, and debate. It remains in print, has sold multiple millions of copies, and may yet sell millions more. It is a book for the ages, one worth discussing as a volume that makes use of a substantial number of deviance disavowal rationales.

Take the violent death of Malcolm's father, Earl Little Sr. in Lansing, Michigan, where Little lived. The community harbored an enclave of the Black Legion, the local equivalent of the Ku Klux Klan, who were violently anti-black, inflicting torture and beatings on "uppity" Negroes. Family lore has it that members of the Black Legion encountered Little, seized him, beat him senseless, dragged him into the street, and shoved him into the path of a trolley car, where he was cut in two. "Earl Little's possible murder may have served the same purpose that lynchings did in the South—to terrorize local blacks and suppress their acts of resistance" (Marable, 2011, p. 31). Events such as these seem almost mythically designed to generate rage in survivors—particularly a five-year-old child—not to mention a lust for revenge. The fact that one of Earl's insurance policies did not pay off, which multiplied a struggling widow's problems raising a poverty-stricken family, rubbed salt in the wound of grief. Throughout his life, in his speeches, and in his *Autobiography,* Malcolm X depicted his father's death as paradigmatic of white American racism and black victimization, and it was a goad to and a justification for his ideological position. *How can you condemn me for being a firebrand,* he seemed to be saying, *when my own father was murdered by racists?*

"The white man is the devil," said Reginald, his brother, as Malcolm sat in Norfolk Prison Colony, serving out a ten-year sentence for a burglary conviction he was convinced was motivated by a racist judge (Malcolm X, 1964/1999, p. 162). "Without any exception?" Malcolm asked. "Without any exception," his brother replied. In desperation, Malcolm searched through his mind in vain for even a single exception that would disprove the rule; Reginald swept away the single exception he managed to come up with. A stream of white faces marched before his mind's eye. The whites who had killed his father; those who called his mother "crazy," causing her to be committed to a mental institution; the judges who had broken up his family, sending him and his siblings to separate households; the teacher who told him to forget becoming a lawyer; his white girlfriends; the white women who wanted categorically to sleep with black men; the whites who slummed in Harlem for a little taste of black soul; the Boston cops; the Jewish merchants and jewelers by whom he believed he had been cheated; the white criminals he had known; the whites with kinky sexual tastes he had been hired to steer to locales where they could engage in appropriately twisted activities; the judge who had given him the ten years; the prisoners; the guards; the officials—he realized that all of them, without exception, were evil: "the devil" (pp. 162–163). Reginald's NOI-inspired claims—new to Malcolm early in his prison sentence—were beginning to make sense, and his later adherence to the racist claims of the Black Muslim faith, spelled out in *The Autobiography,* seemed unequivocally justified.

In a very real sense, Malcolm X's ideology feeds off both specific anecdotes and grand structural narrative, and they in turn justify the ideology. The components fit together like a well-constructed house. "In all my years in the streets," Malcolm X tells us, "I'd been looking at the exploitation that for the first time I really saw and understood. Now I watched brothers entwining themselves in the economic clutches of the white man who went home every night with another bag of the money drained out of the ghetto" (p. 197). In turn, the white man's bags of money supported a house in an expensive, exclusive enclave where the black man could not venture without being harassed, beaten, or chased out. Justification enough to buttress a black nationalist ideology.

The streets were full of "brainwashed brothers and sisters, drinking, cursing, fighting, dancing, carousing, and using dope—the very things that . . . were helping the black to stay under the heel of the white man here in America" (p. 199)—again, a declaration, if true, that both provides the components of a firebrand speech and justification for the overarching ideology that generates such a speech. We are "a thousand and one different colors," he commands an audience. "Turn around, *look* at each other! What shade of black African polluted by devil white man are you? You see me—in the streets they used to call me Detroit Red. Yes! Yes, that raping, red-headed devil was my *grandfather!* That close, yes! My *mother's* father!" (p. 206). These morality tales linking an evil past with a corrupt and demeaning present proved effective in transforming the consciousness of many young men trapped in unemployment, poverty, powerlessness, and confusion to a clearer notion of what their problems were and who was responsible for them—and provided Malcolm X with a vision as to how to shape his pitch, not to mention a justification for that vision. Many audiences found his reasoning enormously appealing, and it undergirds a major swath of his *Autobiography.* We also see a bit of self-mocking irony in his example, since, for him, at this time, all historical miscegenation was rape, yet during his street criminal phase, Malcolm dated several white women and recognized that for many black men, including himself, having sex with white women brought them respect and esteem, not to mention a thumb in the eye of the racist white man.

For Malcolm, slavery is the ultimate justification for his ideological position and for immunity against criticism and condemnation; it provided the cornerstone of black nationalist ideology. "*One hundred million* of us black people! Your grandparents! Mine! *Murdered* by this white man. To get fifteen million of us here to make us his slaves, on the way he murdered one hundred million!" (p. 216). Mankind has never seen, he declared, "such an orgy of greed and lust and murder" (p. 217). "Every time you see a white man, think about the devil you're seeing! Think of how it was on your slave foreparents' bloody, sweaty backs that he *built* this empire that's today the richest of all nations" (p. 217). The *torrent* of accusations, all containing at least a grain of truth, swept up supporters and bystanders alike in its force; factual corrections of niggling details seemed beside the point in those awesomely political, painfully violent times. Malcolm X's righteousness seemed justified by his invocation of the big picture, the historical record, entire institutions built from the ground up on the toxic sludge of racism.

One of the more effective rhetorical strategies Malcolm used in his *Autobiography,* not exactly a mea culpa but a contrivance very much like it, was his admission that he had been wrong about the evil of *every single white person.* This might not seem like much of a concession; after all, even the white racist admits that "some" black people are good and decent—or smart—human beings. But his implacability during his nationalist phase was so relentless that, having encountered its expression, the reader is likely to think that the author will never abandon it. During his pilgrimage, Malcolm encountered men with white skin—who would be regarded as "white" in the United States—who were devout Muslims, united in a brotherhood with all Muslims, and who treated him with enormous respect and decency. Islam is, he realized with shock, a *color-blind* religion, and Muslim societies, socially color-blind as well (p. 345). What he saw, what he experienced, forced him to "*toss aside*" many of his previously held beliefs and "re-arrange" his previously held thought patterns (p. 347). "In the past," he admits, describing his life soon after returning from his pilgrimage to Mecca and adopting the name El-Hajj Malik El-Shabazz, "I have made sweeping indictments of all white people. I will never be guilty of that again. . . . The true Islam has shown me that a blanket indictment of all white people is as wrong as when whites make blanket indictments against blacks" (p. 369). Again, the reader who has stuck by Malcolm through the four-hundred-page-plus experience of the many twists and turns of his behavioral and ideological odyssey is likely to think of him is a more favorable light after such a humbling admission. The fact that it is true increases the empathy factor. Who knows what sort of man he might have become? we think. The confession of this man, who was growing and reaching, yet cut down in the prime of his life, was but a hint of things to come.

In the end (1965), Malcolm comes off as no less a black nationalist than he had in his Minister Malcolm X phase, and no less anti-Semitic—"I know I'll hear 'anti-Semitic' from every direction. . . . But truth is truth" (p. 380), and the truth is that Malcolm is as unfairly derogatory toward Jews, applying a double standard to their behavior, as he had done earlier—and as much of an androcentrist, appropriate to his era and social circles, at the end of the book as in his young adulthood. But he was courageous almost beyond human comprehension; he spoke his mind; he genuinely believed what he said; and, more importantly, he genuinely believed that he was working for the betterment of African Americans. The United States is a racist society, he believed, and it visited iniquity on the body and soul of black folk; its very *system* of social control was based on injustice. But as Ossie Davis says in his eulogy, Malcolm changed the way black men saw themselves; he was a man who enabled black men to see themselves as men. His many apologies, justifications, self-exculpations, denunciations, twists and turns, and contradictions lay out a path that enable the reader who has followed him this far on his long and painful journey to cut the man some slack, withhold ultimate judgment, and abstain from condemning him, feeling, somehow, that he has played out his destiny on earth.

Cathy Wilkerson, "The Intention Was Not to Cause Carnage but Chaos"

On the morning of March 6, 1970, two stupendous explosions erupted in the subbasement of 18 West Eleventh Street, in Manhattan's Greenwich Village; two self-designated revolutionaries working on bombs accidentally detonated the dynamite in a metal pipe, which then touched off an additional bundle of dynamite sticks in a nearby box. Diana Oughton and Terry Robbins, the bomb makers, and Ted Gold, a comrade in a nearby room, were killed. Cathy Wilkerson, a member of the same group, was ironing bed sheets upstairs when a "shock wave shot through the house." The floor collapsed under her, and "a mountain of splintered wood and brick rose up" all around her (2007, p. 1). Cathy, her clothing in tatters, staggered through the dust and debris to find a way out. Kathy Boudin, who was taking a shower in a nearby room, heard her cries for help, and the two clasped hands, located an opening through which they could see daylight, and hand in hand stumbled out onto the sidewalk. Hands reached out of the dust and placed a jacket around Kathy's naked body, and a neighbor offered her apartment as temporary shelter. But knowing that the police would soon arrive, question them, and prosecute and imprison them for conspiring to produce bombs, they both fled and remained in hiding for years.

Cathy Wilkerson had been active in radical politics since the early 1960s and was arrested six times on charges ranging from distributing leaflets on private property without the owner's permission to rioting. During the course of the trial of several Black Panthers early in 1970, members of the Students for a Democratic Society (SDS) made the decision to use bombs to achieve their goals. After the explosion, Wilkerson lived the life of a fugitive for ten years, then turned herself in and served an eleven-month prison sentence. Kathy Boudin remained at large for over a decade and was arrested after a botched Brink's truck robbery in 1981 in which two guards were killed; she remained in prison until 2003. In 1970, both Wilkerson and Boudin had been living in a revolutionary collective in Wilkerson's father's townhouse, which had served as the headquarters of a splinter group of the SDS. The group called itself the Weathermen, a play on a line from Bob Dylan's "Subterranean Homesick Blues": "You don't need a weatherman / to know which way the wind blows." Cathy Wilkerson's *Flying Close to the Sun,* a memoir, relates the tale of how these young people came to choose the path they took—most notably, how they came to be in that building, and in that basement, when the bomb went off and what they were trying to achieve through their revolutionary actions. Unlike Malcolm, Kazan, and Podhoretz (and Augustine), in her memoir, Wilkerson dwells almost entirely in the past and rests her arguments mainly on extenuating circumstances.

Many 1960s radicals have immortalized their opposition to the regime in power with a memoiristic statement. Race, gender, class, the War in Vietnam—these and other lines of conflict in American society inspired movements whose members attempted to change the status quo, and from the perspective of the elite and the cultural mainstream, they often "went too far." The most common justification of their views and actions—which lay outside the lines and attracted challenge and condemnation—was that the politics of the political establishment were inexcusable, unsupportable, and indefensible. Their own defense tended to be straightforward and commonly employed by unconventional politicos: *I'm right and they're wrong; I could not do otherwise; my conscience dictated that I do as I did.*

Authors of political memoirs that seek to win over converts to a cause face a series of dilemmas analogous to those facing all writers of "deviance" memoirs: On the one hand, they must find *common ground* between their potential readers and themselves; on the other, they must explain what makes them special, why they decided to take this unusual path, what qualities they possess that entitles them to lead others to the promised land. Too much hubris, too much arrogance—a too emphatic proclamation of their own enlightenment—and they risk alienating their readers for their "know-it-all" attitude; too little and their readers ask if they have anything special or distinctive to contribute. Too little contact with the people whose lives they are presumably attempting to improve and they risk being labeled revolutionary elitists. On the one hand, how many pages of self-righteous rage can the reader slog through? On the other, intense emotion is one of the chariots to which ideology is hitched; without it, the reader will put down a political memoir out of sheer boredom.

Flying Close to the Sun contains such dilemmas in abundance. Wilkerson's twofold title refers both to the hubris of the Weathermen, a tiny faction of a small but noisy movement whose members imagined that they could bring about a revolution with a few bombs, and that of Western capitalism, uncritically infatuated as it was "with technology coupled with an economic system that disregards humanity's future [which] have led us to fly dangerously close to the sun" (2007, p. 393). As Manning Marable did with Malcolm X, Wilkerson likens herself and the Weathermen to Icarus: They were brought down by a prideful or overweening failed ambition. Originally, the Weathermen sought to recruit a mass movement, large numbers of supporters who would, somehow, de novo, "make" a revolution, but the exacting and extreme demands of the revolutionary can be sustained by only a dedicated few. After failing to rally the masses, the Weathermen sought ever more extravagant methods of achieving their goals, choosing blowing up symbolically important targets, a tactic that led to their own demise. In the end, Cathy Wilkerson later reflected, she had "accepted the same desanctification of human life practiced by Richard Nixon, Henry Kissinger, and William Westmoreland." In the frenzy of her political involvement, she had come to accept their supposition "that in the end, violence is the only effective strategy for social change" (p. 2). And by sharing "qualities with those who I considered implacable, myopic, and selfish"—that is, with "violent human beings"—"I realized just how pompous and arrogant our behavior had been" (p. 384). And in forming a Leninist or elitist revolutionary party, the Weathermen "sought to rescue society from itself" (p. 392)—a minuscule minority attempting to drag a reluctant, even resisting majority toward its own special and particularistic goal—presumably for the common good. In attempting to woo the reader, Wilkerson's dilemma is the almost inevitable choice between *conventionalizing* versus *othering* herself and her peers. How does a political activistwho holds a revolutionary ideology position herself in such a way that she appears sympathetic to the reader? What rhetoric does she use? Wilkerson's neutralization techniques come closest to excusing: We did the terrible things we did (bombing) because the American government was doing even worse things. Our actions were *almost* excused by the monstrous things the American government inflicted on the rest of the world, including the War in Vietnam and the deluge of death and destruction it unleashed on the fine, peaceful, and decent people of Vietnam.

Our motives were upright, says Wilkerson, and we were honorable people. *Flying Close to the Sun* is dedicated to Ted Gold, Diana Oughton, and Terry Robbins, those three young radicals who were killed in the accidental bombing of the townhouse that served as their headquarters. Each of them was motivated—as Cathy herself was—by the desire to provide "adequate food, housing, education, and relative safety" to all of the struggling people on the planet, those "who were desperately trying to climb out of poverty and dislocation" (p. 3). Each of her colleagues in the collective "believed that the only moral choice was to act." To "be passive was to acquiesce in the diminishment of their humanity" (p. 3). The author establishes that she shares the sentiment of all decent members of humanity—compassion for the poor and powerless and needy among us and the desire to help those persons less fortunate than herself: *Who could oppose or criticize such an aspiration? We're all on the same page—aren't we? We fought racism and the War in Vietnam, and our however failed mission inspired all subsequent movements that addressed the exploitation and oppression of women, gays, labor, urban youth, and any and all downtrodden peoples around the globe and managed to inspire reforms of the criminal justice system and achieve rights for GIs, vets, draft resisters, and Native Americans. Aren't these worthy causes?* The government attempted to stamp out, "demonize," and "delegitimize" rightful dissent, and we trained a spotlight on infringements of political and human rights (p. 392), making it more possible for future dissenters everywhere to speak out. Our goals were worthy, though perhaps our strategies were misguided, and perhaps the era had something to do with that, yet we produced some positive results, and we should not be harshly judged by our mistakes. We all did the best we could, Wilkerson tells us, "to realize our fullest humanity during times of terror and great upheaval" (p. 377). Cathy attempts to squelch any potential condemnation of involvement in revolutionary violence by emphasizing her declarations of honorable and righteous motives; her goals are so praiseworthy and her justifications so straightforward that the reader finds it difficult to mount a critical assault against her or her behavior.

Likewise, Wilkerson's willingness to admit to multiple mistakes is disarming; it renders the reader more empathetic to her and her failed mission, more willing to grant her some moral leeway for her flame-throwing revolutionary behavior. Such a verbal strategy represents a strategy of *handicapping,* a clear effort at self-exculpation. "I had made some huge mistakes," she admits. "I had settled for simplistic solutions" and "came to see that there was no quick and easy way to create a more just and sustainable world" (p. 384). The plan—"symbolic bombing"—was "so ill-conceived on so many levels," she concedes, "that the chance of an accident happening . . . was almost inevitable" (p. 2)—an instance of *The Bad News Bears* meets *Reds.* If the bomb had been successful, Cathy says, if it had had the impact we intended it to have, it would have been a "disaster" (p. 354). "We had been into a death trip," she acknowledges (p. 354). While Wilkerson admits to "arrogant mistakes," she continues to harbor hope for the future, drawing "strength from the most generous and courageous impulses of the human heart" (p. 393).

Accounting for Political Transgressions

Political memoirs never invoke their authors' lack of personal control to neutralize the stigma that critics might ascribe to them or their former or current political views and actions, and they never offer excuses for their politics; yes, they cite "extenuating circumstances," which are largely external to themselves, but to most ideologically driven characters, an "excuse" sounds too much like "I had a cold." Such devices would call into question their ideological judgment. Politicos consider "I was duped" and "I'm not responsible" as feeble linguistic contrivances. On the other hand, they often summon up *transcending commitments* as an explanation for their position and policies. We are reminded of Martin Luther's affirmation, "*Ich kann nicht anders*"—"I could not do otherwise." I may have been wrong then, some of our ideologically oriented memoirists declare, but circumstances demanded that I do the right thing. Some of the same injustices still prevail; maybe our solution did not work, but my goals remain the same. Virtually all political narratives generate a *normalization* rhetoric—the argument that existing institutions need to be rearranged according to their authors' formulas. The radical political memoir stands mainstream conventionality on its head, regarding what is considered by conventional standards as deviant *as good,* desirable, benevolent, righteous, and progressive. In addition, some use a redemptive or transformative argument—namely, the way the author saw the world in the past is not the way he or she sees things now. And it virtually goes without saying that political memoirs condemn their condemners—the opponents, critics, and carpers who oppose their views. They also condemn the facilitators and masterminds of the evils of the status quo. Neutralizing politically non-mainstream politics offers an intriguing and penetrating means of examining how ideology works, when and why it does not work, why it fails in some instances, and whether and to what extent explanations of their adoption find favor among readers of such narrations and accounts.

8

Accounting for Deviance

C. WRIGHT MILLS intended "Situated Actions and Vocabularies of Motive" as an analysis of "observable lingual mechanisms of motive imputation and avowal." The very act of explicating motives for our actions *itself has* motives; the reasons why we *do* things are separate and distinct from the reasons why we *explain* the things we do and the *way* we explain the things we do. Under certain circumstances, people are motivated to verbalize their *motives* for doing things. Scott and Lyman (1968) argue that the most important of such circumstances—those that *call for* an account—is that actors believe that audiences will regard the behavior they narrate as objectionable or deviant. Scott and Lyman believe that the ritual of offering *acceptable accounts for unacceptable behavior* helps make the social order possible. Neither Mills nor Scott and Lyman argued that such verbalizations *cause* deviant, untoward, or unconventional behavior. Indeed, the phenomenon they wish to explain is *the very process of rendering such verbalizations.* And some of those verbalizations will be more convincing to specific audiences than others; even though all such devices are conventional efforts to explain unconventional behavior, not all are equally successful in neutralizing deviance.

Sykes and Matza (1957) argue that accepting or believing in the validity of vocabularies of motive that justify or account for deviance *makes delinquent behavior possible*—hence, first the neutralization, then the behavior. This seems to be an unwarranted argument, though actors do know that if others discover or hear or read a description of their unconventional or transgressive behavior, observers or audiences expect them to render an account consisting of justifications, motives, or apologies. In my view, the adoption of stigma neutralization for a deviant act is not a *cause* of deviant behavior; a sensible reading of these accounts indicates that neutralizations are an *accompaniment* or a *consequence* of the enactment of deviant behavior.

The social analyst must be on the lookout for both variety and communalities in these neutralizations. At the very least, different types of behavior generate distinctly different genres of verbalizations—but all are devised for similar motives. Granted, actors are influenced by their social setting or context. In this volume, I focus on one setting in particular: admitting to untoward actions in the actor's memoir and autobiography. I may have harmed some people, authors say—but that was in the past. Or, I did what lots of others did—maybe a little more so—but everyone's hand was in the cookie jar. And the people who condemn me have committed far more serious sins. *He* harmed people; I didn't. Or, I did what was expected of me; it was my heritage, my background. Anyway, I was the victim of circumstance. Or, others pushed me into it; I didn't want to do it, but I just went along. Or, the system is biased against the little guy. I did what I had to do. I couldn't help myself; I was swept away. I wasn't immoral or evil—I was sick, I had an illness. Some people deceived me, took advantage of me. Or, I did the right thing; I struggled for justice; I fought the system; I told the truth. What I did should not be a crime; it doesn't harm anyone. These are neutralizations readers frequently find in memoirs, as all of us do in oral utterances; in fact, except for length, it is difficult to see where the differences might lie.

Common sense tells us that some crimes are so heinous that no offender would attempt to justify them, but common sense is often wrong; pederasts routinely neutralize the stigma of their acts (Durkin and Bryant, 1999; McCaghy, 1967)—still, we virtually never come across a pederastic memoir, only interview studies of anonymous pederasts. One murderer after another explains why he did it (Joey, 1973; Levi, 1981; Hardin, 1961). "I never killed a man who didn't deserve to die" is a common theme in the killer's narration of his illicit actions. Rape? No problem—explain it away; justify it; excuse it; call it fun (Scully, 1990); even rationalize it, *in a memoir,* as an insurrectionary act (Cleaver, 1968). What about bestiality? Even that can be justified and has, by its participants (Maratea, 2011)—though, again, I have never encountered a memoir by an identifiable author with a sexual preference for and sexual experience with animals. Perhaps we can say, closer to the core of human self-consciousness, that the more savagely condemned the act, the greater the necessity for cleansing one's psyche of its taint, but that, contrarily, the greater the stigma of the act, the less likely it is to attract not only enactors but also narrators. William Shakespeare would have us believe, as per *Macbeth,* that madness and compulsive hand washing are the natural offspring of regicide, but the history of humanity teaches us that murdering rulers occasions rhyme, reason, and self-exculpation far more often than deranged compulsivity. Practically any action the human brain can command the body to perform it can likewise sooth itself over with the salve of redemption, convincing its owner that such acts really were not really so bad or they were necessary under the circumstances; indeed, if examined in a certain light, they may even be regarded as praiseworthy.

Still, some of these verbalizations are less persuasive than others, not only for the narrator but also for his or her audiences; as a general rule, the more heinous the act, the less common it is, and the more difficult it is to explain away. The stories we tell one another tend to be morality tales, and when the narrator is the actor, they embed exoneration in their very marrow; this is what activates such tales, and, I argue, they are very essence of memoir. The ordinary, run-of-the-mill, meat-and-potatoes explanations, justifications, and contextualizations that actors offer argue that these actions were not all that bad, even though *certain audiences* disapproved of them. But remember: Deviance neutralizations do not always work; they are *attempts* to mitigate or diminish the condemnation that admitting that one has engaged in a transgressive act is likely to engender. We have a few in our collection that readers are not likely to accept or honor.

How They Account for Themselves

Charles Van Doren's "All the Answers" resembles Augustine's *Confessions.* It has the quality of an apologia in that it is a "secular ritual of expiation" (Tavuchis, 1991, p. viii). "I've remembered that moment for more than forty years," Van Doren tells Columbia University's class of 1968 at their fortieth annual reunion. Yet his apology is steeped in self-exculpation. Van Doren admits violating a norm, expresses embarrassment and sorrow for engaging in wrongdoing, but by positioning himself vis-à-vis Stempel, he attempts to smooth over his sin by asserting his rival's even greater sin; hence, "All the Answers" offers a *partial* mea culpa. "I was seduced into it," Charlie seems to be telling us, "and what I did wasn't as bad as what the other guy did." In short, Van Doren *condemns his facilitators* and *condemns his co-participant,* thereby, presumably, lessening the seriousness of his own sin. But he does not *normalize* his actions, and he does not recommend that a society routinely valorize dishonest quiz shows.

When Bowie Kuhn, commissioner of Major League Baseball, found out what Jim Bouton had written in *Ball Four,* says Bouton, he called him into his office. Bouton explained that Kuhn said he would do a big favor for him: "He said he knew that I realized I had made a terrible mistake and all I had to do was simply sign a statement he had prepared. The statement said, in effect, that the book was a bunch of lies and it blamed everything on my editor. . . . When I politely told the Commissioner what he could do with his statement, he turned a color that went very nicely with the wood paneling" (Bouton, 1981, p. 408). Continuing with his narration, Bouton explains that he and the Commissioner spent three hours wrangling over whether he could reveal what they discussed at that meeting: *I spilled the beans, told the truth, both in the book and about that meeting, and Major League Baseball and its fans ought to thank me. When I pitched for the Yankees and all those other teams, we had to crawl and beg for ten thousand dollar salaries; when I asked for twenty-five, management laughed. My book stirred up a spirit of rebellion and got players talking to one another (and to their agents), and now they have the right to negotiate their own contacts, and they're multi-millionaires. Management has only itself to blame; years ago, they refused to negotiate, and the floodgates opened. Listen, I tell it the way it is, at least as I see it, so I get branded a trouble-maker. I had a good time writing the book—true, some nasty, small-minded people reviled me for it, labeled me a deviant—but it's the most influential sports book of all time. My record speaks for itself. I told the truth,* he tells us, *the hypocrites I exposed didn't, I didn't intend to hurt anyone, and no one was harmed—well, maybe a few reputations were bruised and some wives and girlfriends were angry. But I did no wrong, I committed no sin, and I would have done it again.* As with all politically oriented narratives, Bouton *justifies* his behavior on the grounds that *telling the truth* warrants exposing the sins of the guilty; hence, he does not deserve to be condemned—he *normalizes* truth-telling and whistle-blowing. They are good things for which the actor should not be deviantized, as Bouton was.

A Million Little Pieces—fact or fiction? Who cares? James Frey seems to be saying. What difference does it make? And the author's millions of devoted readers apparently agree. His publisher, likewise, did not pull the plug on the book, in a sense validating the bogus memoir. *Criticize and anathemize* me *for exaggerating and embellishing? It's unfair, unjust, and absurd. What's all the fuss all about? No harm, no foul. Why are you picking on me? Anyway, embellishment is the heart and soul of interesting narrative. Hell,* Frey insists, *I originally tried to sell the book as fiction, and my editors made me package it as a memoir, and it is*—kind *of.* He thereby rolls *condemning his facilitators* and *normalization* into a single verbalization: *I told a more gripping and dramatic story than I could have told had I been technically scrupulous about what happened, but if you want to call it a memoir, that's fine, too.* Moreover, Frey *justifies* his behavior on the basis of art—a kind of *appeal to higher loyalties*—as well as the support of his loyal fans.

"Let us speak of virtuous men," proclaims Joe Bonanno (1905–2002), a member of the mob and a self-proclaimed "man of honor"—"or at least of men who try to be virtuous." *How close have I come to my ideal of virtue?* he asks his reader. "That's not for me to say. It's not for you to say either. It's up to God" (1984, p. 389). But of course Joe Bonanno knows, and the reader knows, that people judge one another and their actions all the time, about multiple matters, and on the basis of varying criteria, and that these judgments have a great deal of influence in the material world. God's judgments—well, they are another matter altogether. Still, judgments do vary according to audiences and according to individual observers. "I've led a productive life," Joe tells us, "not a parasitic one. I've had to protect myself and my people, but I've never been bloodthirsty. I've made mistakes, I'm not perfect, but throughout it all I've remained true to my name and scrupulous to my principles" (p. 389). The reader comes away from Bonanno's memoir sensing—*knowing*—that the author conceals his more shocking wrongdoings though, on some level, believing what he says and that he says what he does to assert the honor and dignity of his name. Bonanno is a deviance neutralizer on an epic scale. *Though it was laid out for me,* he says, *I chose my path. I deny intentionally injuring or victimizing others. My activities have a legitimate place in my society. I am a good and decent man who deserves to be shielded from disgrace and disrepute. I don't harm or victimize anyone, and I* don't *engage in exploitative criminal behavior—such as prostitution, selling narcotics, extortion, or murder. Some do; I don't.* (He did.) *I provide services that my people don't consider criminal; they are merely technically illegal. Condemn me? On what basis? I am a man of honor.* Bonanno comes very close to normalizing organized crime, at least as he lays out what it is, how he says his family practiced it. And by refusing to narrate what are his worst crimes, Joe is engaged in the most primitive of deviance neutralization devices—denial. But if readers knew the low-down on all of his criminal activities, we would have little sympathy for the man, and his narrative would likewise have little credibility for us.

The life of Eddie Bunker (1933–2005), novelist and author of *Education of a Felon,* was like mud, he explains—the material of his life, the muck and slime he lived through, the crimes, the beatings, the betrayals, the deprivations, the incarcerations. He lay in a prison cell, fantasizing about what he could make of his life, how he could redeem himself, exonerate his character, his name. And he wrote his way out of the mud and muck and slime, planting a lotus seed that brought forth life—his books. "Writing a good book would open doors for me," he tells us. "The world would read the truths I would write. I would make a lotus grow from the mud" (2000, p. 294). His dreams from forty years ago began to germinate life in the form of one successful redemptory book after another. "A lotus definitely grows from the mud" (p.

294). Crimes were committed, dishonor fell like a cloak across his shoulders, but dreams were hatched, books were written, release was obtained, success was secured, a man was vindicated, exculpated by means of his own words—note the passive voice in these constructions. Eddie tells us: *I am not a bad man; I did some bad things, but that was then and now is, well, now.* "Whatever happened, happened. . . . I changed as circumstances changed. . . . I am proud of what I am. The traits that made me fight the world are also those that made me prevail" (pp. 297, 299). *Isn't that enough? It's enough for me; how about you?* Eddie Bunker invokes the "even greater good" argument—namely, out of bad, a greater good issued (his criminality provided fertile soil for his books)—and his memoir invokes a redemptive, *transformative* reasoning, as do most memoirs about common crime. Like most common criminals who write memoirs, Bunker does not normalize what he did.

Jack Henry Abbott (1944–2002), chronic offender and inmate and author of *In the Belly of the Beast,* developed a rhetoric of self-justification that played well among sectors of the liberal urban literati; he parlayed his *New York Review of Books* essays and, later, his book into parole and freedom. *I did not commit most of the crimes of which I was accused,* he tells us—"I am not guilty of nine-tenths of the charges" (1981, p. 16)—*and of the few I did commit, I was not responsible for them.* "Responsibility? I am not responsible for what the government—its system of justice, its prisons—has done to me. I did not do this to myself" (p. 17). *And my so-called vices are in fact virtues.* "If I could please Caesar," Abbott says, "I *would,* I gladly would" (p. 15). In Abbott's tale, he is a survivor of an unjust, hellish world in which convict is set against convict and guards brutalize inmates. *The system is wrong, not me.* But in the end, after his murder of an innocent waiter and, three decades later, his own suicide, perhaps the best argument his supporters could muster was that the system corrupted Abbott, and it continues to corrupt convicts. *I've injured only those who have attempted to injure me; I vehemently condemn my condemners and insist that extreme provocation brought me to extreme behavior. My ultimate loyalty is to my code of honor, which may seem obdurate and implacable to some, but it has brought me nothing but pain and suffering. I'm the victim here, not the society.* Abbot *condemns his condemners, condemns his facilitators* (namely, the society at large), and *condemns even worse offenders* (namely, the criminal justice system). *Denial* also plays a role in Abbott's arsenal of deviance neutralization: *I didn't do a lot of the crimes of which I was accused. And I am a better man than most of you out there.*

How can a stock market swindler who ran a "pump and dump" operation that induced tens of thousands of investors to spend, then lose, money on valueless stock, thereby lining his own pockets with millions, justify his larcenous behavior? Jordan Belfort's *The Wolf of Wall Street* does precisely that.

The lavish lifestyle his swindles bought was ostentatious, even vulgar; seducing his young acolytes to follow his schemes train-wrecked many a budding career. Where is the virtue in that? *Listen,* Belfort tells his readers, *everyone was on the gravy train—me, my partners, those young traders, even the merchants and tradesmen we did business with. I lifted everyone out of obscurity, a humdrum existence, and the financial doldrums, and gave everyone their day in the sun. And living a wild life helped transported us through that terrifying roller-coaster ride. Okay, maybe I went overboard—but I had a drug habit; I was hooked. I couldn't have gotten through the craziness without drugs; it was the drugs that made me do it. I took my drugs like a man; no one else could have consumed the quantity and variety of the substances I took and survived. The whole thing was one hell of a wild ride. Who among you petty critics, carpers, and grumblers would have turned down the opportunity to do what I did?* The question answers itself. Belfort *blames his facilitators* (namely, the system of trading on Wall Street), *condemns comparable offenders* (other Wall Street traders), and *excuses* his behavior as resulting from his compulsion to abuse cocaine.

Pete Hamill's *A Drinking Life* narrates the life of a destructive alcoholic who successfully stops drinking. Hamill makes us understand his seduction into the drinking life; participating in it was, he explains, "what men do." Not just drinking, but heavy drinking. Though his dad was an out-and-out alcoholic, giving him, it might be said, a negative role model for alcohol consumption, he set the "magic potion" template for drinking and masculinity. "Drinking gave me strength, confidence, ease, laughter, it made me believe that dreams really could come true" (1994, p. 147). Nearly all his scenes of drinking entail talking—socializing with others. Or seduction. Or sexual frustration and abnegation. He describes with enthusiasm "hard loud whiskey-drinking beer-swilling parties" (p. 211) during his newspaper days. *Who at that age at that time could have said no to such adventures?* "I never thought of myself as a drunk," he tells us. "I was, I thought, . . . a *drinker*" (p. 212). Every description of drinking in Hamill's memoir engenders our empathy; every one helps us understand where he is coming from; every one tamps down our tendency to condemn such a drinker. And when he decides to quit, we understand that, too, and cheer him on, recognizing and valorizing his courage. *A Drinking Life* narrates a dramatic arc from background to seduction to trouble to resolution; though its author did not write it to win us over, it achieves that and more, and we feel satisfied when we put it down. *I have changed,* he tells us. *Early on, I denied my responsibility in drinking too much, but having accepted that responsibility, I've stopped drinking and am no longer a drunk.* Even though Hamill invokes his heritage—that is, he *excuses* it by contending that in his environment, heavy drinking was the rule—and rhetoricizes the palliative effects of heavy drinking, he also invokes the "then versus now" or *transformative* argument, which is the case with *all* alcoholic memoirs. Virtually *no* former alcoholic argues that society would be better off if abusive drinking were the rule, and all dramatize the triumph of their repudiation of heavy drinking. Jack London's *John Barleycorn* (1913/1989) comes close to glorifying what he admits is excessive drinking, but London's life was cut down long before heavy drinking had the chance to trace his lifetime trajectory.

Like Hamill, Susan Cheever tells us that drinking is part of her "heritage." For her, too, alcohol possessed "miraculous" powers. Unlike Hamill, who came from a working-class Irish American Catholic family, Cheever's lineage was white Anglo-Saxon Protestant, characterized by upper-middle-class shabby gentility. While Hamill's clan typically drank in sex-segregated settings, usually bars, men and women among Cheever's folks drank together in a ritual of "six o'clock cocktails," leading to nights of excess and mornings of hangovers. Her father, John, was a famous writer, a famous drunk, and author of suburban tales of alienated lives, most of which were punctuated by heavy drinking, "The Sorrows of Gin" perhaps most notably among them. We need not feel disapproving, or surprised, by the drinking tales contained in *Note Found in a Bottle* or by the news that alcohol was an essential and ordinary part of the author's everyday life. She drank, she says—or so she thought then—"the way everyone I knew drank" (1999, p. 43). Just as her father was "drinking himself to death" (p. 117), she found herself becoming involved with young men who were heavy drinkers—Warren, a beer and whiskey sort of guy; Calvin, a champagne type. She gradually but ineluctably experiences a "slow deterioration" of her sanity (p. 138). Her problems with sexual relationships—for instance, sleeping with three different men in a day—who knew that such behavior had anything to do with drinking? She had children; she stopped drinking. Trapped in a bad marriage, she started drinking again. She got divorced; she got remarried; she had another child. She was not an alcoholic, she told herself. *It was all a huge exaggeration. You know when people in movies are alcoholics; in real life, it's harder to tell. I wasn't on skid row or a falling-down drunk,* she tells us. And then—she stopped. She embraced Alcoholics Anonymous. Cheever watches as her children drift off to sleep, rejoicing in their life and her motherhood. The story comes to a conclusion, the tale is told, deviant practices are discontinued, a wayward life transmogrifies into conventionality, and the reader is satisfied. In sum, Cheever, with Hamill, invokes the "heritage" argument, pointing to her social and cultural *environment* as a facilitator, and, along with most ex-drunks, holds to the *transformation* verbalization: *I've changed; I'm not who I was; I'm a much better person now than I was then.* The remarkable feature of abusive drinking is that since it is an extension of conventional behavior—moderate drinking—actors easily persuade themselves that they are not alcoholics and not engaging in deviant behavior. And, as an advocate of AA, Cheever invokes an illness-like condition that prevents her from drinking moderately and non-abusively.

In spite of his heavy involvement with heroin abuse and thievery, we have a clear sense of where Steve Geng, author of *Thick as Thieves* (2007), is coming from. To begin with, he earns a lot of points for his loving portrait of and loyal dedication to his sister, Veronica. True, he betrayed and alienated her with his career of crime and his drug-saturated life, but as he spins out his tale, we struggle to appreciate why he embarked on the path he took. He renders a roster of literary outlaws appealing and adventurous, and his description of the heroin high is lyrical, its allure made to seem ineluctable. And in the end, his poignant sense of loss at the death of his beloved sister wins us over. Geng leans heavily on the *cultural heroes* argument, though our heart also goes out to him for being such a loving brother. But such arguments only go so far, and in the end, as with all substance abusers, Geng stresses the transformation of his life from self-indulgence and compulsion to abstention. This is a redemptive narrative, and though Steve does not believe he was "sick," he does not attempt to normalize heroin addiction.

William Cope Moyers, a spokesperson for the Hazelden Foundation, a substance abuse treatment program, hews to the view that addiction is a disease rather than the manifestation of immorality. Moyers narrates the tale of his drug dependence, of "starving" for cocaine, of hating himself for his weakness, and "hating the disease" for "sticking" to him "like a leech" (2006, p. 212), of feeling, after seven weeks of abstinence, "like an amputee" (p. 185). Addictive drugs "hijack" the brain, he argues, they grab you, shake you, and will not let go. After four attempts at treatment, he manages to stay clean, and the reader is exhausted by the end of it. His argument represents an attempt to remove the label of deviant from the addict, himself included, and to "break down the wall of shame, stigma, and discrimination that keeps people from finding their paths to recovery" (p. 365). Ultimately, *Broken* is a redemptionist, triumphalist memoir whose narrative wipes away the reader's condemnation of the author, revealing a feel-good emotion. Moyers tells us: *I didn't have sufficient control over myself when I used drugs; I stopped because I'm not responsible for my behavior when I use. Now that I've stopped using, I'm a decent person, a fully functioning human being.*

It's true, Roman Polanski tells us, *I gave champagne and Quaaludes to the thirteen-year-old girl I was photographing, and then I had sex with her. But she told me she* loved *champagne—it was her favorite drink. Honestly, she looked eighteen, she was completely compliant, even seductive, she was sexually experienced, and her mother practically threw her in my arms. States other than California don't penalize people who have sex with minors nearly so harshly as I was penalized, and many offenders elsewhere don't serve any jail time at all.*

Besides, the judge reneged on the deal my lawyer made with him: I had already served *a jail sentence for the technical offense; then he turned the tables on me and tried to reincarcerate me. I was going to get railroaded, and I could see it coming. Why stick around, go back to prison, and then get deported in the bargain? I did what I had to do to protect myself. I've been victimized all my life—why should I allow myself to be victimized again? I didn't do anything seriously wrong and I had no intention of going back to prison* for making love. *And let's face it,* everyone *wants to fuck young girls; I did only what most men dream about.* Polanski *justifies* his behavior; he makes the (blatantly false) inference that *since all men want to do what he did, his act was not wrong.* (The truth is, not all men want to "fuck young girls," and most who want to do so have the self-control not to.) He *justifies* his flight from justice, arguing that he was being unjustly railroaded. He *condemns his facilitators*—namely, Susan, the mother, and Samantha (the so-called victim). He *denies his so-called victim's victimhood.* And he *condemns his condemners.* Specifically, he condemns the judge in this case for giving him jail time that other offenders do not receive. (In truth, relatively few statutory rape cases involve a man in his forties and a thirteen-year-old girl; they usually involve a man in his late teens or early twenties having sex with a girl in her mid-to-late teens.) And he *condemns the offenses against him*—especially those the rabid media committed. Polanski comes *extremely close* to normalizing sex between a middle-aged man and a very early teen; even if it is a sin, he argues, the sin of the criminal justice system was far worse than his. While Polanski may have had the cooperation of facilitators, such justifications are very unusual for convicted child molesters, who usually take the route of denying or excusing their actions.

In *Loose Girl,* Kerry Cohen offers a narrative of addiction-like sexual compulsion; she realizes that she has been engaged in humiliating, self-destructive behavior, reassesses her life, decides to change her errant ways by connecting with the right man, gets married, and resists the sort of temptation she would have succumbed to earlier. *You can forgive me,* Cohen seems to be saying, *because I'm not the deviant person I was before. I've changed; I've mended my ways. The parade of boys has stopped. I wasn't responsible then. I am now.* Cohen leans especially strongly on two forms of neutralization: *excusing* her behavior as a product of insecurity and emphasizing the *transformation* argument: *I'm not the person I was then.*

In sharp contrast, Chelsea Handler jokingly tells us, *I'm promiscuous, and I drink too much, but I'm having fun and not hurting anyone. I'm not sick, compulsive, or self-destructive. What's the big deal?* Her comedy routine, a mixture of satire, jokes, gossip, put-downs, and raunchy or "blue" stories, both portrays her as an inebriated slut and seems to imply that we should not take anything Chelsea Hander says about her wanton sex acts very seriously.

She narrates her memoir, *My Horizontal Life,* for laughs, which automatically neutralizes the very sins that Kerry Cohen and many of the rest of us regard as reprehensible. Her "sleeping around" narrative has limits, however; publicly narrating a past, and possibly current, promiscuous persona may prove to be difficult for her relationships, as indicated by the instability of her self-dramatized dating history. On the other hand, perhaps settling down and living a monogamous existence would be fatal for the comedy niche she has established, given that what we are laughing about is her "horizontal life."

I've seen disgust and disbelief on the faces of people I've told what I did for a living, Melissa Febos tells us, *but I've also see astonishment and wonder. True, toward the end of my employment in the dungeon I began feeling disgusted and humiliated with myself about working as a dominatrix. After a while I just couldn't take it anymore, so I quit, completed my education, got a degree, taught at a college, and wrote a book about my experiences. Actually, I still miss a few things about the job. I did it because I was poor as hell, it paid pretty well, and it got me through some rough patches, and doing it gave me a lot of confidence in my interpersonal ability, soothed my insecurities about my body, and played into my need to dominate and control. I was good at what I did, and the drugs helped me get through the more difficult sessions. Listen, I didn't have to take my clothes off, and I did not have sex with clients. Okay, some of them masturbated because they got so excited with me, and toward the end, I began taking my bra off a lot. But honestly, it was something like therapy—a lot of these men were reliving childhood traumas in the sessions. Well, I'm not that sorry I did it, and it gave me something exciting to write about.* Febos *semi-normalizes* her behavior as not as bad as it seems, *excuses* it on the basis of her poverty and her insecurity about her body and interpersonal competence, and invokes a *transformation* of herself into the clean-living, productive author and professor she is now.

I was different from the other kids, Kirk Read tells us. *I got labeled a faggot, a queer—a deviant. I got stared at a lot and occasionally beaten up. But I fought back and sometimes won. Listen—I was different, true, but I was* special. *I wanted to be true to myself but I also wanted to be accepted. I couldn't be the macho, militaristic male my dad wanted me to be, but I still wanted his love and respect. In the small Virginia town I grew up in, my neighbors and peers did a lot of terrible things to me, but they were decent people, and I wanted them to like me. I had to stand up for my dignity, and it was sometimes very difficult, but I wanted to bond with my community as well. When I go back there, I socialize with them, and they now realize I'm not so bad. They don't insult me anymore, and they accept me for what I am—different, but a good person.* Kirk *normalizes* his behavior and *embraces his former condemners*—by winning them over to his definition of the situation. *Very few* mainstream homosexual memoirs (those outside the evangelical Christian tradition, at any rate) invoke the transformative narrative, and Read follows that tendency, and nearly all normalize the author-actor and his behavior, as Read does.

Few arenas of social life so emphatically demand justification as politics, and for ideological positions that veer away from the normal curve, this is even more emphatically the case. In the 1950s, Elia Kazan (1909–2003), perhaps the most successful film director of his day, became persona non grata—a deviant—among his circle of left-wing intellectuals, artists, and entertainers by appearing before the House Un-American Activities Committee (HUAC) and naming the former Communist Party members he had known in the 1930s. People he had been close with for a generation snubbed him on the street, denounced him in print and in letters, cut off all social relations with him. But Kazan convinced himself that he was right and his critics were wrong: Communism *was* a threat to America and worldwide; freedom, he told himself, was imperiled by Soviet-style communism, which threatened to dominate world politics. And the only way to oppose such subversion was to expose the plot and denounce the parties who were responsible. Kazan accomplished more than he could have imagined as a small boy: He knew a lot of famous people, and he had undreamed-of professional triumphs. But life is treacherous and chancy, he tells himself toward the end of his memoir, and he had more than his share of disappointments, though he does not regret who he was or what he did—he would just like a lot more years of it than he got: *I may have named names, but I didn't harm anyone—those names were already named. I condemned Stalinism just as ex-Stalinists condemned me. My loyalties are to a system of democracy, fairness, equality, and justice—not the Communist Party, and certainly not to ex-communists. I don't deserve the bum rap I got; I should have been revered, not condemned, and my doorstopper of an autobiography explains why.* Political memoirs rely heavily on the "truth is truth" argument, and Kazan's rhetoric follows along this well-trod path.

At some point in his life, Norman Podhoretz realized that the radical and liberal political platform on which his views had previously relied, and those which his closest circle of friends continued to support, was unsustainable. When he rejected the ideology of his intimates, he was shunned, banned, and excommunicated from his crowd. Liberal policies had placed the country—indeed, the entire world—in grave peril. Tolerance for unbridled homosexuality had spread a fatal virus to millions; looking the other way in the face of Soviet policies helped spread terror, murder, and atrocities worldwide; glorifying and romanticizing predatory crime gave license to the slaughter of innocents and undermined the foundation on which a livable society rests. One by one, Podhoretz denounced his friends—the promulgators of these and other absurd and repulsive canons of left-wing thought that he critiqued—and found himself on the outside of their once gratifying company. *What else could I have done?* he asks us. An outcast—a deviant—among his ex-friends, his position nonetheless remains conventional among conservatives. Again, as with other political renegade-neutralizers, the *truth* is Podhoretz's rod and staff.

The task of the Black Muslims was to establish that theirs was the "natural" religion of persons of African descent, and Malcolm X (1925–1965) was its most eloquent spokesperson. But Malcolm came to recognize the racism inherent in the position of the Nation of Islam, and he broke away from it, only to be assassinated for his apostasy less than a year later. Ironically, his message, which he directed to a predominantly black audience, found a readership among whites as well, largely because his scribe, Alex Haley, softened and conventionalized his prose and justified his politics within the context of the American political landscape, thereby rendering him "more palatable for latte-leftist audiences" (Biddle, 2011, p. 79). Malcolm seemed to be saying that though his message might seem offensive to some, the truth as he saw it in the years before he was assassinated had become a less harsh, less abrasive truth by the day he died, and might have softened yet again had he lived to his more mature years. Advocates of unconventional ideologies never neutralize their position by arguing compulsion or a denial of responsibility; indeed, it is their political opponents who are mental slaves to their convictions. "Truth is truth" constitutes Malcolm's central argument, although, ironically, the "truth" he saw before was not the "truth" he saw in his autobiography and would not have been the "truth" he would have seen had he lived substantially longer.

For many idealistic Americans, the 1960s were a time of political and ideological upheaval and hope. A few activists imagined that they could foment a revolution or at least bring about drastic social and political change with violence against the parties they viewed as the "establishment." Cathy Wilkerson was a devoted member of the Weather Underground, a splinter group of Students for a Democratic Society, who disdained mass mobilization to achieve their ends in favor of targeted violence promulgated by a tiny but highly committed number of their ranks. Wilkerson now rejects the Weathermen's tactics but insists that their motives were honorable: *Income distribution was and still is unjust; people were and are struggling for adequate food, shelter, and education; racism then as now prevents millions of people of color from achieving their potential. If our radical solution forty years ago would not work, how does mainstream America propose that they be solved today? I sought to harm no one, only to bring down an unjust system and to bring an end to victimization. I justify our cause, which was deserving, though I feel*

I must apologize for our methods, which were flawed. Wilkerson's memoir departs from many political memoirs in that her neutralization rationale seems to be twofold: *This is the truth I saw then, although, in my maturity, I underwent a transformation and see things differently today.*

Searching for Common Threads

All the categories of deviance discussed here are more protean than we might imagine at first glance. Society hands the transgressor a tool box—the contents of each, somewhat different according to the transgression—and some materials, and he or she constructs an edifice of neutralization with it, but each selects somewhat different tools and materials. Hence, any theory that attempts to draw a straight causal arrow from crime, as a generic entity, to type of neutralization conjured up by participants is doomed to failure and meaninglessness. The paragons of the three types of crime we have limned here—organized crime, street crime, and white collar crime—offer strikingly different verbalizations of their wrongdoing, and different exemplars of the same crimes might very well offer altogether different narratives. Bonanno's fairy tale recitation works only if we buy his story that he is a productive member of the community supplying its members with what they want. The bad guy here is the government, an outsider meddling in our precious lives, telling us what we should and should not want and do. The device is ingenuous to the point of rank duplicity; to buy it, we have to ignore unmentionables that the narrator pretends do not exist. Abbott led a difficult, even horrific life, but he got breaks a lot of men who also suffered did not receive, and they did not end up committing murder—twice. His suicide may have represented the ultimate statement on his awareness that his attempt at self-exculpation did not work. In a way, Bunker's narrative arc is the opposite of Abbott's: The blows inflicted upon the soul of Jack Henry Abbott caused him to justify lashing out at society for abusing him, while Eddie Bunker's image of the mud and slime of life producing a lotus flower conveys the obverse thought. Jack says: *Out of evil, evil comes.* Eddie says: *Out of evil, good comes.* Jordan Belfort shows us that glitz, glamor, enormous piles of cash and cocaine come from malfeasances. *Who could have resisted that? Not I,* says he. The mechanistically minded social scientist becomes frustrated in the search for regularities here. At every turn, we read different justifications: It is not the crime that generates these verbalizations; it is the man. But mainly, Bonanno *normalizes* and *denies*; Bunker *excuses* and *redeems*; Abbott *justifies* and *accuses his accusers*; and Belfort *excuses* (arguing that no normal person could resist the splendiferous temptations) and *accuses his facilitators* (that is, Wall Street's culture of greed).

Where are the common threads in our substance abusers' accounts? Does addiction give birth to common themes? Generally, yes; in their specifics, no. Hamill did as his dad and family and tribe did; he did as men at the time did. Eventually, he looked around, saw alcohol's destructive power, and stopped. No excuses, not much of an apology. *I was a man, so I drank; I'm a man, so I stopped.* Hamill wants us to think well of him, and we do—but that is not why he wrote his memoir. Susan Cheever likewise did as her dad and folks did, saw the problems excessive drinking caused, and stopped. She settles on the disease metaphor, and she does not drink now. Geng's outlaw self-image as a drug abuser takes us only so far, but it does hammer home the multiplicity of self-explanations of abusing psychoactive substances, and whereas most of Geng's outlaw heroes are dead, he suffers from AIDS, and he has maintained on methadone. Moyers tells us his disease made him do it, but closely examined, the disease *is* the addiction, the addiction, the disease. Hamill *condemns his facilitators* (his culture made him do it), *apologizes* to the people he hurt, and *pathologizes,* a little (there must have been something wrong with me that I succumbed but most peers did not). But mostly, Pete accepts responsibility for his sins. Cheever likewise invokes her tradition (he family, her class, her ethnicity), but in the end pathologizes, in line with AA convention. Geng conjures up tough guy hero role models who were junkies; apologizes to his beloved, deceased sister; and in the end settles into the role of a methadone patient—in effect, pathologizes. And Moyers simply *pathologizes.* None of them normalize; after having lived through the destructiveness of a major portion of their lives, they know that substance abuse is not a viable way of life for anyone. The common thread is pathology, and the rhetoric they *avoid* is normalization—telling us that getting loaded day after day is normal, good, and desirable and that everyone should do it.

Scour the literature on pederasts and it would be difficult to come up with the autonarration Polanski leaves us with. The legal definition seems meaningless because Roman does not put himself in that category; he is virtually sui generis. Kerry Cohen is ashamed of her promiscuity and proud of her ability to overcome it. Chelsea Handler finds sleeping around amusing; her audiences find it amusing; and she makes light of it. Melissa Febos puts her bizarre sexual past behind her, uses it to her advantage, and seems almost nostalgic about it. And Read's affirmation of the bonds between his flamboyant and decidedly transgressive self and his former tormenters shows us that every queer has a different story. Where are the commonalities here? Again, positivistic sociology searches in vain for the Holy Grail—a single explanation for neutralizations by type of deviant activity. We do not have a Holy Grail, but Polanski condemns his condemners, including the unfairness of the American criminal justice system, the media, the hypocrisy of American culture; condemns his facilitators (at the very least, Susan and Samantha); accuses his accusers; denies the victimhood of his victim and denies his victim's injury; appeals to higher loyalties; justifies his behavior; denies having done anything wrong—the list is virtually endless. And like Jack London, Pete Hamill, Eddie Bunker, and Jack Henry Abbott, he claims he did what any man would have done—he was a *manly man. Every man wants to fuck young girls,* he claims. *Why am I being railroaded into prison?* Polanski's disingenuousness is almost hallucinatory.

Here is a glimmer of hope for our yearning for *an* explanation for the way our writers acquit themselves. Our politically dissident writers universally agree on a verbalization: "I was right, and you were wrong." All of them arrive at that conclusion, in the end at least. But would they have said the same thing had they written their memoirs during their first, or second, political incarnation? Probably—for them, politics was a long and winding path, and their life story makes the end at which they arrived, through death or old age, seem teleological in nature. Imagine Adolf Hitler writing *Mein Kampf* in his bunker in April 1945. Mind you, I really *do* believe that Kazan, Malcolm, Podhoretz, and Wilkerson were right about some—about many—things they said. But every offbeat political memoirist says much the same thing. And for that we should be grateful, because it gives us optimism for a "theory" of the social construction of deviance neutralization. I hope that this discussion, our close analysis of the life histories of representatives and narrators of these four unconventional activities, has provided something of a first step in that direction.

Looking Back

Nancy Miller (2002) argues that inside every memoir we will hear a clamorous author's voice insisting, "Reader, pay attention to me." Autobiography "remains the act of that solitary ego asserting the right (or need) to take up room in the public spaces of reading and writing" (p. 125). True enough, but authors of deviance memoirs make several demands on their readers aside from attention. Almost contradictorily, they want to excite, impress, surprise, and even shock them, yet at the same time, they want to create a verbal cushion that reassures them that they are not a shoddy, deplorable species of humanity. They seem to beg us for our love *in spite of* their sins. *Papa, forgive me! Mama, forgive me! Uncle Carl, forgive me!* Van Doren cries out in remorse; although most of his readers are strangers, he is doing much the same thing *with us,* his readers. James Frey invents major details about his drug addiction but stirs up his fan club to defend him for his exaggerations. Joe Bonanno sweeps his more heinous sins under the rug, emphasizes that he was not a party to the mob's most exploitative enterprises, and insists that he is *a man of honor.* Memoir writers are less Miller's exhibitionists than, I would argue, self-apologists—defenders of their own decency, even when they narrate unconventional behavior. When Jordan Belfort goes berserk under the influence of massive quantities of mind-altering substances, he tells us what his physician told him—that he is sick, just as a cancer patient is sick. *The cocaine made me do it,* he tells us, even though he knows this is false, even after narrating the illegal acquisition of riches beyond our ability to imagine.

The autobiography is a "moral performance," Bjorklund tells us (1998, p. 158); autobiographers "present a praiseworthy self to their audiences." But autonarrators are both "manipulative" and "sociable," positioning themselves "in terms of what is [considered] good and admirable," presenting the particulars of their lives that they want audiences to hear (p. 159). The self both narrates and justifies; when authors cannot avoid describing behavior that is other that what it should be, they acknowledge their wrongdoing and admit their sins. In recognizing the normative and admitting the struggle against their fallible selves, they acknowledge that their fallibility led to transgressions. The memoir or autobiography is a specific stage on which transgressors enact moral performances. Authors know that sectors of the society disapprove of aspects of their behavior and values and hence, they must mount a preemptory assault against that disapproval.

Does confessing then self-exculpating oneself for one's sins, or putative sins, in memoir and autobiography help knit the society together? Possibly. But the fact is societies do not produce cookie-cutter duplicates of ideal human beings. There is a rambunctious, irrepressible side to humanity. We do not agree on what is right, and even if we grant that something we do is wrong, some of us cannot help doing it. Most violations of society's rules do not do much damage at all, but wholesale and unsanctioned major breaches of the social norms would shred the social fabric and bring down on us chaos, disorder, and disintegration. The apologias, justifications, explanations, and self-absolutions for transgressions we read in memoirs may very well represent attempts by their authors to remind us that we are members of a collectivity, fragments of the whole, and however much we might stray from society's mandates and expectations, we owe our fellow man and woman an accounting for what we did. Exculpation in memoir is a genuflection, though more than that—a sign that the rest of us are curious about what we did, why we it, and how we try to talk our way out of their potential disapproval. It reminds us that we are all bound together in the same human community, and though we do, and approve of, different things, we are always looking over our shoulder at what others think of who we are, what we do, and how we feel. Self-absolution in memoir reminds us that humanity is saturated with a peculiarly human trait—*empathy.*

References

Abbott, Jack Henry. 1981. *In the Belly of the Beast: Letters from Prison.* New York: Random House.

Abbott, Jack Henry, with Naomi Zack. 1987. *My Return.* Buffalo, NY: Prometheus Books.

Abel, Lionel. 1981. "Murder and the Intellectuals: When Foul Looks Fair." *Commentary,* November, pp. 64–68.

Adut, Ari. 2008. *On Scandal: Moral Disturbances in Society, Politics, and Art.* New York: Cambridge University Press.

Agnew, Robert, and Ardith A.R. Peters. 1986. "The Techniques of Neutralization: An Analysis of Predisposing and Situational Factors." *Criminal Justice and Behavior* 13 (March): 81–97.

Amis, Martin. 1993. *Visiting Mrs. Nabokov and Other Excursions.* New York: Harmony Books.

Anonymous. 2008. "After 49 Years, Charles Van Doren Talks." *The New York Times,* July 21.

Atlas, James. 1996. "The Age of the Literary Memoir Is Now." *The New York Times,* May 12, pp. 25–27.

Augustine, St. ca. 400 C.E./1963. *The Confessions of St. Augustine* (trans. Rex Warner). New York: Mentor/Penguin Books.

Barber, Lynn. 2009. *An Education.* London: Penguin Books.

Beah, Ismael. 2007. *A Long Way Gone: Memoirs of a Boy Soldier.* New York: Farrar, Straus and Giroux.

Becker, Howard S. 1963. *Outsiders: Studies in the Sociology of Deviance.* New York: Free Press.

Belfort, Jordan. 2007. *The Wolf of Wall Street.* New York: Bantam Books.

Bentley, Toni. 2004. *The Surrender: An Erotic Memoir.* New York: HarperCollins.

Ben-Yehuda, Nachman. 1990. *The Politics and Morality of Deviance: Moral Panics, Drug Abuse, Deviant Science, and Reversed Stigmatization.* Albany: State University of New York Press.

Berbrier, Mitch. 1999. "Impression Management for the Thinking Racist: A Case Study of Intellectualization as Stigma Transformation in Contemporary White Supremacist Discourse." *The Sociological Quarterly* 40 (3): 411–433.

Best, Joel. 2004. *Deviance: Career of a Concept.* Belmont, CA: Thompson/Wadsworth.

Biddle, RiShawn. 2011. "Malcolm X: All-American." *The American Spectator,* July/August.

Bjorklund, Diane. 1998. *Interpreting the Self: Two Hundred Years of American Autobiography.* Chicago: University of Chicago Press.

Blumer, Herbert. 2004. *George Herbert Mead and Human Conduct* (ed. Thomas J. Morrione). Walnut Creek, CA: Altamira Press.

Blumstein, Philip W. 1974. "The Honoring of Accounts." *The American Sociological Review* 39 (August): 551–566.

Bonanno, Joe, with Sergio Lalli. 1983/1984. *A Man of Honor: The Autobiography of "The Boss of All Bosses."* New York: Simon and Schuster/Pocket Books.

Bouton, Jim. 1970. *Ball Four: My Life and Hard Times Throwing the Knuckleball in the Big Leagues* (ed. Leonard Shecter). New York: World Publishing.

Bouton, Jim. 1981/1985. *Ball Four Plus Ball Five* (orig. ed. Leonard Shecter). New York: Stein and Day/Scarborough House.

Bouton, Jim. 2000. *Ball Four: The Final Pitch.* North Egremont, MA: Bulldog Publishing.

Brann, Ross Ian. 2002. *Power in the Portrayal: Representations of Jews and Muslims in Eleventh and Twelfth Century Islamic Spain.* Princeton, NJ: Princeton University Press.

Breitman, George (ed.). 1965. *Malcolm X Speaks: Selected Speeches and Statements.* New York: Grove Press/Evergreen.

Brooks, Peter. 2000. *Troubling Confessions: Speaking Guilt in Law and Literature.* Chicago: University of Chicago Press.

Buford, Bill. 1996. "The Seductions of Storytelling." *The New Yorker,* June 23, pp. 11–12.

Bunker, Edward. 2000. *Education of a Felon.* New York: St. Martin's Press.

Burroughs, William ["William Lee"]. 1953. *Junkie* (reprinted 1967 as *Junk*). New York: Ace Books.

Burroughs, William. 2003. *Junky: The Definitive Text of "Junk"* (ed. Oliver Harris). London: Penguin.

Cheever, Susan. 1999. *Note Found in a Bottle: My Life as a Drinker.* New York: Simon and Schuster.

Cheever, Susan. 2008. *Desire: Where Sex Meets Addiction.* New York: Simon and Schuster.

Cleaver, Eldridge. 1968. *Soul on Ice.* New York: Random House.

Clinton, Bill. 2004. *My Life.* New York: Alfred Knopf.

Cohen, Albert K. 1955. *Delinquent Boys: The Culture of the Gang.* Glencoe, IL: Free Press.

Cohen, Kerry. 2008. *Loose Girl: A Memoir of Promiscuity.* New York: Hyperion.

Colman, Andrew M. 1991. "Crowd Psychology in South African Murder Trials." *The American Psychologist* 46 (10): 1071–1079.

Conrad, Peter, and Joseph W. Schneider. 1992. *Deviance and Medicalization: From Badness to Sickness* (exp. ed.). Philadelphia: Temple University Press.

Conway, Jill Kerr. 1999. *When Memory Speaks: Exploring the Art of Autobiography.* New York: Alfred Knopf/Vintage Books.

Cressey, Donald R. 1953. *Other People's Money.* New York: Free Press.

Cromwell, Paul, and Quint Thurman. 2003. "The Devil Made Me Do It: Use of Neutralizations by Shoplifters." *Deviant Behavior* 24 (November/December): 535–550.

Crossman, Richard (ed.). 1952. *The God That Failed.* New York: Bantam Books.

Davies, John Booth. 1997. *The Myth of Addiction* (2d ed.). Amsterdam: Harwood Academic Publisher.

De Quincey, Thomas. 1821/1995. *Confessions of an English Opium-Eater.* New York: Dover Publications.

Des Pres, Terrence. 1981. "A Child of the State." *The New York Times Book Review,* July 19, p. 14.

Durkin, Keith F., and Clifton D. Bryant. 1999. "Propagandizing Pederasty: A Thematic Analysis of the On-Line Exculpatory Accounts of Unrepentant Pedophiles." *Deviant Behavior* 20 (April/June): 103–127.

Dyson, Michael Eric. 1996. *Making Malcolm: The Myth and Meaning of Malcolm X.* New York: Oxford University Press.

Farber, A.M. 1981a. "Convict-Author Known by Mailer Is Being Sought in Fatal Stabbing." *The New York Times,* July 20, p. B3.

Farber, A.M. 1981b. "Killing Clouds Ex-Convict Writer's New Life." *The New York Times,* July 26, pp. 1, 26.

Febos, Melissa. 2010. *Whip Smart: A Memoir.* New York: St. Martin's Press/Thomas Dunne Books.

Feeney, Francis X., and Paul Duncan. 2006. *Roman Polanski.* London: Taschen.

Fiddle, Seymour. 1967. *Portraits from a Shooting Gallery: Life Styles from the Drug Addict World.* New York: Harper and Row.

Folkes, Valerie S., and Yun-Oh Whang. 2003. "Account-Giving for a Corporate Transgression Influences Moral Judgment: When Those Who 'Spin' Condone Harm-Doing." *Journal of Applied Psychology* 88 (1): 79–86.

Franklin, Bruce H. 1989. *Prison Literature in America: The Victim as Criminal and Artist* (exp. ed.). New York: Oxford University Press.

Frey, James. 2003. *A Million Little Pieces.* New York: Doubleday.

Friedman, Laurie. 2008. *Angel Girl.* Minneapolis: Carolrhoda Books.

Geng, Steve. 2007. *Thick as Thieves: A Brother, a Sister—A True Story of Two Turbulent Lives.* New York: Henry Holt.

Goffman, Erving. 1959. *The Presentation of Self in Everyday Life.* Garden City, NY: Doubleday Anchor Books.

Goffman, Erving. 1971. *Relations in Public: Microstudies of the Public Order.* New York: Basic Books.

Hamill, Pete. 1994. *A Drinking Life: A Memoir.* New York: Little, Brown/Back Bay Books.

Hampl, Patricia. 1999. *I Could Tell You Stories: Sojourns in the Land of Memory.* New York: W.W. Norton.

Handler, Chelsea. 2005. *My Horizontal Life: A Collection of One-Night Stands.* New York: Bloomsbury.

Handler, Chelsea. 2008. *Are You There, Vodka? It's Me, Chelsea.* New York: Simon Spotlight Entertainment.

Hardin, John Wesley. 1895/1961. *The Life of John Wesley Hardin as Written by Himself.* Norman: University of Oklahoma Press.

Harrell, Jackson, B.L. Ware, and Wil A. Linkugel. 1975. "Failure of Apology in American Politics: Nixon on Watergate." *Speech Monographs* 42 (4): 245–261.

Hemingway, Ernest. 1964/2003. *A Moveable Feast.* New York: Charles Scribner and Sons.

Hendershott, Anne. 2002. *The Politics of Deviance.* San Francisco: Encounter Books.

Hewitt, John P., and Randall Stokes. 1975. "Disclaimers." *The American Sociological Review* 40 (February): 1–11.

Hobsbawm, Eric. 2002. *Interesting Times: A Twentieth-Century Life.* London: Allen Lane.

Hollander, Xaviera, with Robin Moore and Yvonne Dunleavy. 1972/2002. *The Happy Hooker: My Own Story* (1st ed./2d ed.). New York: Dell. Reprint, New York: ReganBooks.

Homans, George Caspar. 1984. *Coming to My Senses: The Autobiography of a Sociologist.* New Brunswick, NJ: Transaction Books.

Howard, Nicole. 2005. *The Book: The Life Story of a Technology.* Westport, CT: Greenwood Press.

Jacobs, Jerry A. 2005. "*ASR*'s Greatest Hits: Editor's Comment." *The American Sociological Review* 70 (1): 1–3.

Jameson, Jenna, with Neil Strauss. 2004. *How to Make Love like a Porn Star: A Cautionary Tale.* New York: HarperCollins.

"Joey," with Dave Fisher. 1973. *Killer: Autobiography of a Hit Man for the Mafia.* Chicago: Playboy Press.

Jones, Margaret B. [Margaret Seltzer]. 2008. *Love and Consequences: A Memoir of Hope and Survival.* New York: Riverhead Books/Penguin.

Juska, Jane. 2004. *A Round-Heeled Woman: My Late-Life Adventures in Sex and Romance.* New York: Villard Trade.

Kahl, Mary. 1984. "*Blind Ambition* Culminates in *Lost Honor*: A Comparative Analysis of John Dean's Apologetic Strategies." *Central States Speech Journal* 35 (Winter): 239–250.

Kakutani, Michiko. 1981. "The Strange Case of the Writer and the Criminal." *The New York Times Book Review,* September 20, pp. 1, 36–39.

Kalab, Kathleen A. 1987. "Student Vocabularies of Motive: Accounts for Absence." *Symbolic Interaction* 10 (1): 71–83.

Karr, Mary. 1995/1996. *The Liar's Club: A Memoir.* New York: Viking/Penguin Books.

Kazan, Elia. 1997. *A Life.* New York: Da Capo Press.

Kazin, Alfred. 1964. "Hemingway as His Own Fable." *The Atlantic,* June, pp. 54–57.

Kipnis, Laura. 2010. *How to Become a Scandal: Adventures in Bad Behavior.* New York: Metropolitan Books.

Kooistra, Paul. 1989. *Criminals as Heroes: Structure, Power, and Identity.* Bowling Green, OH: Bowling Green State University Popular Press.

Kotre, John. 1995. *White Gloves: How We Create Ourselves through Memory.* New York: Free Press.

Laub, John H. 1983. *Criminology in the Making: An Oral History.* Boston: Northeastern University Press.

Lazare, Aaron. 2004. *On Apology.* Oxford, UK: Oxford University Press.

Leaming, Barbara. 1981. *Polanski, a Biography: The Filmmaker as Voyeur.* New York: Simon and Schuster.

Lee, William [William Burroughs]. 1953. *Junky: Confessions of an Unredeemed Drug Addict.* New York: Ace Books.

Lemann, Nicholas. 1999. "The Outcast." *The Washington Monthly* 31 (January/February): pp. 37–40.

Levi, Ken. 1981. "Becoming a Hit Man: Neutralization in a Very Deviant Career." *Urban Life* 10 (April): 47–63.

Liazos, Alexander. 1972. "The Poverty of the Sociology of Deviance: Nuts, Sluts, and Deviated Preverts," *Social Problems* 20 (Summer): 103–120.

Liebow, Elliot. 1967. *Tally's Corner: A Study of Negro Streetcorner Men.* Boston: Little, Brown.

Lindop, Grevel. 1993. *The Opium-Eater: A Life of Thomas De Quincey.* London: Weidenfeld.

Lofland, John, with the assistance of Lyn H. Lofland. 1969. *Deviance and Identity.* Englewood Cliffs, NJ: Prentice-Hall.

Loftus, Elizabeth, and Katherine Ketcham. 1991. *Witness for the Defense: The Accused, the Eyewitness, and the Expert Who Puts Memory on Trial.* New York: St. Martin's Press.

London, Jack. 1913/1989. *John Barleycorn.* New York: Oxford University Press.

Lundgren, Kristina. 2008. "Memorable Literary Hoaxes." *The Los Angeles Times,* March 19.

Luscombe, Belinda. 2009. "World's Most Shocking Apology: Oprah to James Frey." *Time,* May 13.

Maas, Peter. 1968/2003. *The Valachi Papers.* New York: Putnam's. Reprint, New York: Harper Perennial.

Maechler, Stefan (ed.). 2001. *The Wilkomirski Affair: A Study in Biographical Truth.* New York: Schocken Books.

Mailer, Norman. 1959. *Advertisements for Myself.* New York: G.P. Putnam's Sons/Berkley Medallion.

Malcolm X, as told to Alex Haley. 1964/1999. *The Autobiography of Malcolm X.* New York: Ballantine Books.

Malcolm X, with the assistance of Alex Haley. 1966. *The Autobiography of Malcolm X.* New York: Random House/Grove Press.

Marable, Manning, 2011. *Malcolm X: A Life of Reinvention.* New York: Viking Press.

Maratea, R.J. 2011. "Screwing the Pooch: Legitimizing Accounts in a Zoophilia On-Line Community." *Deviant Behavior* 32 (10): 918–943.

Marin, Rick. 2003. *Cad: Confessions of a Toxic Bachelor.* New York: Hyperion.

Martin, John. 1997. "Inventing Sincerity, Refashioning Prudence: The Discovery of the Individual in Renaissance Europe." *American Historical Review* 102 (December): 1309–1342.

Maruna, Shadd, and Heith Copes. 2005. "Excuses, Excuses: What Have We Learned from Five Decades of Neutralization Research?" *Crime and Justice: Annual Review of Research* 32:221–320.

Mayne, Jerome. 2010. *Diary of a White Collar Criminal.* Minneapolis: Planet Earth Publishing.

McCaghy, Charles. 1967. "Child Molesters: A Study of Their Careers as Deviants," in Marshall B. Clinard and Richard Quinney (eds.), *Criminal Behavior Systems.* New York: Holt, Rinehart and Winston, pp. 75–88.

McCourt, Frank. 1996. *Angela's Ashes: A Memoir.* New York: Scribner.

Mead, George Herbert. 1934. *Mind, Self, and Society* (ed. Charles M. Morris). Chicago: University of Chicago Press.

Menchú, Rigoberta. 1984. *I, Rigoberta Menchú: An Indian Woman in Guatemala* (ed. Elisabeth Burgos-Debray; trans. Ann Wright). New York: Verso.

Merton, Robert K. 1957. *Social Theory and Social Structure* (rev. and enlarged ed.). Glencoe, IL: Free Press.

Merton, Robert K. 1979. "Foreword." In Eugene Garfield, *Citation Indexing: Its Theory and Applications in Science, Technology, and Humanities.* New York: John Wiley and Sons, pp. ix–x.

Miller, Arthur G., Anne K. Gordon, and Amy M. Buddie. 1999. "Accounting for Evil and Cruelty: Is to Explain to Condone?" *The Personality and Social Psychology Review* 3 (3): 254–268.

Miller, J. Mitchell, Richard A. Wright, and David Dannels. 2001. "Is Deviance 'Dead'? The Decline of a Sociological Research Specialty." *The American Sociologist* 32 (1): 43–59.

Miller, Nancy. 1997. "Public Statements, Private Lives: Academic Memoirs for the Nineties." *Signs: Journal of Women in Culture and Society* 22 (4): 981–1015.

Miller, Nancy. 2002. *But Enough about Me: Why We Read Other People's Lives.* New York: Columbia University Press.

Millett, Catherine. 2003. *The Sexual Life of Catherine M.* (trans. Adriana Hunter). New York: Grove Press.

Mills, C. Wright. 1940. "Situated Actions and Vocabularies of Motive." *The American Sociological Review* 5 (December): 904–913.

Milner, Christina, and Richard Milner. 1972. *Black Players: The Secret World of Black Pimps.* Boston: Little, Brown.

Minton, Henry L. 2002. *Departing from Deviance: A History of Homosexual Rights and Emancipatory Science in America.* Chicago: University of Chicago Press.

Misch, Georg. 1950. *A History of Autobiography in Antiquity* (3d ed., trans. E. W. Dickes). London: Routledge and Kegan Paul.

Moldea, Dan E. 1983. Review of Joe Bonanno, *A Man of Honor. Washington Post Book World,* May 1.

Morgan, Ted. 1988. *Literary Outlaw: The Life and Times of William Burroughs.* New York: Henry Holt.

Moyers, William Cope, with Katherine Ketcham. 2006. *Broken: My Story of Addiction and Redemption.* New York: Penguin Books.

Mozes, Suzanne. 2010. "James Frey's Fiction Mill." *New York,* November 22, pp. 39–44.

Nussbaum, Felicity. 1987. "Heteroclites: The Gender of Character in the Scandalous Memoirs." In Felicity Nussbaum and Laura Brown (eds.), *The New Eighteenth Century: Theory, Politics, English Literature.* New York: Methuen, pp. 144–167.

O'Connor, Pauline. 2005. "The Jokes Are on Her." *The New York Times,* July 31.

Olney, James. 1999. Review of Diane Bjorklund, *Interpreting the Self: Two Hundred Years of American Autobiography. American Literature* 71 (December): 827–828.

Orbuch, Terri L. 1997. "People's Accounts Count: The Sociology of Accounts." *The Annual Review of Sociology* 23:455–478.

Peele, Stanton. 1998. *The Meaning of Addiction* (2d ed.). San Francisco: Jossey-Bass.

Podhoretz, Norman. 1967. *Making It!* New York: Random House.

Podhoretz, Norman. 1979. *Breaking Ranks: A Political Memoir.* New York: Harper and Row.

Podhoretz, Norman. 2000. *Ex-Friends.* San Francisco: Encounter Books.

Polanski, Roman. *Roman by Polanski.* 1985. New York: Ballantine Books.

Presser, Lois, 2004. "Violent Offenders, Moral Selves: Constructing Identities and Accounts in the Research Interview." *Social Problems* 51 (February): 82–101.

Prose, Francine. 2008. "Books and Circuses: The Politics of Literary Scapegoating." *Harper's Magazine,* September, pp. 87–92.

Raab, Selwyn. 2005. *The Five Families: The Rise, Decline, and Resurgence of America's Most Powerful Mafia Empire.* New York: St. Martin's Press.

Rashbaum, William K. 2011. "Nearly 125 Arrested in Sweeping Mob Roundup." *The New York Times,* January 20, p. A21.

Rauch, Jonathan. 2011. "Gay Is the New Normal." *The Atlantic,* July/August, p. 52.

Read, Kirk. 2001/2003. *How I Learned to Snap: A Small-Town Coming-Out and Coming-of-Age Story.* Athens, GA: Hill Street Press/New York: Penguin.

Resnick, Rachel. 2008. *Love Junkie: A Memoir.* New York: Bloomsbury.

Rohter, Larry. 1998. "Nobel Winner Finds Her Story Challenged." *The New York Times,* December 15, pp. A1, A8.

Rosenblat, Herman. 2009. *Angel at the Fence: The True Story of a Love That Survived.* New York: Penguin Books/Berkley Books (withdrawn before publication).

Ryan, Michael. 1995. *Secret Life: An Autobiography.* New York: Pantheon Books.

Sanford, Christopher. 2007. *Polanski.* London: Palgrave.

Sciolino, Elaine. 2011. "Saluting a Serial Seducer and His Steamy Tell-All." *The New York Times,* November 29, pp. C1, C5.

Scott, Marvin B., and Stanford M. Lyman. 1968. "Accounts." *The American Sociological Review* 33 (February): 46–62.

Scully, Diana. 1990. *Understanding Sexual Violence: A Study of Convicted Rapists.* Boston: Unwin Hyman.

Shabazz, Attallah. 1999. Foreword to *The Autobiography of Malcolm X,* as told to Alex Haley. New York: Ballantine Books, pp. ix–xxiv.

Shaler, Jeffrey A. 2000. *Addiction Is a Choice.* Chicago: Open Court Press.

Sherman, Gabriel. 2008. "The Fog of Memoir: The Feud over the Truthfulness of Ishmael Beah's *A Long Way Gone.*" *Slate,* March 6.

Shover, Neal. 2012. "Life Histories and Autobiographies as Ethnographic Data." In David Gadd, Susanne Karstedt, and Steven F. Messner (eds.), *The Sage Handbook of Criminological Research Methods.* New York: Sage, pp. 11–22.

Silverman, Sue. 2001. *Love Sick: One Woman's Journey through Sexual Addiction.* New York: W.W. Norton.

Snyder, C.R., Raymond Higgins, and Rita J. Stucky. 1983. *Excuses: Masquerades in Search of Grace.* New York: John Wiley and Sons.

Spence, Donald P. 1982. *Narrative Truth and Historical Truth: Meaning and Interpretation in Psychoanalysis.* New York: W.W. Norton.

Stanley, Alessandra. 2012. "Season of Equal-Opportunity Sexism." *The New York Times,* January 11, pp. C1, C7.

Stokes, Randall, and John F. Hewitt. 1976. "Aligning Actions." *The American Sociological Review* 41 (October): 838–849.

Stoll, David. 1998. *Rigoberta Menchú and the Story of All Poor Guatemalans.* New York: Westview.
Sumner, Colin. 1994. *The Sociology of Deviance: An Obituary.* Buckingham, UK: Open University Press.
Sykes, Gresham M., and David Matza. 1957. "Techniques of Neutralization: A Theory of Delinquency." *The American Sociological Review* 22 (December): 664–670.
Symonds, John Addington. 1892/1984. *The Memoirs of John Addington Symonds* (ed. Phyllis Grosskurth). London: Hutchinson/Random House.
Tanenbaum, Leora. 2000. *Slut! Growing Up with a Bad Reputation.* New York: Harper-Collins.
Tavuchis, Nicholas. 1991. *Mea Culpa: A Sociology of Apology and Reconciliation.* Stanford, CA: Stanford University Press.
Taylor, Ian, Paul Walton, and Jock Young. 1973. *The New Criminology: For a Social Theory of Deviance.* London: Routledge and Kegan Paul.
Toobin, Jeffrey, 2010. "The Celebrity Defense." In Stephen J. Dubner (ed.), *The Best American Crime Reporting.* New York: HarperCollins/Ecco, pp. 139–171.
Topalli, Volkan, 2005. "When Being Good Is Bad: An Expansion of Neutralization Theory." *Criminology* 43 (August): 797–835.
Van Doren, Charles. 2008. "All the Answers." *The New Yorker,* July 28, pp. 63–69.
Vidal, Gore. 1995. *Palimpsest: A Memoir.* London: André Deutsch.
Wells, Jane. 2007. "Who's Jordan Belfort? I'll Tell You Exactly Who He Is." Available at http://funnybusiness.cnbc.com.
Wilkerson, Cathy. 2007. *Flying Close to the Sun: My Life as a Weatherman.* New York: Seven Stories Press.
Wilkomirski, Binjamin. 1996. *Fragments: Memories of a Wartime Childhood* (trans. Carol Brown Janeway). New York: Schocken Books.
Wu, Pei-Yi. 1990. *The Confucian's Progress: Autobiographical Writings in Traditional China.* Princeton, NJ: Princeton University Press.
Yagoda, Ben. 2009. *Memoir: A History.* New York: Riverhead Books.
Zeigler, Henry A. 1970. *Sam the Plumber.* New York: Signet Books.
Zeller, Tom, Jr. 2006. "Before the Fame, a Million Little Skeptics." *The New York Times,* January 23.
Zinsser, William (ed.). 1998. *Inventing the Truth: The Art and Craft of Memoir* (rev. and exp. ed.). Boston: Houghton Mifflin.

Index

ERICH GOODE is Professor of Sociology Emeritus at Stony Brook University. He has published ten books, including *Moral Panics* (coauthored with Nachman Ben-Yehuda), *The Paranormal, Deviant Behavior,* and *Drugs in American Society*; seven anthologies; and articles in magazines, newspapers, and an array of academic journals. He is a Guggenheim Fellowship recipient, and he has taught at half a dozen universities, including the University of Maryland, New York University, and the University of North Carolina.